GREAT HIGHWAYS OF THE WORLD

25

SPECTACULAR JOURNEYS

ACROSS SOME OF THE WORLD'S MOST BREATHTAKING SCENERY

GREAT HIGHWAYS OF THE WORLD

Copy editor: Wendy Lawson

Designers: T T Designs. Tony & Stuart Truscott

List of contributors:
John M Baxter, Rosemary Burton, Elizabeth Cruwys, Ben Davies, Adi Kraus, Pip Leahy, Anne Matthews, Tony Pinchuck, Beau Riffenburgh, Richard Sale, David Scott, Melissa Shales.

Produced by AA Publishing

First published 1995. Reprinted 1998

Published by AA Publishing
(a trading name of Automobile Association Developments Limited, whose registered office is Norfolk House, Priestley Road, Basingstoke, Hampshire RG24 9NY; registered number 1878835).

ISBN 0 7495 1055 2 (hardback); 0 7495 1966 5 (softback)

A CIP catalogue record for this book is available from the British Library.

Colour separation by Fotographics Ltd

Printed in Spain by Gráficas Estella, S.A.

Contents

Great Highways of the World

THE ROMANCE OF THE OPEN ROAD has always been a favourite theme of novelists and poets, songwriters and film-makers; there is something intensely exciting about setting out on a journey. There is the inviting prospect of new experiences, interesting encounters and the amazing variety of the natural world around us; we are never sure how much we will be changed, between the start and end points of the journey, by the actual experience of travelling.

In the words of Robert Louis Stevenson, 'To travel hopefully is a better thing than to arrive', and the authors of this book have all given accounts of the fascinating sights and sounds

along the way, whether the journey is from Bangkok to Singapore through tropical Malaysia, or through the awe-inspiring vastness of the Canadian wilderness on the Trans-Canada Highway. 'Road movies' and country songs celebrate the cult of travel; on the road we feel somehow separate from the everyday life around us as we speed by, the landscape is a source of enjoyment but it is static, unlike the traveller who can move on to discover new delights.

Great highways of the world have included the straight paved roads built by the Romans in the heyday of their empire, the shifting desert sands traversed by traders in silk and spices, and the perilous rocky tracks along which thousands rushed in the quest for gold. Multi-laned expressways like those of America or Singapore have come to symbolise efficiency and modernity – the car has

RIGHT, *America's network of highways makes long distance travel in remote areas less daunting*

BELOW, *the grandeur of the Eastern Sierras forms the backdrop to a drive along this California highway*

RIGHT, *in search of solitude and magnificent scenery in Big Sur National Park*

replaced the camel, but the urge to trade, to make contact and to experience different ways of life from our own, is universal. Sometimes a road can take us on a journey through time, as when we walk on the very stones that Roman soldiers trod as they marched along the Appian Way.

Highways tell stories of heroic endurance, of the determination of pioneers like John McDouall Stuart to open up continents despite the hardships they confronted. The story of Route 66 evokes the hopes and trials of people leaving their homes in search of a better life for their families. Sometimes, however, the call of the road ahead is irresistible just for its own sake; in the words of the pilgrims on the Golden Road to Samarkand,

'...we shall go
Always a little further: it may be
Beyond that last blue mountain...'

Map Symbols

Great Highway - Europe

Great Highway - South/South-east Asia

Great Highway - North America/ South America

Great Highway - Northern Asia

Great Highway - Africa/Middle East

Great Highway - Australia/New Zealand

Motorway

Main road

Other road

TOMINTOUL Highway start/finish

International boundary

International boundary (disputed)

National boundary

Urban area

National/State Park area

Airport

Castle

Historic house

Museum

Distillery

Abbey/monastery/church

Cemetery

Memorial

Prehistoric site

Roman site

Site of ancient Inca settlement

Garden

National/State Park

Marine National Park

Wildlife reserve

Bird reserve

Cave

Other place of interest

Viewpoint

LEFT, *the road twists and turns across the hilly landscape of Tibet*

Arctic Ocean
Arctic Circle
Dawson City
Whitehorse
CANADA
Victoria
Saint John's
Chicago
Leggett
USA
North Pacific Ocean
Los Angeles
North Atlantic Ocean
See inset area
Equator
Quito
ECUADOR
PERU
South Atlantic Ocean
Santiago
CHILE
Keith
Tomintoul
Bushmills
Larne
UK
GERMANY
CZECH REPUBLIC
Würzburg
Praha
Zell am See
Füssen
Budapest
HUNGARY
FRANCE
Lienz
AUSTRIA
Santiago de Compostela
Marseille
Menton
ITALY
Roncesvalles
Roma
Brindisi
SPAIN
Antarctic Circle

Arctic Ocean
Arctic Circle
RUSSIAN FEDERATION
Sankt-Peterburg
UKRAINE
Odessa
KAZAKHSTAN
UZBEKISTAN
Samarkand
KYRGYZSTAN
TURKMENISTAN
Halab
SYRIA
Dimashq
Tel-Aviv-Yafo
ISRAEL
Yerushalayim
Baghdād
IRAN
AFGHANISTAN
PAKISTAN
NEPAL
Lhasa
Kathmandu
INDIA
CHINA
Xi'an
JAPAN
Tōkyō
Kyōto
Pacific Ocean
Mangalore
Kanniyakumari
THAILAND
Bangkok
MALAYSIA
Singapore
Equator
KENYA
Lamu
TANZANIA
Dar es Salaam
Indian Ocean
Darwin
AUSTRALIA
Adelaide
SOUTH AFRICA
Stormsrivier
Mossel Bay
NEW ZEALAND
Skippers
Queenstown
Southern Ocean
Antarctic Circle

ABOVE, *the poet Horace was a traveller on the Appian Way in 38/37* BC, *and an account of his experiences appears in the 'Satires'*

The Appian Way from Rome to Brindisi

ROSEMARY BURTON

Twenty-three centuries ago the magistrate Appius Claudius built a road south-east from Rome to Capua. Later extended through Benevento and Taranto to Brindisi, the Via Appia was described in poetry as the 'queen of roads', and it marked the beginning of a process which would culminate in a huge network of highways across the Roman Empire. The Via Appia (named after its builder) linked sea to sea – Mediterranean to Adriatic – and it can also be said to have linked Rome with the Hellenic world, for Brindisi was, and still is, the place to take ship for Greece.

MENTION THE VIA APPIA and the images captured by 18th-century artists come to mind – a stretch of ancient road, dotted with crumbling brick and marble tombs, shaded by pines and cypresses and with an occasional goatherd in the distance. Such romantic rural scenes (give or take the goatherds) can still be found on the outskirts of Rome today, but anyone who makes a journey in search of the rest of the Via Appia will discover other memorable images – the brilliant colours of a Roman painting in an underground temple at Capua; a mosaic showing the grape harvest in the region which produced some of the most prized wines of antiquity; or the arches of a Roman bridge still carrying motor traffic over a river at Benevento.

BELOW, *leaving Rome, the road passes the 3rd-century Aurelian Walls*

That first tomb-lined stretch of the Via Appia is simply the beginning of a route which leads from the style and sophistication of Rome through the heart of Italy into a distinctive southern land of small communities, each with its own olive groves and vineyards, almond and tobacco plantations. Southern Italy was known as Magna Graecia (Great Greece) from the large number of Greek colonies there – Taranto, for example, was founded by Sparta in the 8th century BC – and today some of the southern townships with white-washed houses overlooking azure seas retain much of that Greek flavour. The original Via Appia ran south-east from Rome along the coastal plain below the Alban Hills (Colli Albani), and then inland to Capua. The date of construction is recorded as 312 BC, but the work must have

LEFT, *the Arch of Trajan at Benevento is decorated with reliefs detailing the emperor's achievements*

BELOW, *ruined buildings in the shade of the trees, beside a stretch of the old Via Appia*

Roman roads are famous for being straight, but the evolution of the Via Appia meant that it was straight in sections only, and to follow its far-from-direct line from start to finish today is not easy. In the 1880s there was talk of a grand scheme, to be implemented over many years, which would eventually turn the entire route into a kind of national archaeological park and long-distance trail. This idealism came to nothing, and centuries of neglect combined with the effects of wartime bombing and post-war development have meant that parts of the road are lost beyond recall. Another complication lies in the fact that as early as the first century BC travellers from Rome to Brindisi often favoured another route, avoiding Taranto altogether and striking north-east from Benevento. The poet Horace travelled this route (also known as the Via Traiana) in the first century BC. There is much to be said for choosing to follow this simpler itinerary, which does, after all, include the whole of Appius Claudius's original route between Rome and Capua.

A selective approach might involve travelling from Rome to Terracina and Santa Maria Capua Vetere along the SS7, and then following the same road on to Benevento. From this point one could travel on minor roads south through Aeclanum and Venosa, picking up the SS7 where it coincides with the ancient route again on the outskirts of Taranto, and then on through Oria and Mesagne to Brindisi. The Via Traiana route runs through Ordona, Canosa, Ruvo di Puglia and Egnazia. For a swifter alternative, and one which gives a driver rather more opportunity to appreciate the dramatic and changing landscape, take the motorway from Benevento to Bari and then explore Egnazia, Brindisi and Taranto on separate excursions.

ABOVE, *the Quirinal Hill in Rome, seen from the Palatine, as depicted in a 19th-century engraving by Pinelli*

BELOW, *this ruined brick-built temple is one of many Roman remains along the route*

involved the incorporation and upgrading of a number of existing tracks and is likely to have taken several years. Appius Claudius, the city magistrate responsible for the work, was in effect building the prototype Roman road, the forerunner of a vast international network of highways designed to guarantee swift military and civilian communications across huge distances.

The first official Roman road ('the queen of roads', according to the poet Statius) was a work of advanced engineering, although in time it would be improved, by-passed and partly superseded. Well-drained and surfaced (though perhaps not paved at first), supplied with milestones and with service stations at regular intervals offering food, a change of horses and a bed for the night, it penetrated the territory of the Latin tribes immediately to the south and demonstrated Rome's supremacy over them. As Rome's power spread during the next century, the road was extended in stages from Capua through the Apennines to Benevento, Taranto and Brindisi, 365 Roman miles (530 km) away on the south-east coast, and this piecemeal development accounts for the way the road wanders about before it reaches a final destination never envisaged by Appius Claudius.

LEAVING ROME

The Via Appia left Rome at the Porta Capena, a gate in the city's republican walls, and ran past the tomb of the Scipio family, which can still be visited, to the Porta San Sebastiano in the Aurelian Walls, which date from the 3rd century AD. Subsequent development has left the precise course of this first section less than clear, and it is beyond the Porta San Sebastiano, named after the nearby Christian catacombs of San Sebastiano, that the real journey begins. The road here is steeped in the early history of Christianity – the catacombs themselves attract thousands of visitors to see elaborate sarcophagi preserved in networks of underground corridors, and one of the most celebrated stories about the Via Appia concerns a vision of Christ.

ABOVE, *a section of the original paving of the Via Appia Antica, such as can be seen at Terracina*

Leaving Rome to escape martyrdom, Peter saw Christ travelling the other way and asked him 'Domine, quo vadis?' (Lord, where are you going?). On hearing the reply that Christ was going to Rome to be crucified a second time, Peter realized that Christ would be taking his place, and turned back to be crucified himself. The Church of Domine Quo Vadis, only a short distance from the Porta San Sebastiano, commemorates this encounter and contains the stone in which Christ is said to have left his footprint when the encounter took place.

The Via Appia Antica (not to be confused with the Via Appia Nuova, a more recent construction within Rome, often running quite close to the original road) still carries heavy traffic along its first short stretch, which is called the Hill of Mars (Clivus Martis) in memory of a vanished temple to that god which stood near by. Most of the traffic is oblivious to the milestone which stands by the roadside and, to be fair, this is a replica – the real one has been moved to the Piazza del Campidoglio in the heart of the city. Many of the original milestones are now in museums, but at a few places along the route, at Arpaia for example, between Capua and Benevento, Roman milestones can still be seen by the roadside close to their original position. After a few hundred yards, beyond the hill of Mars, the majority of traffic turns off, and the ancient road leads ahead for several miles. Sadly, 20th-century road builders made few concessions to antiquity. After about 5 miles (8 km) the Appia Antica is casually sliced in two by Rome's outer ring road.

According to Roman law, burials had to take place outside a city's walls, and that is why the land to each side of the Via Appia beyond the limits of Rome is filled with funerary monuments such as the huge cylindrical Tomb of Cecilia Metella. Most of the rich marble which once adorned the tombs disappeared long ago, leaving odd-shaped brick structures and only a hint of their original magnificence. Different types of monument can still be made out, particularly the sort which were known as *columbaria* (dovecots), because their many niches for the ashes of different

RIGHT AND BELOW, *the Tomb of Cecilia Metella on the Via Appia outside Rome, as it looks today, and in an 18th-century engraving by Piranesi*

family members resembled pigeon-holes. The high brick walls of the Circus of Maxentius, a stadium dating from the 4th century AD, loom over this first stretch of the route, and it is also possible to see the fragmentary remains of excavated villas. Here and there the ancient paved road surface survives. The smooth and shiny black stone is volcanic, a legacy of the lava flow from the Alban Hills, and it presents a challenge to any car, calling for good suspension and very slow speeds. It's a bumpy enough ride in a modern vehicle, and the discomfort of travel in an ancient carriage – of the type which cut the deep wheel-ruts visible in the stone – is scarcely imaginable. Little wonder that, despite mosquitoes and drunken sailors, travellers such as Horace preferred to cover part of the long journey by boat, along a canal beside the road between Faiti (ancient Forum Appii) and Terracina (Anxur).

Horace's first overnight stop was at a modest inn at Ariccia, 16 miles (26 km) from Rome, where today there is a Roman maritime museum. After Ariccia the modern road, the SS7, deviates from the ancient route, winding round the base of the Alban Hills, but beyond Cisterna di Latina it coincides exactly with the course of the Roman road, running absolutely straight for 24 miles (38 km) towards Terracina and the coastal area which became a favourite retreat for wealthy Romans. This road, planned 2,300 years ago and still very much in use today, has been compared to a modern motorway. It was designed not to serve individual hill settlements such as Cori and Norma (where there are Roman and even older ruins), but to take traffic directly and efficiently from one major centre to another. It runs across the area of the Pomptine Marshes, which were the subject of various drainage projects over the centuries. It was not until Mussolini's time that the marshes were thoroughly and successfully drained, and they must have presented one of the major challenges for Appius Claudius's engineers.

A canal, like that used by Horace, can be seen beside the road between Faiti and Terracina and, despite the volume of 20th-century traffic, a drive along this unique length of Roman road can be one of the most evocative experiences of the Via Appia today. It is often on the outskirts of a town that a good straight stretch of the Via Appia can still be found. People who

RIGHT, *a funerary monument at the roadside*

approach Taranto and Brindisi today on the SS7 are following the course of the original road.

For Horace, Terracina (actually the citadel of Anxur above the old town of Terracina) was conspicuous because of its shining white rocks, but the impression now is rather one of greenness, as vegetation seems to have taken hold. The lower town, with hotels along the beach, is a popular holiday resort, just as this area was in ancient times. The old town on the slopes below the citadel is a charming place, with the line of the Via Appia still forming one of the main streets. A stretch of ancient paving is preserved here, and you can still make out the letters of a Roman inscription cut into the flags of the forum outside the cathedral.

After his arrival here by boat from Forum Apii, Horace says that he washed his face and hands in Feronia's fair spring – something which can still be done, although the spring is very well hidden. The search for it involves a drive of about 3½ miles (5.6 km) north-east from the railway station along a significant but neglected stretch of the Appia Antica where, again, ancient paving can still be seen. Where this road swings left to join the main road (SS7), the spring is to be found down a track to the right, just beyond a modern mill.

BUILDING A BY-PASS

Terracina offers dramatic evidence of the development of Roman road-building skills. At the time of Horace's journey the Appia still followed its old laborious course from Feronia uphill to the temple of Anxur – and he recalls three miles of miserable slow progress in carriages (today it is simply a matter of driving along the Via Panoramica for a visit to the ruins above, and a spectacular view of the old and new town below). In the first century AD the Emperor Domitian ordered the building of a by-pass along the coast, which reduced what had been a whole day's journey to a matter of two hours. Domitian's engineers drove the new road right through the rocky outcrop known as Pisco Montana, and Roman numerals incised into the side of the rock indicate the 120 foot (36 m) depth of the cutting, measured at intervals of 10 Roman feet. It was not until the 1950s that a road was built all the way along the coast from Terracina to Formia and beyond, and it is interesting to

BELOW, *the 4th-century circus built by the Emperor Maxentius for chariot racing is still well-preserved*

ABOVE, *the impressive construction of the aqueduct at Minturno has stood the test of time*

FAR RIGHT, *the original column marking the end of the Via Appia at Brindisi*

BELOW, *Gnathian ware dating from the 4th century* BC *is displayed in the museum at Taranto*

compare this highway, sweeping through tunnels and galleries above the sea, with Domitian's early achievement. The modern coast road also has the advantage of taking you to Sperlonga, where an unusual seaside grotto and villa complex of the Emperor Tiberius have been discovered. Fragments of some monumental statue groups have been found here, which are displayed in the purpose-built museum.

The course of the Via Appia, however, lies inland from Terracina and right through the pleasing little town of Fondi, dominated by its castle. Fondi retains its ancient street plan, with the church of San Pietro standing on the site of the Roman forum. Inside the church there is an elaborate early pulpit, supported by crouching carved lions and a ram, and approached up a steep metal ladder. Another church, San Francesco, has a cloister turned into a museum, with an impressive display of Roman relics including a Via Appia milestone.

The road, still called the Via Appia at Fondi and beyond, carries international traffic to and from Formia, a short distance further on. On the way you pass a milestone and the remains of a tomb, which might be that of the great Roman republican orator, Cicero. Like many other successful Romans Cicero had a villa in this now large and busy town, and it is possible to look down on what are said to be its ruins. On a famous occasion Julius Caesar and his entourage called on Cicero here, sending the host into considerable panic. Formia has one extraordinary Roman relic still in use today – the former Roman theatre, now known as il Cancello, has been turned into a whitewashed block of flats, with washing lines strung across its arches.

From Formia the SS7 follows the course of the Appia directly to Minturno, where a substantial Roman aqueduct stands just outside the archaeological site of ancient Minturnae. Here a 300-yard stretch of the original paved road can be seen, together with an elaborate bath building, a market complex, a communal latrine and a much-damaged but still charming mosaic. This unassuming piece of art, not even mentioned in the guide book, shows winged cupids swinging athletically in the branches of a vine, cutting and collecting fruit, while others tread the grapes and the liquid runs out of the tanks into waiting jars. The scene is particularly appropriate on the edge of the region which produced the Falernian and Caecuban wines prized by the Romans.

AN EASTERN RELIGION UNDERGROUND

An even more magnificent relic of Roman life awaits the traveller at Santa Maria Capua Vetere. The colossal amphitheatre, with its connotations of butchery and brutality, is the best known monument in a city which was a famous training ground for gladiators; but the real delight lies hidden underground. Access to Capua's temple of Mithras, a Persian sun god much worshipped by soldiers, can be arranged with the amphitheatre custodian. An insignificant door opens on to some metal steps leading down to a small chamber with stars on the ceiling. On the left-hand wall there is an exquisite miniature marble carving depicting Cupid and Psyche and, at the far end, a startling wall painting showing the ritual Mithraic scene in which the god, with distinctive Persian cap and vivid red cloak and leggings, sacrifices a bull, attended by a dog, a snake and a scorpion. There are temples to Mithras all over the Roman world , even as far north as Hadrian's Wall in Britain, and the better preserved ones have fine marble carvings of this standard scene, but it would be difficult to find anything to equal this.

Somewhere beyond Capua in a narrow defile near modern Arpaia, the fearful humiliation of the Romans at the Caudine Forks took place in 321BC. An army of the local Samnite people defeated a Roman force battling for supremacy in this region and compelled them to walk beneath the *iugum* or yoke. The disgrace was heightened because this was the traditional Roman method of humiliating an enemy, and the origin of the term 'subjugation'. The episode was never forgotten, but the Romans recovered to beat the Samnites into submission. The Via Appia was extended and Benevento became a Roman colony in 268 BC. It was here that Horace's host cooked thrushes for his guests' supper and nearly set the house on fire in the process. Today the city has a considerable museum, and a triumphal arch across the line of the Via Appia with sculptured panels facing towards and away from Rome, commemorating home and foreign policy, respectively. Less well known, but well worth seeking out, is the Ponte Leproso, a Roman bridge still carrying motor traffic over the River Sabato.

THE WAY DIVIDES

Beyond Benevento an attempt to travel close to the original route of the Via Appia involves an upland journey on minor roads through Horace's birthplace of Venosa to Taranto, and calls for some hard driving. Taranto itself, however, is a fine place with a museum containing an outstanding collection of Greek vases. The old city has an imposing castle and stands on an island linked by two bridges to the mainland, creating what is virtually an inland sea.

A highlight of the more northerly Via Traiana route is the archaeological site of Egnazia, which features in Horace's poem and has a number of tombs that belong to the Messapian civilization, which existed here long before the arrival of the Romans. Once known as Gnathia, it gave its name to Gnathian ware – a distinctive type of pottery made during the second half of the 4th century BC with red, white and yellow colours painted onto a black background glaze. Examples can be seen in the museum here and at Taranto. A harbour was built here during the Roman Empire and there are remains of substantial Christian buildings, but the excavations pose some unanswered questions. What was the purpose of the oval area which looks vaguely like an amphitheatre, but clearly couldn't have been one given its position so close to the forum? And what was the Cryptoporticus – four underground corridors forming a rectangle – used for?

The two routes from Benevento had Brindisi as their common destination and, as the Via Appia (again the SS7) runs straight into the city today, the names of the side streets on the right provide a catalogue of all the famous writers of Roman literature. Unfortunately a one-way system diverts drivers shortly before the road reaches its goal, close to the city's Stazione Marittima. The end of the long journey from Rome is marked by a column and a column base (the rest of it stands in the city of Lecce) at the top of a broad flight of steps where, as if to prove that one journey's end is only another's beginning, people sit gazing out to sea, waiting for the ferry which will take them to Greece.

PRACTICAL INFORMATION

■ The journey will take between five days and a fortnight. If you want to see every surviving relic of the road the essential guidebook is by Lorenzo Quilici and published (in Italian only) in two volumes: I, *Via Appia da Porta Capena ai Colli Albani* and II, *Via Appia Dalla Pianura Pontina a Brindisi* by Fratelli Palombi Editori (1989). These books contain maps and detailed discussions of the various sections, and the second volume also covers the alternative route along the Via Traiana from Benevento to Brindisi.

■ Information is available from the Italian Tourist Board at 1 Princes Street, London W1R 8AY, Tel: 0171 408 1254. In USA, contact: 630, 5th Avenue, Suite 1565, NY 10111. Tel: 2454 822.

The Way of St James from Roncesvalles to Santiago de Compostela

PIP LEAHY

ABOVE, *the stone figure of St James at Compostela wears a pilgrim's cloak and the distinctive hat with cockle-shell symbols*

It's over a millennium since the relics of St James the Apostle were said to have been discovered in the isolated, north-western corner of the Iberian Peninsula, but remarkably three million people still visit his shrine each year. Many of those only pay a fleeting visit, curious to see what the fuss is all about; others, who make the journey to Santiago de Compostela, travelling across the northern territories of Spain from the Pyrenees, follow one of the greatest routes in history, trodden by countless pilgrims for a thousand years and known as the Way of St James.

ST JAMES THE APOSTLE spent seven years in Spain preaching Christianity before returning to Judaea, only to be martyred by King Herod in AD44. His body was put in a marble sepulchre and, guided by an angel, was carried across the seas to the mouth of the River Ulla in the Kingdom of Asturias, where it lay undiscovered for hundreds of years.

RIGHT, *the cathedral at Santiago de Compostela rises above the red roofs of the town*

Early in the 9th century a group of shepherds (in other versions, a pious hermit) were guided to its resting place by a supernatural light. The rediscovered tomb soon became the object of local veneration, a church was built on the site and the town of Santiago de Compostela grew up around it.

Christian Spain was by now in turmoil: Muslims from North Africa

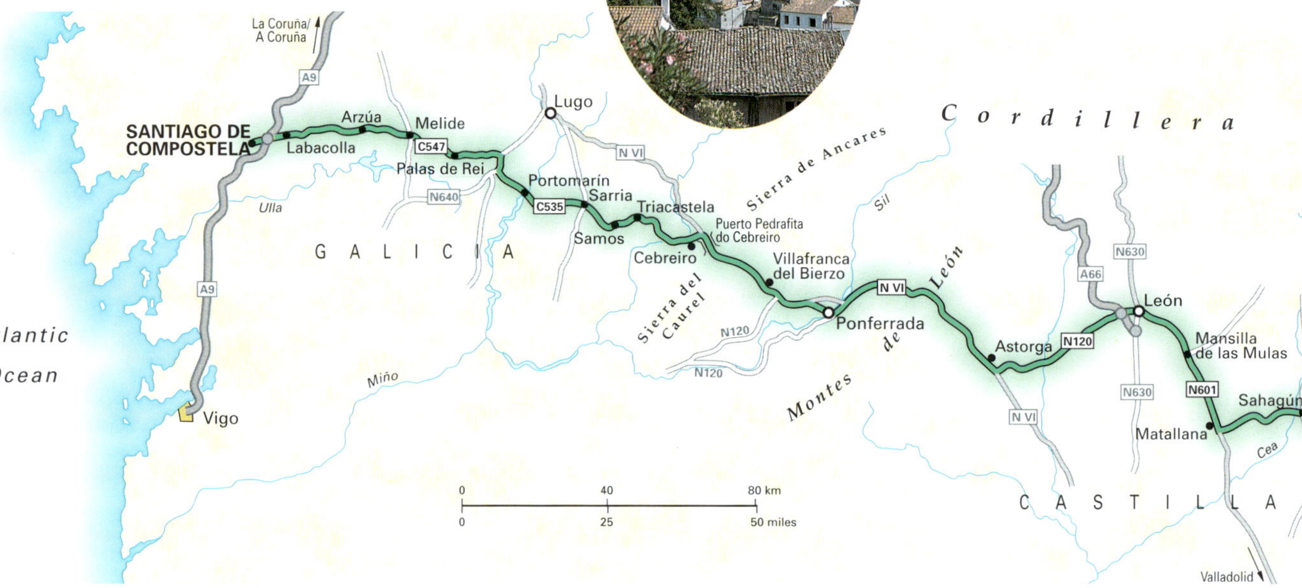

had invaded the country in AD711, swiftly conquering the entire peninsula. It was to take seven centuries before the infidels were finally banished, but the Reconquest had already started. In AD844 St James miraculously appeared as a knight in armour on a battlefield at Clavijo and led the Christian army to victory over the Moors. Spain had found itself a new patron saint.

Not unnaturally, the French were very interested – the Moors had been repulsed at Poitiers in 732 – and the image of St James as Matamoros (Slayer of the Moors) must have appealed to them too. Indeed so many Franks came to venerate the relics of the Apostle that the main route linking the Pyrenees with Galicia became known as the Camino Francés (the French Way). Frankish influence is still in evidence in many of the cities and villages along the route. Most of the roads to Santiago de Compostela were used, at one time or another, by pilgrims from all over Christendom but it is the Camino Francés which is now called the Camino de Santiago or Way of St James.

Through a mixture of politics and devotion, the cult of St James spread throughout Europe: pilgrims not just from France, but also from England, Germany, Italy and Scandinavia began to make the journey to the shrine at Compostela. Eventually Santiago ranked equally with Rome and Jerusalem as a place of pilgrimage, and in its heyday the Camino Francés was one of the busiest highways in Christendom. An estimated 500,000 to 2 million people a year travelled its length, and the economic and artistic legacy of such an influx changed the face of northern Spain forever.

Written in the first half of the 12th century, the world's first 'tourist guide' was about the journey to Santiago. The account has been attributed to a French cleric, Aimery Picaud, and is attached to a tome of five volumes, known as the *Codex Calixtimus* or *Liber Santi Jacobi*. One version of the

Although medieval pilgrims followed various routes across northern Spain to Santiago, it's the route over the Ibañeta Pass near Roncesvalles through Pamplona, Burgos and León which is generally thought of as the Way of St James in Spain. No doubt contemporary travellers can expect a far shorter and less arduous journey than their counterparts in the Middle Ages, but it is still possible to capture the atmosphere of those times and, even along the modern roads, follow almost exactly the route they would have taken.

In some places the old Way is only accessible to walkers and riders, but equally it often follows the busy main roads and motorways which link the main centres. You can be sure that if you walk up the Calle Mayor in the smaller towns and villages along the Way you are on the pilgrims' route – many of the towns owe their existence to the pilgrimage and grew up beside the road that the pilgrims travelled. The Way is not only historic, it is tremendously beautiful, taking you through the foothills of the Pyrenees, along the edge of the great plains of Castile and into the lush wooded scenery of Galicia. Each city, town or village has something of interest to offer the traveller and usually a reminder, if only brief, that you are on the road to Santiago.

From Roncesvalles the main N135 runs directly to Pamplona and the route follows the fast roads (often dual carriageway) of the national and international road network all the way to Burgos. Between Burgos and León the terrain becomes more uncertain and the journey slower: you have to follow narrow minor roads to and from Castrojeriz but will rejoin the reasonable N120 again at Carrión de los Condes. Only one other small section of the route after the Pedrafita Pass leaves the main road.

ABOVE, *rooftops jostle for space in the narrow streets of the old town in Santiago de Compostela*

Codex – there are four – is preserved in the archives of Santiago cathedral. Aside from the religious detail and the fact that it offers a fairly biased view (Picaud was obviously a cultured man and regarded many of the people he encountered along the Way as little short of barbaric), the guide offered useful practical information to anyone undertaking the journey. It gives a detailed account of the route through France and Spain with descriptions of the land and rivers. In the early days, travellers would often have to wade through rivers and rely on them as the only source of drinking water.

All kinds of people embarked on the journey to Compostela (which would have taken months, even years if a detour or two interrupted the itinerary), although not everyone was on the road for spiritual reasons. Frequently the pilgrimage was imposed as a punishment. Some even travelled on an 'all expenses paid' basis, the journey dedicated to the absolution of a client.

BELOW, *the baroque façade of the cathedral at Santiago de Compostela dates from 1750, but behind it is a Romanesque church which remains much as the pilgrims would have known it.*

Almost always travelling in groups to ward off the brigands and thieves who lurked on the quieter stretches of the Way, the pilgrims adopted a uniform of a tunic, short cape, and a wide brimmed hat for protection against wind, rain and sun. They carried a staff and hollow gourd which served both as flask and bowl. Usually their hats were adorned with scallop shells – the symbol of the pilgrimage to Santiago. According to legend St James saved a man and his horse from drowning and they emerged from the sea unscathed but covered in shells. Buildings all along the way are carved with this symbol: the largest carved shell is the font in the church of Santiago at Villafranca de Montes de Oca.

The pilgrimage to Santiago lost its mass appeal towards the end of the 15th century and when, in 1589, Drake attacked Corunna and the bishop removed the Apostle's relics from the cathedral, the point of it was lost altogether. Lost too were the relics, for nearly three centuries, until 1879 when they were rediscovered and the pilgrimage resumed, although on a lesser scale.

The Start of the Pilgrims' Journey

There are two major crossing points over the Pyrenees, one at Somport and the other further to the west at Roncesvalles. Those pilgrims who crossed at Somport would have taken a route which is followed, more or less, by today's main N330 to Jaca, whose Romanesque cathedral is one of the oldest in Spain. Crossing over the River Aragón on the Puente de San Miguel they would have proceeded to the Monasterio de Leyre, where the monks still run an inn.

Roncesvalles, though, was the busier of the crossing points and an important north–south route over the Pyrenees, even in ancient times. Events in August 778 put it on the map as the site of an epic historical tale. It was here that the rearguard of Charlemagne's army, led by his nephew Roland and fleeing back across the border to France, was massacred by the Basques. Legendary tales of Roland's heroism, his enchanted horn 'Olifant' and unbreakable sword 'Durandal' were embellished and retold, culminating in the first French epic poem, the 12th-century 'Chanson de Roland'. The little church of San Salvador de Ibañeta is reputed to stand on the site of Roland's tomb, and is also thought to be the place where an 11th-century hermit set up his cell so he could toll a bell to guide the pilgrims over the Pass in misty weather and at night.

A massive monastery with zinc-lined roofs dominates the village of Roncesvalles. It once housed one of the greatest hospices on the Way, where pilgrims were allowed free food and lodging for three days to recuperate after their journey across the Pyrenees. Doctors, apothecaries, cobblers, farriers and tradesmen of all descriptions would have been on hand to tend the travellers. Navarre's ruler, Sancho el Fuerte, founded the abbey church in the 13th century: this impressively proportioned man was buried here with his wife. The church also contains the Madonna of Roncesvalles, a 12–13th-century carving which was supposedly discovered because a deer with shining antlers pointed to its remote hiding place. Early pilgrims would have worshipped in the Romanesque Chapel of Spiritus Sancti, Roncesvalles' oldest building.

Pamplona / Iruñea, founded by the Romans and since early times the most important city in the Spanish Pyrenees, was the beginning of the third stage of the pilgrim's journey . What remains of medieval Pamplona centres on its Gothic cathedral, in whose right tower hangs Spain's largest bell. Although nothing remains of its Romanesque origins and it has acquired a Classical façade, the beautiful 14th-century cloisters should not be missed. Medieval pilgrims would have eaten in the refectory here, famous for its sculpted frescoes: it is still possible to view the great open fireplaces in the kitchens. There is a good deal to see in Pamplona, including numerous palaces of noble families and the lavish baroque façade of the Ayuntamiento, but perhaps the city is best known for its *fiesta* in July. Each morning for six days bulls (and people) are run through the town's narrow, cobbled streets amidst a fever of excitement, in preparation for the evening's *corrida* or bullfight. The *fiesta* and the city were immortalized by Hemingway in his novel *The Sun Also Rises* and there is a statue of him outside the bullring.

ABOVE, *the Romanesque chapel where the pilgrims worshipped is the oldest building in Roncesvalles*

On the way to Puente la Reina, where several of the pilgrimage routes converged and which derives its name from the 11th-century, six-arched bridge that still spans the rio Arga, is the Romanesque church of Nuestra Señora de Eunate. Standing apart in a trough of wooded hills, its octagonal shape suggests that it may have been a copy of the Holy Sepulchre in Jerusalem, an idea further compounded by the fact that it was built by the Knights Templar. It was almost certainly a funerary chapel, one of many along the Way which catered for unfortunate travellers who didn't make their final destination.

Another church built by the Knights Templar lies just outside the old town walls. The Iglesia del Crucifijo contains a famous Y-shaped crucifix which was brought from Germany by a pilgrim in the 14th century.

BELOW, *once the fortified capital of of Navarre, Pamplona today has decorative squares and spacious parks and gardens*

MAIN PICTURE, *the bridge at Puenta la Reina, where two main pilgrim routes converged*

The next major stopping place was Estella, or 'Estella la Bella' as the pilgrims called it. A modern church marks the site where pilgrims stopped to venerate Our Lady on the Hill: a statue of the Virgin found by shepherds guided by falling stars. In the 11th century the town was colonized by the French, encouraged to settle here after making a pilgrimage to Santiago to form a bastion against the Moors. Later, when the Jews were being expelled from other parts of Spain, they too were welcomed and the town became a prosperous trading centre. A Romanesque palace in the Plaza de San Martin is one of the oldest secular buildings in Spain, built by the kings of Navarre in the 12th century. St Andrew's relics have been proudly displayed in San Pedro, Estella's oldest church, since the 13th century.

Just south of Estella, at the foot of Montejurra, is one of the country's National Monuments, the Monasterio de Irache. The monks were so devoted to helping those travelling the Way that an abbot of the monastery, St Veremundo, was adopted as the pilgrims' patron saint. Until the last century Irache was also known for its university where medicine, theology and art were studied.

Stucco, sculptures and paintings virtually cover

the nave of the parish church of the Assumption (Asunción) in Los Arcos. Its diverse styles – Renaissance bell tower, Plateresque façade, Baroque interior and Gothic cloister – vividly illustrate Spanish art and architecture through several centuries. Peculiar to Spain, the Plateresque style developed in the early 16th century: buildings were decorated with carvings so intricate they resembled the work of a silversmith.

Since his lengthy description of Navarre and its inhabitants is not at all complimentary, Aimery Picaud must have been pleased when at last he crossed the border into what is now the province of La Rioja. Famous for its wine, the countryside turns a rich red and is dotted with vineyards. About 7 miles (11 km) south of Logroño, a busy provincial capital and manufacturing centre, is Clavijo, the site of St James' miraculous appearance in a battle with the Moors.

Santo Domingo de la Calzada (St Dominic of the Road or Causeway) became an important stage on the way after a hermit, St Dominic, devoted his life to improving the pilgrims' journey. He built the 24-arched bridge which today spans the River Oja, and founded a hospice which still takes in travellers as one of Spain's famous

BELOW LEFT, *a pilgrim staff features prominently on this tomb at Santa Dominga de la Calzada*

BELOW, *harvesting grapes for the famous wines of La Rioja*

RIGHT, *the windows in León cathedral are so large that several restorations have been needed to strengthen the walls supporting them*

Paradors. St Dominic is buried in the town's cathedral, which has been home to countless pairs of white-feathered chickens, kept there ever since a miracle caused a roasted cock and hen to jump off their dish and cluck and crow in front of a doubting magistrate. Pilgrims still collect the birds' white feathers as a mascot for their journey.

Off the main road from here to Burgos is the monastery of San Juan de Ortega, a follower of St Dominic, who also devoted his life to building roads on the Way.

EL CID

El Cid is Spain's most famous hero and Burgos is essentially his town. He was born just 6 miles (10 km) away at Vivar, and is buried, together with his wife Ximena, in the city's splendid Gothic cathedral. Europe's greatest architects and artists came to Burgos to work on this spectacular building, the country's third largest cathedral after Seville and Toledo. St James is not entirely forgotten in Burgos; there is a chapel dedicated to him in the cathedral and another at the Real Monasteria de las Huelgas, the summer palace and pantheon of the Kings of Castile. Members of the Order of Santiago were knighted by the statue of Santiago at Las Huelgas: it has jointed arms and sits on a throne with a sword in the right hand.

A short detour from Burgos will bring you to the monastery of Santo Domingo de Silos, known for its outstanding two-storeyed cloister and Gregorian chants; Benedictine monks have lived here since the 11th century.

Another Benedictine monastery, now long gone, was responsible for one of the best examples of Romanesque architecture you see along the Way. The church of San Martín at Fromista dates from around 1066 and the decorative bands which line the edges of the roof became the hallmark of Romanesque churches on the route. An equally fine illustration of a different style of architecture lies a short way from Mansilla de las Mulas, a faded medieval town between Sahagún and León. San Miguel de Escalada was built, early in the 10th century, by a group of monks fleeing the dominance of the Moors in the south. Obviously influenced by their previous rulers, they built the church in Mozarabic style with horseshoe arches and Moorish motifs.

Medieval pilgrims were bidden by Picaud to pay homage to the relics of St Facundo and St Primitivo at Sahagún. Thanks to the presence of the powerful San Benito monastery (now in ruins), the town was one of the richest and busiest along the Way. Poplars which grow along its river banks are said to be descended from the lances of Charlemagne's knights, which miraculously took root and put out leaves.

St Isidore was Archbishop of Seville and Primate of all Spain, and his relics were taken from the Moors in 1063 and brought to León from Toledo. The Collegiate church, dedicated to him and where he now rests, is known as 'the Sistine chapel of Romanesque art' because of its 12th-century frescoes. It was one of the main goals for pilgrims on the Camino de Santiago. León's pure

BELOW, *the striking brickwork patterns of the church of St Martín at Fromista*

Gothic cathedral is thought by many to be one of the finest: its beautiful stained glass windows (some dating back to the 13th century) are probably unique in Spain. On the main doorway a column supporting a statue of Santiago has been worn down by the hands of countless pilgrims. St James, as Matamoros, appears on the centre of the monumental Plateresque façade of the Convent of San Marcos, a former pilgrims' hospital set up by the military-religious order of the Knights of Santiago.

There were more than 20 hospices in Astorga where the Via de la Plata, the pilgrims' route from southern Spain and Portugal, joined the Camino Francés. An interesting museum dedicated to the pilgrim routes can be explored in Astorga's Episcopal Palace. The building was designed by Antoni Gaudi, a turn of the century architect chiefly known for the unfinished Expiatory Church of the Holy Family in Barcelona.

ENTERING GALICIA

Further along the route at Ponferrada is a Templar castle, a mighty ruin of medieval military architecture. The town was named after a Roman bridge over the River Sil, strengthened with iron for the pilgrim traffic. After Villafranca del Bierzo you will be in Galicia, and nearing the end of the journey. The lush wooded landscape of hills and valleys is probably not so very different to the way Picaud described it in the 12th century.

At Cebreiro, above the Pedrafita Pass, a small mountain church displays what is known as the Galician Holy Grail: a chalice and paten from the 13th or 14th century which became objects of veneration after the bread and wine they contained were transformed into flesh. When they reached Triacastela the medieval pilgrims took a stone from the foot of the mountain and carried it to Castañeda 'to make lime for the building of the Apostle's church'. A glamorous Baroque façade adorns the nearby monastery church of Samos.

This last leg of the journey will take you through Galician villages and towns full of reminders of the ancient Way of St James: Sarria, Portomarín (which remarkably was moved stone by stone when its original site was flooded to make a reservoir in the 1960s) through Palas de Rey, full of splendid Romanesque buildings, Melide and Arzúa. Finally, at Labacolla, where planes fly into Santiago's modern airport, it's worth remembering the medieval pilgrims who used to wash here in preparation for their journey's end.

Sick and weary travellers arriving in Santiago headed for the Hospital Real, now the Hotel de los Reyes Católicos, which stands in the magnificent Plaza de Obradoiro facing the cathedral. It was founded by the Catholic monarchs Ferdinand and Isabella, who finally reunited Spain under Christian rule. The hospital still welcomes travellers through its magnificent Plateresque doorway, although it is now a luxury hotel. According to Picaud 'money changers, inn keepers and diverse merchants' used to line the Rua del Franco, which runs off the Plaza de Obradoiro: boutiques and cafes have taken their place today, but little else has changed. The city still retains its medieval character and at its heart, today as always, is the cathedral, built layer upon layer down the centuries, all for the glory of St James.

LEFT, *the Hotel de los Reyes Católicos in Santiago, once a resting place and hospital for pilgrims, has a doorway in the Plateresque style*

PRACTICAL INFORMATION

■ The journey from Roncesvalles to Santiago is about 500 miles (804 km). It is best undertaken at a leisurely pace (allow about two weeks in a car) as the route is brimming with history and you will pass through some of Spain's great cities.

■ Further information can be obtained from the Spanish Tourist Office, 57 St James' St, London SW1A 1ZD, Tel. (0171) 499 0901, Fax 629 4257, or from the Confraternity of St James, 3 Stamford Street, London SE1 9NT (please enclose s.a.e.), who have an extensive booklist. Tel: 0171 5930013. The tourist office in Santiago is at Rua del Vila, Tel. (81) 58 41 81.

The Malt Whisky Trail around Speyside

JOHN M BAXTER

Wherever you travel in Scotland you cannot fail to notice a curl of smoke from a distillery chimney. No two of Scotland's famous malt whiskies are the same. The Malt Whisky Trail in Speyside is a signposted road tour which takes in an area where there are a great number of distilleries, most of which welcome visitors. In addition there is a wealth of natural beauty, crisp clean air and cultural heritage to explore and enjoy.

ABOVE AND CENTRE, *decorative labels from two of the distilleries along the route*

BELOW, *near Craigellachie Bridge the road runs close to the River Avon, with Ben Avon in the distance*

MALT WHISKY, until recently, has been one of Scotland's best kept secrets. Although there are many spirits distilled throughout the world, there is none to match the subtlety of variation in flavour and texture of malt whisky. The secret of whisky may well have come to Scotland with the monks as they carried the message of Christianity around Europe. This water of life, or *uisge-beatha* in Gaelic, is now an intrinsic part of Scottish culture, as mysterious as the dark glens from which the essential waters flow and inextricably linked with the momentous events of Scottish history, as at Culloden, when it was used instead of wine to serve Communion.

There are over 100 distilleries in operation in Scotland, and the heartland of this industry is undoubtedly Speyside, although there is also a smaller concentration

of distilleries in the Western Isles, in particular Islay. The Malt Whisky Trail is a signposted road tour which takes in eight participating distilleries, but the country through which this route takes you is home to at least 30 distilleries, with yet more on the fringes.

The Malt Whisky Trail has no actual starting or finishing point. The small village of Tomintoul lies at a height of 1160 feet (351 m) above sea level and is the highest village in the Highlands; it is an ideal starting and finishing point for this round tour. It was built at the behest of the fourth Duke of Gordon in 1754 after the Battle of Culloden, when the Hanoverian presence in the Highlands was still strong. It stands on an old military route that linked Fort George on the Moray coast with Edinburgh.

Heading north out of Tomintoul down its long straight main street from the village square, the A939 wends its way high above the River Avon (pronounced Aan), which lies in a birch and alder wooded valley. A little way out of the village you

ABOVE, *the River Avon near Tomintoul winds beneath the old Bridge of Avon*

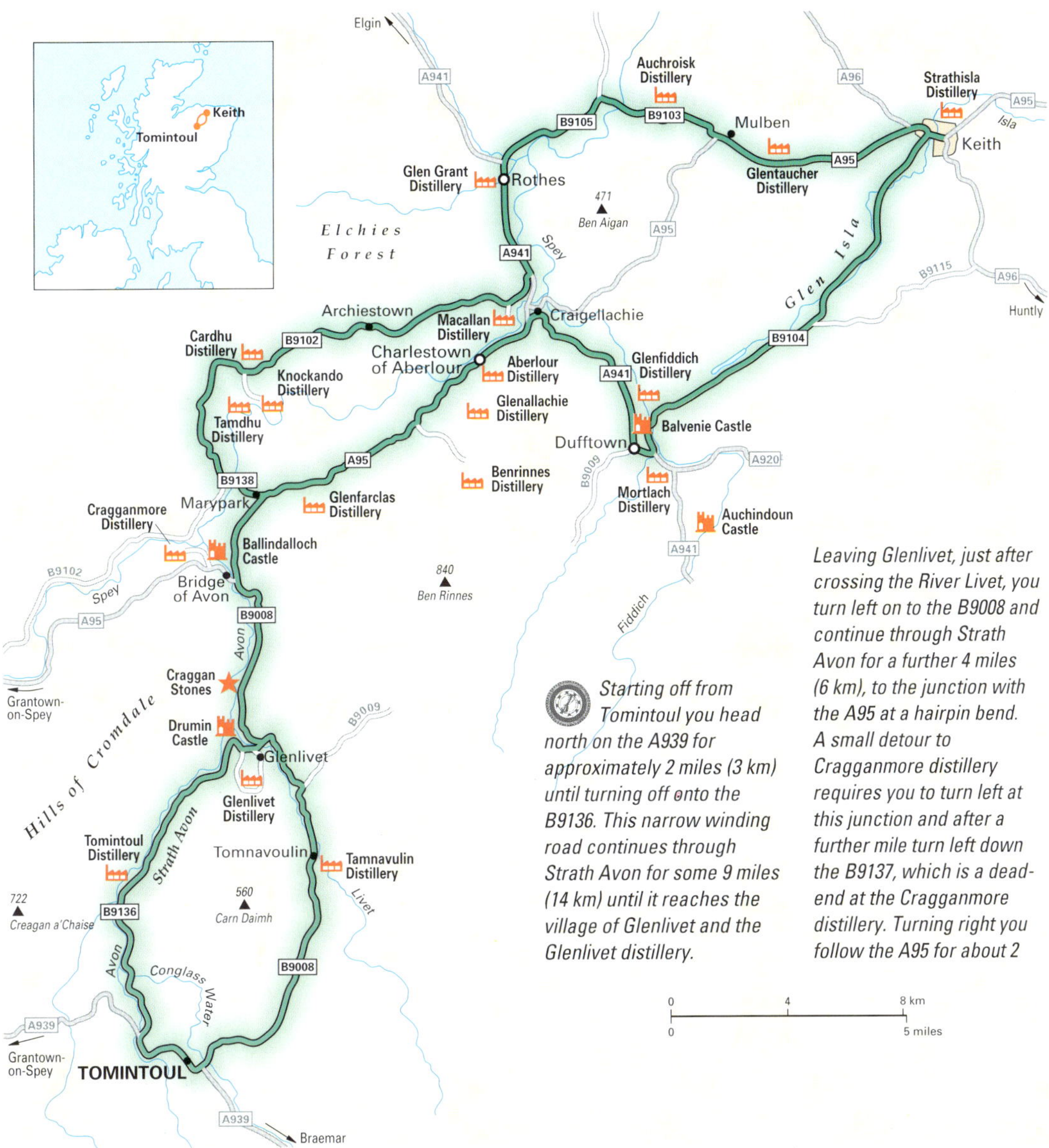

Starting off from Tomintoul you head north on the A939 for approximately 2 miles (3 km) until turning off onto the B9136. This narrow winding road continues through Strath Avon for some 9 miles (14 km) until it reaches the village of Glenlivet and the Glenlivet distillery.

Leaving Glenlivet, just after crossing the River Livet, you turn left on to the B9008 and continue through Strath Avon for a further 4 miles (6 km), to the junction with the A95 at a hairpin bend. A small detour to Cragganmore distillery requires you to turn left at this junction and after a further mile turn left down the B9137, which is a dead-end at the Cragganmore distillery. Turning right you follow the A95 for about 2 miles (3.5 km) before taking a left turn on to the B9138, and shortly afterwards at the junction with the B9102 you turn right. This road takes you past the Tamdhu and Cardhu distilleries. The road passes Craigellachie on the opposite bank of the River Spey and joins the A941 heading north to Rothes-on-Spey, where the Glen Grant distillery is to be found. From Rothes-on-Spey the route follows the B9105, B9103 and finally the A95 on its way to Keith and the Strathisla distillery. From Keith you follow the B9104, which passes through Strathisla to Dufftown, with its seven distilleries, including Glenfiddich, before heading northwards again on the A941 to Craigellachie where you join the A95, and thence to Aberlour. After about 4 miles (7 km), you come to the Glenfarclas distillery. From here you begin to retrace your path, turning left onto the B9008 and following this road through Glenlivet to the Tamnavulin distillery, and from there back to Tomintoul and the end of the round trip of some 80 miles (128 km).

take the B9136 and continue with the river to your left. It is a river of deep peaceful pools, interspersed with rushing muddled streams where families of goosanders can be seen in the summer and dippers flit from stone to stone. Just past this junction, the A939 crosses the River Avon. The road is now carried by a new bridge which stands just upstream of the old Bridge of Avon, built during the construction of the military road in 1754. In the valley the land has been improved: cattle and sheep graze here and crops of barley, oats and turnips are grown. Just after crossing the Conglass Water and rounding a corner you come to Tomintoul distillery, which sits next to the road surrounded by its white painted fence. It was only the third new distillery to be built this century and produced its first distillation in 1965.

Past Moor and Mountain

The road continues through wonderful scenery with pasture down by the river, and a strip of dense semi-natural birch wood with a rich and varied understorey of plants and fungi supports a wide variety of birds, including redpoll, siskin, Scottish crossbill and buzzard. Above are the peaks of Carn Daimh (1848 feet, 560 m) and Carn Liath (1812 feet, 549 m) to the east and Creagan a' Chaise (2383 feet, 722 m) to the west, covered in heather moor over which red and roe deer roam and flocks of sheep are scattered. This is a breeding ground for snipe, redshank, curlew and short-eared owls.

The ruins of Drumin Castle, the former stronghold of Alexander Stewart, the 'Wolf of Badenoch', can be seen from the road shortly before it crosses the River Livet, a tributary of the River Avon, which itself empties into the mighty River Spey. Glenlivet has been synonymous with Speyside whisky for as long as the amber liquid has been produced either legally or illegally. The first record of whisky is from 1494, when a listing of 'eight bolls of malt to Friar John Cor wherewith to make aquavitae' is found in the Scottish Exchequer Rolls. After the Act of Union in 1707 both malt and whisky became taxable at such extortionate levels that many illicit stills sprung up, and only after the 1823 Excise Act was passed did they eventually disappear (more or less). The reputation of the illicit whisky produced in Glenlivet was so great that even King George IV ensured he was kept in good supply. The Glenlivet distillery was the first to be granted a licence under the 1823 Act. The present distillery is at

BELOW, *from a vantage point high on Ben Rinnes, Glen Livet can be seen across the wild landscape*

Minmore, having moved there in 1858.

From Glenlivet the B9008 north takes you through wooded countryside with the River Avon running in a deep valley to your left. Just before Craggan Farm, and set into an alcove in the fence, are the Craggan Stones which were used for clandestine open-air preaching by dissenters from the Church of Scotland in 1843. From these meetings the Free Church of Scotland, known as 'The Wee Free', resulted.

Just on from here you come to a junction marked by a war memorial; left is sign-posted to Grantown-on-Spey, right to Charlestown of Aberlour. The Malt Whisky Trail route takes you right, but if you permit yourself a short detour, go left through Bridge of Avon. As you cross the new bridge, you can admire the old one set down to the right, with a turreted gatehouse which guards one of the entrances to Ballindalloch Castle. This fine house is an example of the 16th-century Scottish Baronial style. The house stands in grounds which are contained by both the River Avon and the River Spey. Just past Bridge of Avon you turn right onto the B9137, which takes you to the Cragganmore distillery lying nestled in a dip surrounded by Scots pine. Founded in 1869, this small distillery produces a 12-year old malt with an almost herbal bouquet – an aristocrat amongst the malt whiskies of Speyside.

Rejoining the Malt Whisky Trail proper, taking the A95 towards Charlestown of Abelour, turn left on to the B9138, crossing the River Spey, and then turn right at the junction with the B9102, the road to Archiestown and Craigellachie. Knockando distillery lies off the road on the high wooded bank of the River Spey, resplendent in its whitewash with the pagoda head rising through the trees. The road continues on through pasture land and coniferous forest framed by the ever present surrounding mountains. Tamdhu and Cardhu distilleries come in quick succession, both official stops on the Malt Whisky Trail. Tamdhu was built in 1896, and is situated on a great sweeping bend in the River Spey, surrounded by dense woodland. The long-disused Victorian railway station at Knockando has been converted into the reception centre for the distillery. Cardhu distillery was first licensed in 1824, only one year after the Excise Act was passed, although the owner, John Cumming, was a notorious whisky smuggler and had been distilling whisky at the site since 1811. The 12-year-old malt is light and smooth with a hint of sweet peat smoke.

Approaching Craigellachie, on a small hill overlooking the River Spey is the site of the Macallan distillery, where whisky has been distilled since the late 1700s. The first licensed distillation at Macallan, however, took place in 1824, and to this day great care is taken in the selection of the sherry casks in which the spirit is laid down to age. The result is a range of malt whiskies which exude richness, complexity and finesse. The 18-year-old malt is a dram for the true connoisseur, with its deep amber colour and full flavour recalling the years spent lying in the cask with its mixture of sherry and oak.

Heading north on the A941 along the valley of the River Spey, the skyline on your right is dominated by Ben Aigan, whose bare peak at 1554 feet (471 m) protrudes through a skirt of conifers, whilst to the left is the sprawling mass of Elchins Forest. The village of Rothes-on-Spey is surrounded by five distilleries: Glen Grant (the official stop on the Whisky Trail), Glenrothes, Glen Spey, Speyburn and Caperdonich. King Edward I passed south through the Glen of

ABOVE, *the River Spey, here seen at Craigellachie, is a constant feature of the Malt Whisky Trail*

BELOW, *the distinctive pagoda-like tower of the Strathisla distillery at Keith is typical of the older kilns*

Rothes in 1296 and again in his great invasion of 1303, but the village was not founded until 20 years after the defeat of the Clans at Culloden in 1746.

The Glen Grant distillery opened in 1840. As with so many of the older distilleries, its founders, the Grant brothers, John and James, were erstwhile whisky smugglers. The son of James Grant, Major James, built a second distillery in 1898, known as Glen Grant No. 2, on the other side of the road and joined the two together by a pipe running above the road. This distillery closed in 1902 and only reopened in 1965 as Caperdonich distillery, which produces mainly whisky for blending rather than its own malt. The other distilleries all have their tales to tell. Speyburn distillery is built on the site where Rothes criminals were executed, and the place is reputed to be haunted by the ghosts of some of these unfortunates. Glenrothes distillery came into production in 1891 and the first whisky came off the stills on the night of the great Tay Bridge disaster. The Glen Spey distillery stands on the bank of the Rothes Burn and is overlooked by the ruins of Castle Rothes, which for centuries was the stronghold of the Leslies, Earls of Rothes, who led the Covenanters against Cromwell.

From Rothes-on-Spey the Malt Whisky Trail follows the B9015 north-eastwards, but lovers of fine whisky may be tempted to make a detour to the ancient cathedral city of Elgin. This road takes you through rolling country-side and past six distilleries which lie in the Glen of Lossie, including Linkwood with its smoky, light whisky with a spicy apple tang, and Longmorn.

Keith itself, with its solid stone-built houses, is the archetypal Highland town, and is the very hub of life in the area. There are records of a settlement on this site since AD700, and in 1195 it was included in the charter of lands granted to the Abbey of Kinloss by William the Lion. The current town is based on plans set down by the local laird in 1750 in the wake of the Jacobite Rebellion. Next to the churchyard on the banks of the River Isla is the small stone packhorse bridge, which dates from 1609 and was once the only means of crossing the river. The Strathisla distillery is an official stop on the Malt Whisky Trail. It is arguably the oldest distillery in Scotland, starting as Milltown distillery in 1786. The distillery draws its water from a spring, the

BELOW, *years of ageing in oak casks result in the smooth taste of the mature whisky – discarded barrels are seen here near Keith*

Fons Buliens, which was documented by the Dominican monks who lived here in the 12th century. The 12-year-old malt has a fruity yet malty palate. In contrast, Glen Keith distillery, a converted meal mill, was a very recent addition to the industry in 1960. It lies on the opposite side of the River Isla.

Keith marks the north-eastern extremity of the Malt Whisky Trail, and the B9014 now takes you south-westwards towards Dufftown. The road travels through the picturesque Glen Isla, with its meadows, forests and mountains. On the outskirts of Keith lies a third distillery, Strathmill, which nestles down on the banks of the River Isla. It was established in 1891 and was formerly called the Glenisla-Glenlivet distillery. The road between Keith and Dufftown is a wilderness in terms of distilleries, but the wild unspoilt countryside is worthy of your attention and appreciation.

DUFFTOWN – A TOWN BUILT ON SEVEN STILLS

Dufftown has been likened to Rome. Where Rome was built on seven hills, Dufftown prospered on the proceeds of seven stills. Dufftown is a robust settlement which only began to take shape in 1817 at the instigation of the local laird, the Earl of Fife, James Duff. The Town House Tower, built in 1836, is at the hub of this bustling little town and is the dominating feature as you enter the town from any direction. On the Tower there is a plaque to the memory of George Stephen, a son of the town who gained fame as the co-founder of the Canadian-Pacific Railway.

Mortlach is the oldest distillery in Dufftown, having been established in 1823. It is centred

ABOVE, *Dufftown's famous Town House Tower is set against the green moorland landscape of the Grampians*

ABOVE, *at Glenfiddich, north of Dufftown, whisky is both distilled and bottled on site by an old-established family company*

RIGHT, *a nature trail at Tomintoul provides a chance to explore at the beginning or end of the journey*

BELOW, *these copper whisky stills in the Glenfiddich distillery at Dufftown are beaten by hand into onion shapes*

around a well and, although now producing a fine malt whisky, for many years it was a stop–start operation, the buildings being used in the intervening periods as a barley store, a place of worship for members of the Free Church of Scotland, and as a brewery.

For many years Mortlach was the only distillery in Dufftown, but in the late 1800s there was a spate of developments, including the establishment of the distillery which produces what is probably the best known malt whisky in the world, Glenfiddich. This distillery was built in 1887 and is now one of only three where the whisky is still bottled where it is made. The other five of the original seven distilleries associated with Dufftown are Balvenie, Convalmore, Parkmore, Dufftown and Glendullan. Newer additions are Pittyvaich and the newest of all Scottish distilleries, Kininvie, founded in 1992.

The more ancient history of the area is reflected in the evocative remains of Balvenie Castle, which has for more than seven centuries commanded the high ground above Dufftown. The castle has a unique double-leaf yett, the Scottish equivalent of a portcullis, with horizontal bars criss-crossed with vertical ones making it almost impossible to dismantle. The castle has known a number of famous visitors – Edward I was there in 1304, Mary, Queen of Scots visited in 1562 and the Duke of Cumberland billeted troops there prior to the battle at Culloden. Another castle of note near Dufftown, a few miles down the A941 towards Rhynie, is that of Auchindoun, the stronghold of Adam Gordon. He was responsible for the burning of Corgarff Castle in 1571, as part of the squabble between the Gordons and the Forbes, who were on opposing sides of the Catholic–Protestant divide during the Reformation. Corgarff Castle has survived, but Auchindoun Castle is no more than a broken shell as a result of it being sacked and burned in 1592. The remains stand on the protective earthen mound with the imposing slopes of The Scalp rising to 1634 feet (495 m) at its back.

Heading north out of Dufftown you soon come to the village of Craigellachie, which sits at the junction of the River Fiddich with the River Spey. This village lies on the side of a hill with its rows of cottages terraced into the hillside. One of Thomas Telford's many bridges, dating from 1814, spans the River Spey here with its cast iron span and turreted granite supports. The Craigellachie distillery opened in 1891, but the building now on the site is the result of a rebuilding programme in 1964–5.

A few miles further on is the village of Charlestown of Aberlour, which lies at the very heart of the Malt Whisky Trail. Like so many of the Highland villages it has a long main street and a village square at the hub. It lies on the banks of the River Spey and in the shadow of the Conval Hills, with the dominating peak of Ben Rinnes

at 2755 feet (840 m). It is claimed that on a clear, calm day you can see the smoke of 43 distilleries from its summit.

Heading out of Charlestown of Aberlour south-west on the A95 you are treated to further majestic views up the broad valley of the mighty River Spey,winding on its way down from the Monadhliath Mountains; no two views are the same and each is as awe-inspiring and refreshing as the last. Aberlour distillery was first built in 1826 and, although it has burned down twice, it survives to this day to produce a fine 12-year-old malt, Aberlour-Glenlivet with its distinctive sweet, spicy flavour and smooth, creamy finish. Further down the road, set well back in the shadow of Ben Rinnes, are the Glenallachie and Benrinnes distilleries. Glenfarclas distillery, nestling beneath the slopes of Cairn Guish (1634 feet, 495m) with Ben Rinnes behind it, produces some highly acclaimed whisky, most notably the 8-year-old malt, Glenfarclas 105, which is the strongest malt in an official bottling.

Glenfarclas is the penultimate stop on the official Malt Whisky Trail. From here you retrace your steps along the B9008, which gives you the opportunity to admire and enjoy the view you had at your back, looking up Strath Avon to the Cairngorms and Grampian Mountains with the dominating peak of Ben Avon at 3868 feet (1172m), which even in the height of summer can have snow lying in some of the more sheltered corries. At Glenlivet you continue on the B9008, following the River Livet. Beyond the village, and off to left in what is now a forestry plantation, is the land where the Battle of Glenlivet was fought in 1594. A force of about 2000 local men who supported the Catholic Earls of Errol and Huntly routed 10,000 highlanders under the Protestant Earl of Argyll.

Shortly you come to the Tamnavulin distillery, the last official stop on the Malt Whisky Trail. The first official stop was Glenlivet, one of the oldest legal stills, and it is perhaps fitting that the last stop is one of the newest, having been built in 1966. The road from Tamnavulin takes you through the Braes of Glenlivet and thence back to where you started in the centre of Tomintoul and maybe a wee dram – but where do you start?

PRACTICAL INFORMATION

- A map of the Malt Whisky Trail and some useful information is available from Tourist Information Offices, including the Aviemore and Spey Valley Tourist Board, Aviemore PH22 1PP, Tel. 01479 810363
- Most of the distilleries on this route welcome visitors for different periods of the year. Details for all of them and others besides are contained in the excellent book by Gordon Brown *The Whisky Trails*, A Prion Guide (1993).
- The scenery changes with the seasons and there is much to recommend the different times of the year. However, heavy snow falls in winter make some roads impassable.

The Antrim Coast Road from Bushmills to Larne

JOHN M BAXTER

The glens of Antrim and the surrounding coast from Bushmills to Larne contain some of the most beautiful and spectacular scenery in Northern Ireland. Originally intended for military use, the Coast Road was completed in the 1830s and now provides an artery along which travellers can experience the long history of war, settlement, and religion. Prehistoric relics, raths, mounds and castles, churches and friaries recall earlier times and conflicts, together with remains of the industrial age.

ABOVE, *Larne's industrial landscape conceals remains from the Neolithic period*

BELOW RIGHT, *the whole of Glenariff has been designated a forest park, with wonderful moor and mountain views*

BELOW, *stormy skies over Cushendun, a favourite haunt of the poet John Masefield*

THE GLENS OF ANTRIM and the surrounding coast from Larne in the south to Bushmills in the north contain some of the most spectacular scenery in Northern Ireland, and this route is rightly proclaimed as one of the most beautiful journeys in the world.

The starting point is Larne, a grey town, which can trace its history back to the Vikings, who named Larne Lough, 'Ulfrecksfjord'. It is notable as standing near the place where Edward Bruce landed in 1315 in his abortive attempt to free Ireland of English rule and forge a Celtic alliance. Edward was the brother of Robert Bruce, King of Scotland, who inflicted defeat on King Edward's army at the Battle of Bannockburn after reputedly having been inspired by watching a spider try and try again to weave a web in an cave on the island of Rathlin, where he was hiding after defeat at the hands of the English in 1306.

Larne is today still the landing point for many more peaceful visitors who make the ferry crossing from Stranraer or Cairnryan. For these and many others, Larne is the gateway at the start of this wonderful journey, which takes in secluded, white sandy bays, dramatic headlands, towering cliffs and outstanding sea views,with the ever present evidence of millennia of history to be savoured and explored.

The A2 leading north out of Larne hugs the coast of Drains Bay and moves on to Ballygalley.

The road has been built on an ancient raised beach from which the sea has long retreated. A persistent search will reveal flint implements among the pebbles, a reminder of the settlers who lived here some 9000 years ago. This area yielded the best flint in highland Britain, with plentiful supplies either freed by erosion of the chalk cliffs or unearthed by open cast quarrying, as at a site on Ballygalley Hill. Ballygalley Castle, now a hotel, is a fine example of a 17th-century Scottish Baronial style castle, built around 1625 by James Shaw of Greenock. This is one of the few 17th-century buildings still in use in Northern Ireland.

The road continues its flirtation with the sea as it wends further north. It is periodically closed by mud slides from the hills. You are treated to panoramas of patchworks of fields and proud headlands which appear stacked one on another as they disappear into the distance. On a clear, bright day the outline of the Rhinns of Galloway and the Mull of Kintyre can be picked out.

BELOW, *an exhilarating drive along the coast road at Ballygalley gives views of the ruined Carne Castle from the headland*

The route starts in Larne, which may be your arrival port if coming from mainland Britain, or it can be easily reached by road from Belfast by either following the A2 coast road through Carrickfergus and Whitehead or cutting inland on the A8 via Ballynure. From Larne the A2 heads north along the coast. It is a relatively narrow and winding road which can be very busy, particularly in the summer months. The road is also susceptible to being closed by landslides, caused by the heavy rains which occur in the autumn and winter months.

The village of Glenarm marks the beginning of the glens of Antrim and, if the fancy takes you, any of these glens are worth a detour, each having its own unique character and charm worth savouring.

You continue on the A2 through Carnlough, around Garron Point where there is a car park which lets you stop to marvel at the view, and then drive on to Cushendall where there is a tourist information office. From Cushendall you continue on the A2 over the Glendun Viaduct, and shortly after this you turn right onto the B92 into Cushendun. From there, you take the unclassified coastal road to Torr Head. This is not for drivers of a nervous disposition as the road is very narrow with passing places and often with precipitous drops to the sea below.

There are a number of very steep inclines and declines punctuated by a series of hairpin bends.

You join the A2 again at Ballyvoy, but then on leaving Ballycastle you should take the B15 past Carrick-a-Rede. Rejoin the A2 for a short distance before turning onto the B146 to the Giant's Causeway, then join the A2 again for the last few miles into Bushmills.

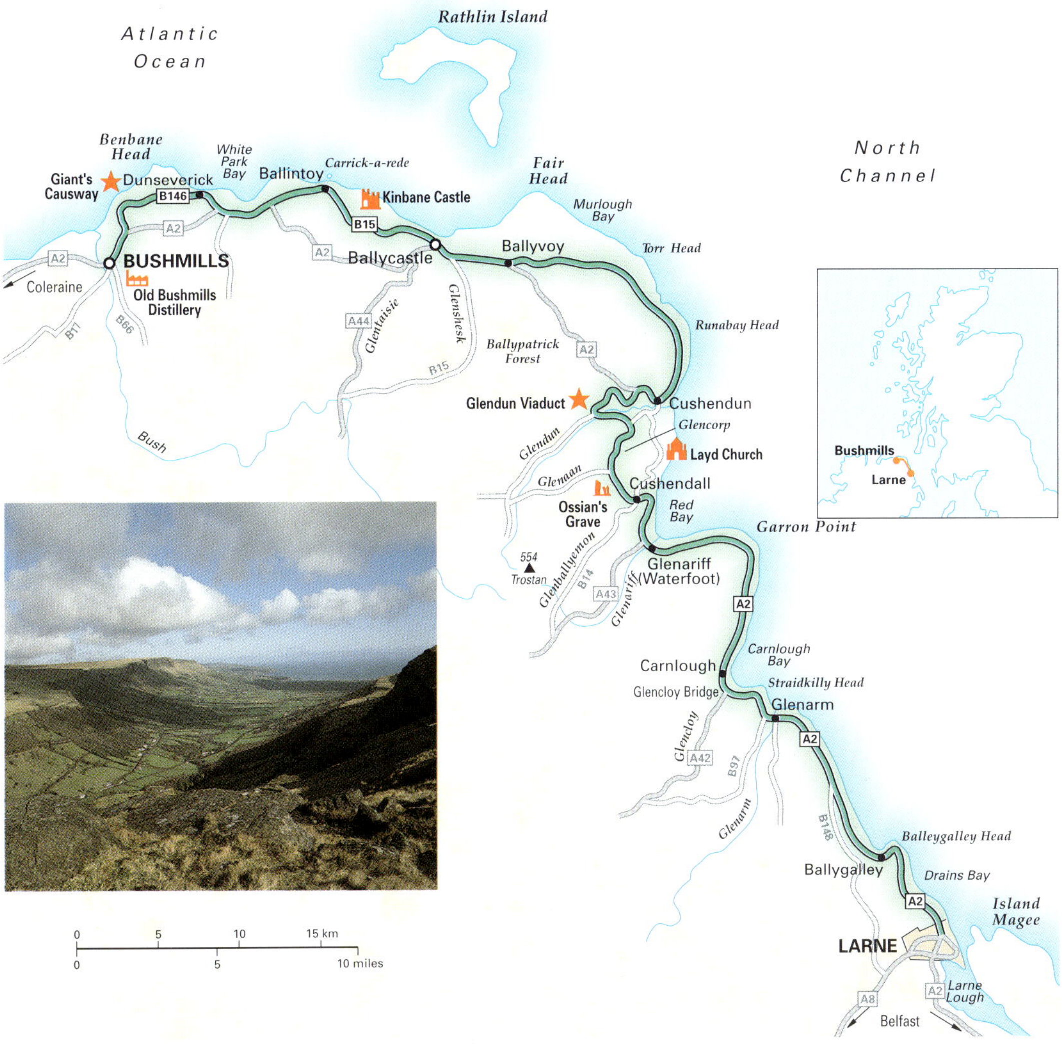

RIGHT, *the tiny harbour at Carnlough is enclosed by high stone walls*

THE GLENS OF ANTRIM

The village of Glenarm, which lies nestled in the elbow of Glenarm Bay, signals the start of the nine glens of Antrim, all worth exploring, each with its own special charm and character. Glenarm is a quaint village with its origins in medieval times, having grown up around a 15th-century Franciscan friary established by the Bisset family, and a later 16th-century castle. Some remains of the friary nave, chancel, transept and cloister survive to this day in the graveyard of St Patrick's parish church.

Northwards from Glenarm, the road rounds Straidkilly Point and crosses Glencloy Bridge, which marks the seaward end of Glencloy – 'the glen of hedges'. From here it is a short drive to Carnlough, a sprawl of terraced houses resolutely facing the Irish Sea, together with its quaint and picturesque harbour. The rock faces of the limestone quarry form a backdrop to the village. The Londonderry Arms Hotel dominates the village. It was built in 1848 as a coaching inn during the great potato blight of 1845-1849 by Frances Anne Vane Tempest , Marchioness of Londonderry, who inherited great tracts of land between Glenarm and Cushendall from her mother, the Countess of Antrim. The Marchioness and her husband, Charles William, Lord Stewart, the third Marquis of Londonderry, were notable as responsible landlords who initiated much building work during the Great Famine to try to provide employment for their tenants. After her death her grandson inherited the Carnlough estate, and on his death the estate and hotel passed to his second cousin, Sir Winston Churchill.

The road north from Carnlough continues to hug the coast, with the hills behind rising up to the Antrim Plateau at around 1148 feet (350m). As the road rounds Garron Point and heads west

BELOW, *the village of Glenarm is set among green hills sweeping down to the sea*

along the bottom of Red Bay you cannot fail to be in awe of the majesty of the sweeping slopes criss-crossed with hedge-lined fields, suddenly breaking into the vertical rock faces of the scarp. The long history of conflict in this area can be seen with the 16th-century stone castles, many of them built on the remains of mottes, earthwork defences characteristic of the early Anglo-Norman conquests of the 12th century.

A short distance north is the small, sleepy village of Cushendall. On the plateau behind the village between Glenballyemon and Glenaan lies the stone age axe factory at Tievebulliagh, where there is a plentiful supply of porcellanite, a hard, tough, bluish-grey rock. This is such a rare rock type that it can be fairly certain that any porcellanite blade found in the British Isles comes from County Antrim. The only other significant source is at Brockley on Rathlin Island. Records of porcellanite implements range from as far afield as Aberdeenshire in the north to Kent and Dorset in the south.

On leaving Cushendall, there is a choice of either following the small coast road to Cushendun or remaining on the A2 as it takes a short digression inland to follow the line of Glencorp. The former route presents the opportunity of further marvellous sea views, and has the added attraction of the fine ruins of Layd Church standing in its graveyard beside a fast flowing stream above Port Obe. Traditionally a Franciscan foundation, it was a parish church in 1306 and continued in use until 1790. There are many fine gravestones in the yard including memorials to the MacDonnells. Following the A2 instead of the coast road, it is worth a short detour along the Cushendall – Ballymoney road to visit Ossian's grave. From the car park at the side of the road a footpath leads uphill to this Neolithic court tomb, with its semicircular forecourt opening into a two-chambered burial gallery, romantically named after the early Christian warrior poet. As a bonus, there are glorious views from here of Glendun, Glenaan and further afield across the water to Scotland. Returning to the A2 and continuing north, the road passes through Glencorp across the Glendun Viaduct, designed by Charles Lanyon, which spans the rushing waters of the Glendun river, and finally descends into Cushendun, a sleepy peaceful place. Cave House, now a Catholic retreat, was once the holiday home of the poet John Masefield. In what might be called the centre of Cushendun there is a pub which is reputedly one of the smallest in the world – McBride's Bar. Cushendun is an ideal place to stop, relax, and reflect on what you have seen so on the journey so far.

At this point the A2 strikes out to the north-west across the plateau, bordered by peat bog and skirting the great Ballypatrick Forest. It is better to take the coast road, although it is most certainly not for the faint hearted nor those in a hurry. The road is a collection of twists and turns, steep inclines and declines which demand your full attention, which is a problem if you are driving, as the most marvellous views are there to be enjoyed. A small diversion on this road brings you to the auxiliary coast guard station at Torr Head; here, when standing at the sea edge, you are only 12 miles (19 km) from the Mull of Kintyre across the North Channel, the nearest point on Ireland to the Scottish mainland.

The road from Torr Head strikes west towards Ballycastle, rejoining the main A2 again at Ballyvoy. Taking this route and ignoring the inviting little side roads to Murlough Bay and Benmore or Fair Head will deny you some of the greatest jewels of this journey. The headland and chalk grasslands at Fair Head and above Murlough Bay are part of the largest tract of wild coastline remaining in Northern Ireland. There is an intriguing mixture of plants, adapted to the varying conditions created by the influence of the salt spray and underlying rock types. Ling, bell heather, dwarf whin and harebell are to be found, together with various species of orchid. The cliffs at Fair Head are awe inspiring, with their sheer drop of 396 feet (120 m) to boulder scree below, comprising blocks of up to 26 feet (8 m) in diameter, prized off the cliff face as the ice thawed at the end of the last Ice Age. These cliffs are not only a superb vantage point for views across Rathlin Sound to the island of that name and beyond, but also provide nesting sites for a range of birds including guillemot, puffin, razorbill, fulmar and kittiwake together with peregrine falcon and buzzard.

ABOVE, *the road emerges from the trees to cross the Glendun viaduct spanning the fast-flowing river*

BELOW, *peaceful Cushendun has a sandy beach and good river fishing*

ABOVE, *the island of Carrick-a-Rede can be seen from the road, but to visit it you must cross a rope bridge*

BELOW, *the extraordinary formations of the Giant's Causeway, said to be the stepping stones of the giant Finn MacCoul*

A VIEW OF THE PAST

The country through which the route has taken you holds many insights into the past, with extensive remains of early Christian settlements from around 400 to 1100 AD. Remains of fortified, enclosed farmsteads known as raths are common. Settlements were also built on artificial islands of brushwood, timbers and stones, known as crannogs. These settlements were more defensible than the raths and are more common in some of the lakeland areas of Ireland. Although rare in Antrim, a good example of a stone-revetted crannog can be seen at Lough-na-Cranagh at Fair Head.

Ballycastle is located at the confluence of Glenshesk and Glentaisie. The harbour at Ballycastle was once important for the shipment of coal won from the surrounding hills, but this industry is now extinct. The harbour, however, still provides the vital daily link by ferry, when the weather permits, between the mainland and Rathlin Island. The link between Ballycastle and Rathlin was also exploited by Marconi during his early experiments with radio. He established a transmitter on the shore at Colliery Bay just east of Ballycastle and a receiver on Rathlin Island. Reminders of more ancient history are to be seen in the remains of the Bonamargy Friary. Founded in about 1500 by Rory McQuillan, this Third Order Franciscan friary was used until the middle of the 17th century. The gatehouse is set in an earth bank and the remains of the long narrow church still display the flamboyant tracery in the windows. A vault running south from the church is the burial place of the MacDonnells, the Earls of Antrim.

Heading out of Ballycastle on the B15 a short detour takes you to the evocative ruins of Kinbane Castle, perched on a limestone promontory. This 16th-century castle was a stronghold of the MacDonnells and was vital in the struggle for power between the Gaelic families of the MacDonnells and MacQuillans in North Antrim. From here the road continues west along the coast with more spectacular views out over the sea, which is dotted with isolated stacks and small islands. Of these Sheep Island and Carrick-a-Rede (which means 'the rock in the road', for it blocks the way of returning salmon as they make their way along the coast,) are the most notable for their breeding birds, including large numbers of cormorant, razorbill, guillemot and kittiwake, with flocks of oystercatcher and eider scattered

along the coast. You may be very lucky and catch sight of a chough – a member of the crow family. It is very distinctive with its long curved red beak, and is now very rare in Northern Ireland with only a few pairs nesting on the more inaccessible cliff faces. Although it should not be attempted by the faint-hearted, it is possible to make a trip across the narrow rope bridge which links Carrick-a-Rede to the mainland, providing access for the salmon fishermen to their nets.

The road wends on to Ballintoy with its striking white church, which stands out in vivid contrast to the blue of the Atlantic Ocean on a sunny summer's day. The harbour was built to accommodate the schooners which carried the burnt limestone from the adjacent kilns and quarries.

West of Ballintoy you will come to White Park Bay, a magnificent sweep of white sand backed by sand dunes, seen at its best when the great Atlantic breakers are crashing in. The sand dunes hide much about the earliest inhabitants of the area and are rich in wildlife, with several species of orchid and a number of rare snails and insects. The bay can be reached from the car park and there is little more exhilarating than a walk along the white sands with the wind in your face and the sound of crashing Atlantic breakers competing with the cries of the circling seabirds.

The Giant's Causeway

Revived, you can head west once again on the B146, which enables you to keep to the coast, passing the stark ruins of Dunseverick Castle, traditionally the capital of the ancient kingdom of Dalriada. A few miles further along the road is the Giant's Causeway Visitor Centre, a focal point for any visit to the Giant's Causeway coast, which is both a National Nature Reserve and a World Heritage Site. The Causeway is a most striking array of basalt columns and outcrops formed about 60 million years ago by the cooling of lava.

This area of the Northern Ireland coast has been visited by many distinguished visitors, including Mark Twain and Sir Walter Scott. The coast is rugged and storm swept and has claimed many ship wrecks, but perhaps none as famous as the Spanish galleass *Girona*, a survivor from the ill-fated Spanish Armada, which was wrecked off the coast with only five survivors out of 1300 on board. Much of the treasure she was carrying remains on the sea bed, but some has been recovered and can be seen on display in the Ulster Museum in Belfast.

The end of the journey is in sight as you approach the town of Bushmills, lying on the River Bush. Here you can watch local and visitor alike trying to catch salmon in the river. The town has been the centre of industry since the 17th century. In 1633, Sir Randall MacDonnell leased a site for a woollen mill, later used as a paper mill then a linen mill before being converted in 1883 into what is said to have been the first hydro-electric power station in the world. Of all the industries which have come and gone, by far the most famous must be the distillery. It was established in 1608 and is the oldest licensed whiskey distillery in the world. The products, Bushmills Malt together with Old Bushmills and Black Bush, delight the palate and are rightly acclaimed as some of the smoothest whiskeys known to man. There is no better place to end this journey than with a tour of the distillery and a sample of its amber liquid.

Practical Information

- The route can be travelled in a day, even allowing time for stops at some of the landmarks and monuments along the way. It is possible to a take more leisurely trip over a number of days and there are any number of small hotels and friendly bed and breakfast houses in many of the villages and towns.

- The main office of the Northern Ireland Tourist Board at St Anne's Court, 59 North Street, Belfast (Tel: 01232 231221) can provide a wealth of information about many of the places of interest.

The Corniche from Marseille to Menton

PIP LEAHY

For glamour you won't better it, for Modern Art lovers it will be a joy and of course there are the spectacular and varied views. This is surely one of the most beautiful journeys in the world, although you won't be enjoying it alone. Since the middle of the 19th century this small section of France's coastline has attracted both society's elite and most of the great artists of the time: their glittering legacy has endowed this stretch of coast with a mystique and allure that still endures today.

ABOVE, *a graceful statue outside 'Les Collettes', the home of the artist Renoir at Cagnes-sur-Mer*

RIGHT, *the fortified hill village of St Paul de Vence is crowned by its medieval church*

BELOW, *an unusual view of the coast road sweeping down to Monte-Carlo, free of high season traffic*

OUR ROUTE begins in France's second city and most important port: Marseille. It hasn't the glamour of resorts further along the coast, but it's a lively, cosmopolitan city nevertheless and there are plenty of reasons to spend some time exploring. Marseille has been in the business of trading, with varying changes of fortune, ever since it was founded by the ancient Greeks. Unsurprisingly, its heart is in the Vieux Port, but its hallmark has for a long time been the Canabière, the most famous of the city's main streets, where sailors and Sultans once rubbed shoulders. Running the length of Marseille's coastline is the Corniche Président J F Kennedy and if you look out to sea from here you'll get a good view of the Château d'If, built on one of the Frioul islands and made famous by Alexandre Dumas' tale *The Count of Monte-Cristo*.

After Marseille, it is more or less impossible to follow the coast by road (except for a drive to the end of the Cap Croisette and back) until Cassis, a

small, lively and attractive fishing port which caught the eye of artists such as Dufy and Matisse. It is also noted for the *calanques* (creeks) which lie just to the west, fine examples of a coastal feature which stretches from Marseille to Toulon. From Cassis to la Ciotat the road will take you on around Cap Canaille on the Corniche des Crêtes and past the highest cliffs in France, rising from the sea to 1188 feet (360 m).

The road from la Ciotat to Toulon runs through the pleasant resorts of les Lecques, Bandol and Sanary-sur-Mer and then cuts across the Cap Sicié peninsula to Toulon, France's leading naval base. All along this stretch of coast you will see the vineyards which produce the full-bodied Bandol wines. Hyères, which lies about 11 miles (18 km) to the east of Toulon, is the oldest resort on the Côte d'Azur and its grand villas are a legacy of the time when it was patronized by royalty and the cream of society. Today it is chiefly known for the palm trees and pot plants which it exports all over the world.

BELOW, *Hyères, in its sheltered setting, is the most southerly as well as the oldest of the Riviera resorts*

Once you leave the Président J F Kennedy Corniche in Marseille, follow the D559 to Cassis and then turn on to the D40 which follows the coast around Cap Canaille to la Ciotat. After la Ciotat rejoin the D559, leaving it only to visit the resorts of les Lecques and Bandol.
At Sanary-sur-Mer take the D616 around Cap Sicié to la Seyne and then Toulon. After Toulon a minor road, the D86, will take you around the Cap Carqueiranne rejoining the D559 at Carqueiranne itself and shortly after turning inland to Hyères. It is impossible to drive around Cap Bénat in a loop, so take the N98 out of Hyères and just before Bormes les Mimosas turn back on to the D559. At Bormes les Mimosas turn on to the D298 to explore Cap Bénat. From le Lavandou the D559 follows the coast to Cavalaire-sur-Mer and starts to cross the head of the Ramatuelle peninsula. At la Croix-Valmer turn on to the D93 which winds over the Col de Collebasse, after which you turn left on to the D61 through Ramatuelle and Gassin (it is possible to stay on the D93 to St-Tropez). At the end of the D61 turn right into the resort of St-Tropez. After you have visited St-Tropez join the N98 in the direction of Fréjus – this will take you along the Corniche des Maures through the coastal resorts of Port-Grimaud, Ste-Maxime and les Issambres to Fréjus Plage. After exploring Fréjus and neighbouring St-Raphäel rejoin the N98 (the Riviera road) which more or less hugs the coast to Menton, through the great Riviera resorts of Antibes, Cannes and Nice. The D2559 will take you around Cap d'Antibes. Biot is about 4 km from the coast on the D4 from la Brague; St Paul and Vence are reached via the D36 or minor D2 road from Cagnes-sur-Mer.

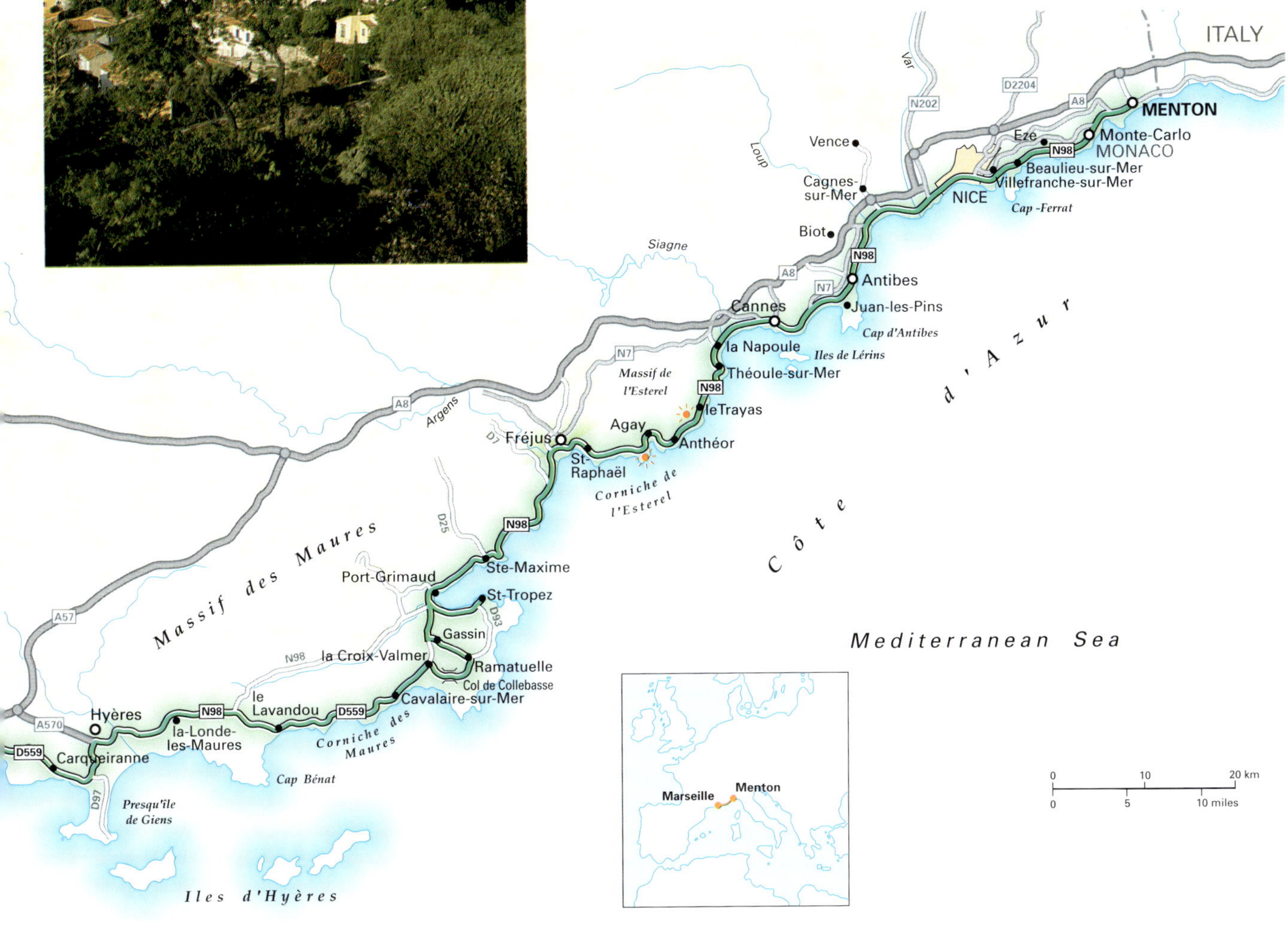

ABOVE, *St-Tropez, named after a martyred Roman centurion, was once a small republic with its own army and navy*

Old Hyères is a splendid medieval walled town clinging to the slopes of Castéou Hill, and to the south are the lagoon and salt marshes of the Giens Peninsula (Presqu'île de Giens.) More salt marshes are passed as you leave Hyères on the N98 and head for le Lavandou on the other side of the Cap Bénat.

Life in le Lavandou revolves around the busy marina and, like so many of the famous coastal resorts on the Riviera, it was once just a small fishing port. You will rarely see a genuine working boat now. The resort marks the start of the Corniche des Maures, named after the Maures Mountains which run down to the sea. A string of coastal villages merge into one another along this stretch of road; it was on the fine sandy beaches and small coves around Cavalaire-sur-Mer that the Allied forces landed in August 1944. Turning off the main road at la Croix-Valmer, a winding road will take you over the Collebasse Pass. Here there are superb views of the Baie de Cavalaire and the Hyères Islands, which lie just off the coast and are often known as the Iles d'Or, because of the golden hue of their steep cliffs. Turn left on yet another winding road to Ramatuelle, a typical old Provençal town, past the ruins of the Moulins de Paillas and on to the hilltop village of Gassin. On a clear day the distant peaks of the Alps are visible from Gassin.

ST-TROPEZ

At the other side of the Ramatuelle Promontory is St-Tropez, a resort which in recent years has been at the centre of controversy: its most famous resident Brigitte Bardot denounced the influx of tourists which descend on it each year. Certainly it gets almost unbearably crowded in the height of summer, but it is still possible to see the appeal it had for the likes of Matisse, Bonnard, Dufy and Seurat when it was just another quiet fishing village. In any case, it was Bardot who caused the place to become something of a cult town when she starred in Vadim's *And God Created Woman,* which was filmed here. It is worth fighting through the crowds to see the fine collection of paintings in the Musée de l'Annonciade.

The next resort along the coast is Port-Grimaud, an imitation Provençal fishing village built in the 1960s as an upmarket holiday complex – if you're lucky you might rub shoulders with a film star or two, but only the seriously wealthy can afford the houses here.

Less glitzy but nevertheless popular is Ste-Maxime, which faces St-Tropez across the bay. Rocky coves dent the shore from here to Fréjus Plage, the seaside annexe of one of the most historically interesting towns along the route.

Fréjus proper is a short way inland, its ancient harbour having been silted up by the River Argens. It was founded by Julius Caesar as a trading post on the Aurelian Way, the great road which the Romans built from Rome to Arles. It became an important Roman naval base, and at one time had a population greater than the 42,000 who inhabit it today. There are extensive Roman remains to explore.

Nearby St-Raphaël also has ancient origins; it was a holiday resort even in Roman times. After a period in the doldrums, thanks to the Saracens who plundered the coast in the 8th century, St-Raphaël became a fashionable resort once more at the end of the last century. Here is the beginning of one of the most beautiful and least built-up sections of the route, the Corniche de l'Esterel, also called the Corniche d'Or. Between here and la Napoule the coast is characterized by small coves and creeks, rugged promontories and minute bays. Agay, about 4½ miles (7 km) to the east of St-Raphaël, is the only resort of any size along this stretch, the others are well contained by their geography. Just before you reach Agay, look out for a turning to le Dramont semaphore. From here you will get a wonderful view of the Massif des Maures, the two rocks guarding the entrance to the Golfe de Fréjus (the Lion de Mer and the Lion de Terre) and the tiny Iles d'Or. It's also possible to see Mont Vinaigre, the highest peak of the Esterel Mountains. Another marvellous view can be enjoyed from the Pic du Cap Roux, which stands between Anthéor and le Trayas, a resort built on the highest point of the Corniche. The vivid red tints of the Esterels are displayed at their best on three peaks of the Cap Roux Range.

CANNES

Towards the end of the Corniche d'Or is the small resort of Théoule-sur-Mer – an important harbour in the 17th century – and after this la Napoule. There is no denying where you are, for across the bay is glittering, glitzy Cannes. It was an Englishman, Lord Brougham, who was responsible for turning the village into a sophisticated international resort. He set the fashion for wintering here in the middle of the 19th century and his example was soon followed by wealthy socialites, aristocrats and European royalty. La Croisette, Cannes' renowned seafront boulevard, was established during this time and became lined with luxury hotels and smart shops. It is still at the heart of the city and you will find the locals strolling here among the tourists. Old Canois (as it was then called) grew up around a watchtower built at the summit of Mont Chevalier. At its foot is the Vieux Port, laid out shortly after Lord Brougham began to attract his cronies here. Two new marinas have been added at the eastern end of the Boulevard de la Croisette, close to the now defunct Palm Beach Casino. Each year Hollywood descends on Cannes for the International Film Festival and the eyes and cameras of the world turn to the city. An aptly named suburb, la Californie, is the site of the Super-Cannes Observatory, where one of the finest views on the entire Côte d'Azur can be enjoyed.

BELOW, *Meryl Streep is one of the many stars who have left their imprint on Cannes*

To your right as you drive along the Golfe de la Napoule, and in striking contrast to the hullabaloo on the coast, are the peaceful Iles de Lérins. The monastery on the smaller of the two islands, St-Honorat, was once one of the most powerful in Christendom and supposedly produced 600 bishops and 20 saints.

Between Cannes and Antibes the road skirts the Cap d'Antibes, a peninsula which separates the Golfe Juan and the Baie des Anges. At its highest point is one of the most powerful lighthouses on the coast. Antibes' major claim to fame is the Musée Picasso, housed in the medieval château which for many years in the 14th and 15th centuries was the residence of the town's rulers at the time, the Grimaldis. Picasso, who was staying in Antibes, was allowed to use part of the château as a studio and he donated the work he completed there to the museum. Other great artists including Miró, de Stael, Ernst and Modigliani are also represented.

Just north of the town is the state-of-the-art

BELOW, *the sophisticated resort of Cannes is equally glittering by day or night*

INSET, *the architecture of the world-famous Casino at Monte-Carlo is extremely decorative*

TOP RIGHT, *Eze is one of the 'perched villages' of the Alpes Maritimes, built by peasants from local stone*

BELOW, *Monaco's exotic gardens flourish in the hot sun of the Mediterranean*

business park Sophia Antipolis, one of several in the area which have earned it the title of 'Silicon Valley of France'. Business income now outstrips tourism on the Côte d'Azur.

From Antibes the road takes you inexorably on towards Nice, the so-called Queen of the Riviera, passing expensive but nondescript sea-side conurbations. The more interesting villages are just inland: Biot with its Fernand Léger Museum, medieval Cagnes-sur-Mer, where Renoir lived and which has a fine collection of his work in the town's art museum, and still further inland from Cagnes, the hill villages of St-Paul and Vence, where Chagall lived until the end of his life.

NICE

Despite the hordes of tourists, Nice still manages to sparkle, and the jewel in her crown is undoubtedly the palm-lined Promenade des Anglais, with its views across the bay on one hand and sophisticated 'Belle Epoch' architecture on the other. As well as the evidence of Nice's Roman history, there are two notable museums in the town's smart suburb of Cimiez. The Musée Matisse shows a fine collection of the artist's works, while Chagall is represented in the Musée National du Message Biblique Marc Chagall.

PRACTICAL INFORMATION

■ If you attempt this journey in the summer months beware of traffic jams: many French people head south in August and unless you have booked well in advance it may be difficult to get accommodation. June or September are often the best times for a hassle-free visit in virtually guaranteed sunshine.

■ More information can be obtained from the Comité Régional du Tourisme (French Riviera Tourist Board), 55 Promenade des Anglais, 06000 Nice, Tel: 93 87 07 07, Fax: 9392 82 98, or the Provence-Alpes-Côte d'Azur office, 2 rue Henri-Barbusse, 13241 Marseille, Tel. 91 39 38 00, Fax 91 56 66 61.

At Nice you have to make a choice between the three Corniche roads which run to Menton. Napoleon's Grande Corniche offers long distance views, the Moyenne Corniche has dramatic bridges, or you can stay closer to sea level on the Corniche Inférieure.

The lowest of the three roads runs through Villefranche-sur-Mer, which stands at the entrance to dazzling Cap-Ferrat. Villefranche's medieval Chapelle de St-Pierre was decorated by Jean Cocteau. At Beaulieu-sur-Mer there is a faithful reproduction of an ancient Greek villa built and lived in for 20 years by an archaeologist: it is now open to the public. The perched village of Eze is approached from the Moyenne Corniche, but the coast road runs through its seaside extension and on to Monaco and Monte-Carlo. Perhaps more than anywhere else along the Riviera, this tiny principality is swathed in glamour and mystique: this is largely thanks to the late Grace Kelly, who turned every girl's dream into reality by marrying a prince and living in a fairytale castle surrounded by rich and beautiful people. It was Grace Kelly and Cary Grant who immortalized the coastal roads of the Riviera in Hitchcock's film *To Catch a Thief.*

It is possible to see the sumptuous state apartments of Monaco's 'pink palace' when the Grimaldis are not in residence, and the Musée Océanographique is also worth a visit, but the *pièce de résistance* is Monte-Carlo's flamboyant Grand Casino. Soon after it was built, at the end of the 19th century, the casino was earning one hundred per cent of the principality's revenue. Today, although it still draws the crowds, its contribution is much reduced.

MENTON

The three Corniche roads converge just before Menton, the last resort on the French Riviera before the border with Italy. Until the middle of the last century the town belonged to the principality of Monaco, but was sold to France in 1860. Menton doesn't sparkle in the way that Nice and Cannes or Monaco do, neither has it the notoriety of St-Tropez, but its genteel air captures something of the atmosphere of the Riviera in its heyday: a fine and beautiful corner of the world, discovered but not yet spoiled.

BELOW, *Menton is a warm sun-trap, sheltered by the mountains*

The Romantische Strasse from Füssen to Würzburg

ADI KRAUS

ABOVE, *Dinkelsbühl's children's festival, held at the Kinderzeche*

BELOW, *autumn colours add a special beauty to the wooded setting of the castle of Neuschwanstein*

The idea of the Romantische Strasse was first conceived in 1950 to guide the tourist through many romantic little villages and towns of historical interest in the south of Germany. The road links the Bavarian Alps with the River Main, visiting places which were important in medieval times. A wealth of castles and churches, mainly in the baroque style, can be seen along the way, and art objects of immeasurable value are sometimes housed in a simple village church.

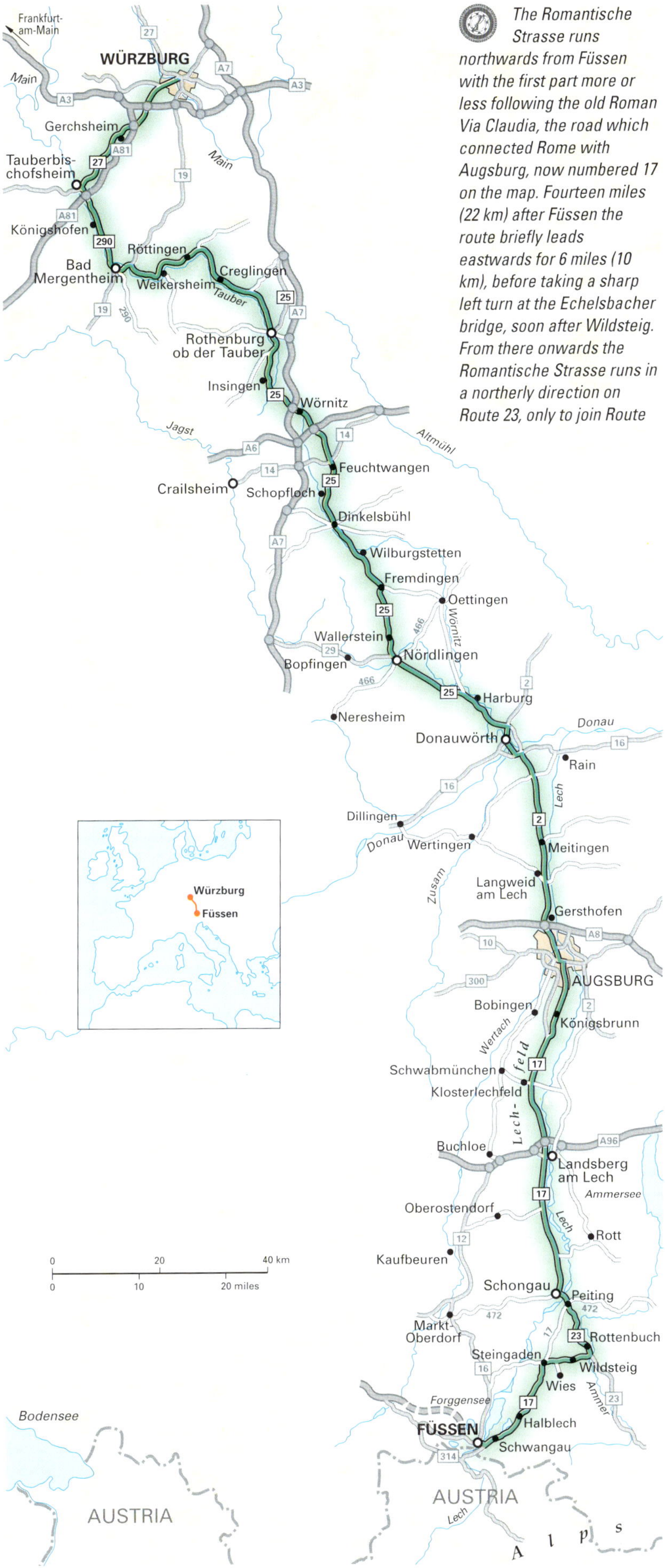

The Romantische Strasse runs northwards from Füssen with the first part more or less following the old Roman Via Claudia, the road which connected Rome with Augsburg, now numbered 17 on the map. Fourteen miles (22 km) after Füssen the route briefly leads eastwards for 6 miles (10 km), before taking a sharp left turn at the Echelsbacher bridge, soon after Wildsteig. From there onwards the Romantische Strasse runs in a northerly direction on Route 23, only to join Route 17 again at Peiting, and continues for the next 20 miles (32 km) along the Lech River reservoirs to Landsberg am Lech. With historical Lechfeld on your left and the Lech River on your right you follow Route 17 north for 23 miles (37 km) on a straight course to Augsburg.

Leaving Augsburg you take Route 2 north to Donauwörth for 25 miles (40 km), and continue for a short distance until the road bends. There you take the left fork for Harburg and Nordlingen; the road now becomes Route 25. From Donauwörth to Nördlingen is 17 miles (27 km). You now follow Route 25 for 20 miles (32 km) to Dinkelsbühl. From there it is 8 miles (13 km) to Feuchtwangen and 19 miles (30 km) to Rothenburg ob der Tauber. Leave Rothenburg on the Bezoldweg along the northern town wall for the Tauber valley and Bad Mergentheim. The route passes through Creglingen, Rottingen and Weikersheim over a distance of 28 miles (45 km). From Bad Mergentheim take Route 290 to Tauberbischofsheim, a distance of 11 miles (18 km) and then continue on Route 27 northeast for 19 miles (30 km) to Würzburg.

THE ROMANTISCHE STRASSE begins at Füssen in the northern foothills of the Alps. The area was first inhabited by the Celts; they were followed by the Romans, who built an important road across the Alps to link Rome with the frontier of their empire on the Danube (Donau). Today the stretch between Füssen and Augsburg follows the basic direction of the Via Claudia, the original Roman Road.

Present day Füssen has its origins around the Benedictine Monastery of St Magnus. The monastery now serves as the Rathaus (town hall), and inside it the Fürstensaal (hall of the princes) and the Papstzimmer (Pope's chamber) are well worth visiting. The Hohes Schloss, the castle which dominates the town, is also interesting.

FAIRY-TALE CASTLES

The two main attractions near Füssen are the castles of Hohenschwangau and Neuschwanstein. Standing right above the village of Schwangau, and reached by a steep walkway, Hohenschwangau was built in the 12th century and remodelled by Crown Prince Maximilian of Bavaria. The interior features wall paintings of old German sagas and parts of the legends used by the composer Richard Wagner for his operas. Wagner often stayed there and was greatly admired by Ludwig, Maximilian's son. There are fine views from the castle terraces, especially of the much photographed castle of Neuschwanstein.

ABOVE, *the church known as 'The Wonder of Wies' is extravagantly decorated in the rococo style*

CENTRE, *the town square in Augsburg, birthplace of Rudolf Diesel who invented the diesel engine*

BELOW, *a statue commemorating one of Augsburg's benefactors, Jakob Fugger*

King Ludwig II had the magnificent castle of Neuschwanstein built towards the end of the last century. A stage designer was chosen for the plans, whose task it was to translate the king's dream into reality. It was worked on for over 17 years but was still not completed when Ludwig died. The unfortunate king enjoyed only 102 days in his castle, as mental illness forced him into permanent medical supervision elsewhere.

The route now leads northwards, bypassing the small Bannwald See. A pleasant drive through attractive woodland leads towards Steingaden and its church of St John the Baptist. Its exterior Romanesque features belie the lavishly decorated baroque interior.

The abbot of Steingaden was also responsible for the erection of the pilgrim church at Wies, called the 'Wieskirche', literally translated as 'church on a meadow'. Only by its size can you guess from the outside that you are about to see one of the finest buildings of its kind in Europe. The background to the building of the church is interesting. In about 1730 the owner of the meadow was looking at a figure of the Scourging of Christ, when he noticed tears on the face of Christ. He persuaded the abbot of Steingaden to build a chapel in the field, but the story of this miracle led to an unexpected surge of pilgrims, and the decision was taken to erect a church on the site. One of the famous Zimmermann brothers, Dominikus, was commissioned for the work, and created a rococo masterpiece.

From Wies it is a short journey back to Kohlhofen, where you turn right. Passing several reservoirs of the Lech River, after 20 miles (32 km) you reach the historically important town of Landsberg am Lech. A beautifully decorated gate, the 'Bayerntor', erected in 1425, forms the entry into the town. The tower-gate was once part of the defence system of Landsberg. From the top you have an extensive view over the whole town. The main square, which is also the market place, is adorned by the graceful Maria Brunnen fountain. Dominikus Zimmermann was responsible for decorating the façade of the Rathaus and the rosary altar in the church of Maria Himmelfahrt. He also contributed to the rococo Johanniskirche from 1750 to 1752 and was Mayor of Landsberg for five years. The old town wall, with its gates and many towers, and the churches and old houses with gabled roofs all create a romantic medieval atmosphere.

Leaving Landsberg for Augsburg, the road is flanked on one side by a plain, called the Lechfeld, and on the other side by the River Lech itself.

AUGSBURG

One of the oldest and most distinguished towns in Bavarian Swabia, Augsburg was founded by the Roman Emperor Augustus as a military camp about 15BC. In the first century it became known as Augusta Vindelicorum and was the capital of the Roman province of Raetia. During the 300 years or so of Roman rule, trade and commerce blossomed, facilitated by the Via Claudia. After the withdrawal of the Romans the town was subjected to frequent intrusions by the Huns from Eastern Europe. Finally King Otto I went to battle with the Huns in AD955 on the Lechfeld. He scored a decisive victory which had wide-spread consequences.

The defeat of the marauders encouraged merchants to set up business in Augsburg, and prosperity returned to the town. Two families were primarily responsible for the creation of wealth in the town, the Fuggers and the Welsers, reaching the height of their success in the 15th and 16th centuries. As early as 1519 the Fuggers founded what would now be called a social

The royal Maximilianstrasse, flanked on either side by medieval houses, is a beautiful example of a street dating from the Middle Ages. The massive building of the Rathaus and the nearby Perlachturm (tower) form the centre of Augsburg, and from the top of the Perlachturm there is a splendid view over the town. If a yellow flag is hoisted on a clear day, it signifies that the panorama extends right up to the Alps. Leopold Mozart, the father of Wolfgang Amadeus, was born in Augsburg and his birthplace at Frauentorstrasse 30 has become a museum.

Donauwörth is the next town on the road, another centre of the Fugger family. The large house they built there has hosted, amongst others, the Swedish King Gustaf Adolf and Emperor Karl VI. The Reichsstrasse is flanked on either side by impressive looking houses which document the importance of the town in the Middle Ages.

Soon after Donauwörth the route turns left to Harburg, and you will soon see its castle standing on a crag high above the road. Once the seat of the Staufen Kings, the castle was never conquered and is well preserved. The chapel, ramparts, keep and banqueting hall can all be visited. Art collections include the works of goldsmiths and woodcarvers, and decorative objects of enamel and ivory. The splendid setting of the castle attracts many painters, photographers and historians, and the lovely Wörnitz River winding around the town completes an idyllic scene.

The road now takes you further along the romantic trail to the town of Nördlingen, where the original medieval town walls are still complete. You can walk all the way along the ramparts in a

housing estate. Some conditions were imposed upon the beneficiaries: you had to be married, a citizen of Augsburg, Catholic, poor and of unblemished character to qualify for the low rents of one Rhenish guilder per year for an apartment of two and a half rooms. This estate, called the Fuggerei, is still standing and the rents are still the same, equivalent to DM 1.71 per year.

Augsburg has some remarkable buildings, starting with the Stadtpalast (town palace), which was initiated by Jakob Fugger, 'der Reiche' (the rich one) between 1512 and 1515. Although destroyed during the last war, it was rebuilt by the family. Of special note are the asymmetric arcades in the Ladies' Courtyard.

The Dom (cathedral) was started around AD807 and later the austere Romanesque building received many art treasures. Five of its stained-glass windows picture five prophets; believed to be the oldest of their kind in the world, they were constructed in the second half of the 11th century. Two lions support a bishop's throne, carved in stone; and Hans Holbein the Elder, a citizen of Augsburg, created the altar paintings.

BELOW, *Harburg is a popular stopping place, with its quaint houses beside the River Wörnitz*

INSET LEFT, *Nördlingen and villages near by host the Rieser Cultural Season every two years; many other towns on the Romantische Strasse have annual arts festivals*

circle around the town, past five gates and 11 towers. The complete walk is about 2 miles (3 km) long. Looking towards the town centre you will always see the 'Daniel', the 295 foot (89 m) steeple of St Georg's church. Nördlingen is also the centre of a natural phenomenon, the Ries crater. Scientists set the time of its formation at about 15 million years ago, when a meteorite struck the area.

REMINDERS OF THE THIRTY YEARS WAR

The next point of call is the town of Dinkelsbühl, where you are joined again by the Wörnitz River. Old walls and towers surround Dinkelsbühl, which has found a happy compromise between the historic past and modern-day living. A pleasant stroll through the old town starts at the market place, which is dominated by the Deutsches Haus, one of the most impressive examples of half-timbered buildings in Franconia. It now hosts a hotel and restaurant and is flanked by other old buildings, all characterised by the typical high-gabled roofs.

Nearby St Georg's church is noted for its unpretentious exterior and intricate net-vaulting supported by slender pillars inside. The positioning of the houses in the old streets is also interesting, jutting out one by one, so that all the residents had a clear view of the town gates. The Segringerstrasse leads past the new town hall to the Segringer Gate and its baroque tower. You can now walk along the fortifications to the Green Tower, turning right down the steps to the Schmiedeviertel, the smiths' quarter.

Old lanes lead to the Rothenburger Gate. Passing through the gate offers one of the most rewarding views of the Dinkelsbühl fortification network. Further lanes through the

MAIN PICTURE, *peaceful Dinkelsbühl still retains its medieval walls and towers; there is even a moat*

Priesterviertel (priests' quarter) at the back of St Georg's Church lead to the old town hall, its square and the Kinderzeche, the venue of a yearly festival in mid-July which commemorates the saving of the town from destruction during the Thirty Years War. A group of very brave children walked through the gate of the besieged town to plead with the conquerors to spare their homes. The plea was granted and Dinkelsbühl was saved.

You will most likely leave the town through the Rothenburger Gate and continue through Feuchtwangen, a small attractive market town with large medieval burgher's houses on either side of its main square. The massive Stiftskirche, a former collegiate church, dominates the centre and the former cloister is on the south side of the buildings. Two of its wings are still preserved in the original state and are used as the setting for plays during the summer season.

Few towns in Germany have been able to preserve their history and appearance so well as Rothenburg ob der Tauber. The town was seriously threatened only once, in 1631, during the Thirty Years War when, as with Dinkelsbühl, luck and a gamble saved the town from destruction. As the Imperial troops, under General Tilly, were about to begin wrecking the town, the former Mayor Nusch was offered a bet by the General: if he could drink 3.5 litres (6 pints) of wine in one go, the town would be spared. He fulfilled the bargain and the town remained intact. The occasion is commemorated in the centre of Rothenburg at the Ratstrinkstube (Councillors' Tavern), which houses the clock and reminds citizens and visitors alike of the hero who saved the town. The original goblet is displayed at the Reichsstadtmuseum.

ABOVE, *a decorative house façade in the medieval town of Nördlingen*

ABOVE CENTRE, *on the road approaching Rothenburg ob der Tauber – 'the red castle on the Tauber'*

BELOW, *the bright morning sun casts shadows in Rothenburg's narrow gabled streets*

The Rathaus stands next door to the famous tavern and shows a combination of the original Gothic and later Renaissance styles. The view from the top of the tower is especially fine, taking in the attractive buildings of the town centre and also the gentle valley of the Tauber River beyond.

The St Jakob church is a Gothic structure and should be visited for the treasure which is housed inside: the Heiligenblutaltar, altar of the sacred blood, carved by the master craftsman Tilman Riemenschneider. As well as the high altar and beautifully stained glass windows, the church is notable for its serene atmosphere. Before leaving the centre, don't miss the rare museum in the Burggasse – its interesting collection of old coats of arms, seals, legal symbols and torture and punishment devices offers a fascinating insight into medieval crime and punishment.

The Klingenbastei in the north of the city is a covered walkway and part of the fortifications, built at a later date, around 1587. Through a fortified medieval gate, the Burgtor, you can enter the gardens and take in all the splendour of ancient history. You may not wish to leave such a romantic place as Rothenburg so soon, but you are now presented with one of the most scenic drives of the whole route, as the journey leads through an enchanting part of the Tauber valley, the Taubergrund.

Driving further along the Tauber trail brings you to the small town of Weikersheim, with the Schloss Weikersheim, originally a moated castle first mentioned in 1152. A museum has been installed there and the splendid knight's hall, with its elaborately decorated ceiling, is used as a venue for staging chamber concerts.

Continuing with the journey, after a few bends the road reaches Bad Mergentheim, having left the state of Bavaria for a brief incursion into

neighbouring Baden-Württemberg. On the main square in Bad Mergentheim, known as the Deutschordensplatz, stands the castle of the Order of the German Knights. It was the residence of the Grand Master from 1529 to 1809, when the Order was dissolved on the orders of Napoleon. The buildings which stand there now were erected between 1565 and 1570. Today part of the castle is a museum dedicated to the Order, and the castle's church houses the tombs of former important members.

The market square is dominated by the Rathaus, built in the middle of the 16th century. The centre of the square is adorned by a fountain bearing a statue of Wolfgang Schutzbar holding a flag and shield, commemorating the former member of the German Order.

The next stop is Tauberbischofsheim, with its attractive castle situated on a hill. When you enter you are surrounded by medieval buildings dating from 1250. Beautiful half-timbered houses stand at different angles to each other, not in line as is usual with other castle buildings, and the effect is that of a village rather than a castle. The mighty keep, the Türmersturm, is a massive round tower on one side of the castle yard, and its foundations date back to the 13th century. Down in the village the parish church of St Martin was a fairly recent addition in 1910, but it is graced by several works by pupils of Tilman Riemenschneider. The picturesque half-timbered houses of the castle are echoed in the market square and the Liobastrasse.

From Tauberbischofsheim you return to the part of Bavaria known as Franconia, and its main centre, the town of Würzburg. Würzburg invites a longer stay, especially for those interested in history and architecture. It is an old settlement, and the earliest available records speak of a 'Castellum Virteburg' in AD704. A few years earlier three missionaries of Irish descent, Kilian, Kolonat and Totnam, were murdered here. Duke-bishops ruled later, successfully combining of worldly and religious powers and commissioning outstanding works of art. In 1156 Friedrich I Barbarossa married Beatrice of Burgundy in Würzburg, and later increasing wealth brought famous artists to the town. Bombing raids at the end of World War II destroyed most of the town, but much of it has been painstakingly rebuilt.

A green belt, the Ringpark, surrounds the old town. Its centre is the garden behind the Residenz, which is mainly of south German baroque style and executed by three architects, Neumann, Welsch and Hildebrand, the latter from Vienna. It took 25 years to complete the building and, although badly damaged by bombs and fire, some important parts remained intact and the stones of the rubble were re-used for rebuilding the rest. The Kaisersaal (Emperor's hall) should be seen; the frescoes are by the Venetian Tiepolo, and the hall now offers an ideal setting for Mozart concerts and serenades. The first cathedral was built in Würzburg on the graveside of St Kilian and was consecrated in AD788 by the Emperor Karl der Grosse (Charlemagne). Two of the tombs of prince-bishops inside the cathedral were carved by Tilman Riemenschneider, who became the adopted son of the town, a council member and Bürgermeister. However, in 1525, during the Peasants' Revolt, he sided with the suppressed farmers. After torture and a court case which went against him he lost all his wealth and subsequently died on 7 July, 1531. His work can be admired in various churches in the area, and also in the Mainfränkisches museum housed in the fortress of Marienburg, Würzburg's main landmark.

The Marienkirche stands on a hill on the other side of the River Main. It was consecrated in AD706 and later formed the basis of a fortress. The keep also dates back to this period and the main castle is surrounded by a well-preserved wall. Towards the end of the 15th century the defences were strengthened by the Bishop of Scherenberg, after whom the great entrance gate was named.

Near the cathedral stands the Rathaus, which has functioned since 1316 . There is also a former Carmelite convent; a delightful end to your journey along the Romantische Strasse.

PRACTICAL INFORMATION

■ The central office for the Romantische Strasse is at D 91550 Dinkelsbühl, Marktplatz (Tel. 09851 90271, Fax 09851 90279). This office also supplies a useful list of hotels, *pensions* and local inns at places *en route*, with prices in local currency (DM).

■ The Romantische Strasse is about 220 miles (352 km) long. The whole journey by private car should take about one week, depending on how many stopping places are selected. The best time to travel is in early spring or late September. Weekends and the summer season are busy and should be avoided whenever possible.

BELOW, *the Old Town in Würzburg provides many examples of the rococo and baroque architecture for which the town is famous*

The Road of the Emperors from Budapest to Prague

ELIZABETH CRUWYS AND BEAU RIFFENBURGH

The Road of the Emperors links some of the most beautiful capital cities in the world. Beginning in Budapest, the capital of Hungary, it runs north-west towards Bratislava. Moving west, the route visits Vienna (Wien), majestic capital of the Austro-Hungarian Empire and then moves north-west, ending in Prague (Praha), the beautiful capital of the Czech Republic. The Road of the Emperors no longer exists: it became fragmented through the years when the Habsburgs began to lose power and no longer needed to travel between the cities. Yet the links between these great cities are still present, in their history, their music, and their beauty.

ABOVE, *the monument on Gellért Hill in Budapest commemorates the Soviet army of liberation*

FAR RIGHT, *these figures of Magyar chiefs on horseback stand at the base of the 36m high column in Heroes Square*

BELOW, *there has been a fortress on the Visegrád citadel since Roman times*

STRETCHING ACROSS the very heart of Europe, the Road of the Emperors travels between the capital cities of Hungary and the Czech Republic, passing through the ancient settlement of Brno, beautiful Vienna, and Bratislava, the capital of the Slovak Republic. Recent years have seen dramatic changes in this part of Europe. Yet these changes are only the latest stage in a history of fluctuating borders and waxing and waning fortunes that has continued for hundreds of years. As the Habsburg (or Hapsburg) emperors

united Austria, Hungary, Bohemia, Moravia and many other smaller states into the great Austro-Hungarian Empire, they forged a dominion that was to last until World War I. Austria, Hungary and Czechoslovakia were separated after that war, and Czechoslovakia divided again into the independent republics of Czech and Slovakia not long after the bloodless 'Velvet Revolution' ousted its Communist rulers.

And so the Road of the Emperors that once linked great cities in a unified Empire now winds through four independent countries, but although borders have changed, parts of the cities have remained untouched. Budapest is often called the Paris of Eastern Europe because of its wealth of culture and architecture. Vienna is unsurpassed in its musical culture and the elegance of its buildings and palaces. Bratislava's grim fortress frowns over the rapidly growing new capital of the Slovak Republic, while Prague (Praha), with its winding medieval streets and quiet cobbled squares is a jewel among cities. Each

The Road of the Emperors – a journey of roughly 350 miles (560 km) – begins in Budapest.
The magnificent Royal Palace overlooking the wide, brown flow of the River Danube is a good place to start. The Habsburgs were of Germanic extraction, rather than Magyar, and, although the Royal Palace (heavily restored following serious damage during World War II) is a residence fit for kings, the royal family never lived here for any length of time. In other parts of Budapest, visitors can explore the many art museums, stroll through the Old City, or visit the curious Fisherman's Bastion. For the more adventurous, Budapest has many thermal baths ranging from those built during Turkish times to gleaming new ones.
The road out of the old town of Buda heads for Györ (Raab in German), 68 miles (109 km) distant. It then bends north-west into the Slovak Republic and Bratislava. From Bratislava, the traveller heads west on Route 9 towards Vienna, for many years the centre of the vast Austro-Hungarian Empire. Vienna is a vibrant city, offering concerts and live performances to cater for almost every musical taste, as well as an enormous number of buildings, palaces and museums, and the famous amusement park at the Prater.
Route 7 takes the traveller directly north from Vienna towards the Czech Republic border near Mikulov, and on into Brno (Brünn). After Brno, a multi-laned road travels north-west towards Prague, passing Velke Mezirící before reaching the city of Jihlava, by-passing Humpolec, and then into the outskirts of Prague. As in Vienna, there is much to absorb the traveller in Prague, including concerts, quiet medieval streets and an impressive array of architectural styles.

ABOVE, *the Palace on Castle Hill is reflected in the Danube, with the 19th-century Chain Bridge which replaced an earlier pontoon bridge*

city – like its country – is different, yet they are connected by a history that stretches back hundreds of years, even before the great Habsburg Empire that once upon a time united them.

Budapest and Hungary

The Emperor's Road begins in Budapest, now a large, rapidly westernizing city with a population of more than two million people. Budapest is, in fact, two cities, separated by the Danube (Duna), which flows through the heart of the modern metropolis. The old city is Buda and stands on the west side of the river, while Pest (pronounced 'Pesht') is on the east. In the 13th century, King Bela IV built a fortress at Buda, and his successors began to use it as their capital. Its history, like that of Hungary as a whole, is a violent one. Since the Magyars first crossed the Carpathians from the western steppes and entered the area that is now Hungary in 896, the kingdoms of the middle basin of the Danube were engaged in a seemingly continuous series of struggles and battles, fighting, among others, the Kuman from the steppes in the 1080s, the Mongols in 1241, and the Austrians and the Moravians in the mid-14th century. In 1526 Hungary was defeated by the Ottoman Turks led by Suliemen the Magnificent, who occupied Buda. In the following decades, the lands were divided between the Turks and the Habsburgs. When the Turks were expelled in the 1690s, the Habsburgs moved in, and a Hungarian rebellion (1703–11) against their new occupiers ended in Habsburg domination. Another revolution in 1848–49 resulted in bloody reprisals by Emperor Franz Josef. As both international and internal economic difficulties mounted, Franz Josef saw the advantage of making concessions to the Hungarians, and in 1867 the establishment of the 'Dual Monarchy' gave Hungary more internal independence than it had enjoyed since before the conquest by the Turks.

When war broke out in Europe in 1914, Hungary sided with Germany, and when the Central Powers lost, Hungary forfeited much of its territory. Admiral Horthy was elected as leader, and when World War II began, he collaborated with Hitler's regime. The Allies exacted a terrible price from Budapest, and many historic buildings and homes were bombed. All the city's seven bridges were destroyed, and even today the marks of shells and bullets can be seen on some buildings. Some of the scars resulted from the 1956 uprising against the Moscow-dominated Communist regime, when efforts were made to establish a neutral multi-party government. The Russians reacted quickly, and thousands were killed in street fighting and the ensuing reprisals.

Despite its bloody history, and the fact that so many of its buildings were damaged or destroyed,

and trucks. Situated at the confluence of three rivers, it dates back to Celtic times, although many of the buildings that can be seen today were raised in the 17th and 18th centuries. Also interesting are the cathedral with 11th-century foundations (it was blown up in the 16th century by the Turks), and the splendid Bishop's Castle, first built in the 13th century. Several small towns near Györ boast fine examples of Romanesque architecture and Benedictine abbeys.

BELOW, *the Fishermen's Bastion in Budapest was designed to be both decorative and functional, since it served as a lookout over the Danube*

Bratislava and the Slovak Republic

From Györ, the road slips briefly across the border into the Slovak Republic, heading towards Bratislava. Although the people of the two new republics that arose from divided Czechoslovakia speak similar languages, they are culturally distinct, and their histories are different. While the Slovaks were under Hungarian rule for centuries, the Czechs enjoyed freedom and political influence until they came under Habsburg control in the 17th century. After the Thirty Years War (1618–48), the Habsburgs began to strengthen their hold over the Czechs, while the Slovaks were divided between the Habsburgs and a much reduced Hungary. After World War I the Czechs and the Slovaks were joined together to form Czechoslovakia. In 1993, these two nations separated peacefully, forming independent republics.

Bratislava is now the capital of the young Slovak Republic, and stands on the Danube (Dunaj), which in defiance of the title of Strauss's waltz is not blue but brown. The castle, a great square edifice standing on a rocky promontory, overlooks the town and river. Although little survives but its walls, it still appears impressive, and it houses an informative museum. St Margaret's cathedral stands near by, where many Hungarian kings were crowned.

Budapest still boasts fine baroque, neoclassical and Art Nouveau architecture. The castle district has been lovingly restored, incorporating the remains of the medieval town. Parts of the synagogue at Tancsics Mihaly date from the 14th century, while the caves that riddle the rock under Castle Hill were said to have been used by the Turks, and acted as air-raid shelters in World War II. The current Royal Palace dates from the 18th and 19th centuries, being rebuilt after 1945, although it stands on the site of a far earlier castle. It houses the Ludwig Collection of Modern Art.

Budapest is a city that changes constantly. At night, its splendid buildings are illuminated in gold and green, sending reflections dancing in the dark waters of the Danube. In summer and spring, it is bathed in a warm, yellow light, quite different from the harsh grey skies of winter. The road out of the old town of Buda runs south following the course of the Danube, until a modern road curves away to the west, heading towards the small town of Bicske. It then turns directly to Györ, cutting through the Hungarian countryside. Hungary's economy is still strongly rural, and the land is heavily farmed. In the rolling hills, small red-roofed villages stand among cultivated fields, and it is well worth stopping at some of them to savour their peace after the energetic bustle of Budapest.

Györ, Hungary's third industrial city, has far more to offer the visitor than textiles, rolling stock

ABOVE, *Vienna's National Library was designed for the Emperor Charles VI by Johann Bernhard Fischer von Erlach, in the high baroque style*

VIENNA AND AUSTRIA

The visit of the Road of the Emperors to the Slovak Republic is brief, and the route heads west from Bratislava across the border with Austria. About 37 miles (59 km) from Bratislava lies the great city of Vienna, once the imperial capital of one of the most powerful and longest lasting dynasties in the world. When the Habsburg monarchy finally crumbled in 1918, the great Austro-Hungarian empire was dismembered, and Austria emerged very much smaller. It became part of the German Reich in 1938, and reverted to independent status in 1945 at the end of World War II.

Although Allied bombs fell on Vienna at the end of the War, buildings that were destroyed or damaged were painstakingly repaired, and the Vienna of the late 20th century is every bit as splendid as it was during the age of empire. The old Inner City is encircled by a ring of roads that pass some of the most elegant buildings in Europe. Chief among these is the carefully rebuilt State Opera House, which is an essential part of the itinerary for opera lovers worldwide. Behind the imposing exterior lies a vast arena fringed with flower-draped balconies and extravagant decorations. Equally imposing is the vast palace complex of the Hofburg, the winter residence of the Habsburgs, whose crescent-shaped façade is a well-known landmark in this extraordinary city. The Hofburg houses several museums and the Spanish Riding School. This was established in the 16th century in order to provide the emperors with suitably trained horses. Few visitors can fail to be impressed by the sight of the great white Lipizzaner horses prancing in the chandeliered Renaissance halls.

During the summer, the Habsburgs resided in the Schönbrunn, a fabulous palace of pale yellow stone set among manicured gardens. Rooms vary between the small chamber with the uncomfortable-looking bed on which Napoleon Bonaparte's son died at 21, to the glittering Great Gallery, a long cream and gold hall dripping with chandeliers. The Empress Maria Theresa brought up her 16 children (including the fifteenth, Marie Antoinette, who was executed during the French Revolution) at Schönbrunn, while Emperor Franz Josef (her great, great grandson) ruled his empire from here for 68 years. Franz Josef, Maria Theresa and 135 other Habsburgs lie in the eerie vaults below the Capuchin church. Visitors can descend into the chill, musty rooms and wander past the coffins, some highly ornate, others plain.

But Vienna is perhaps most famous for its music. Beethoven, Mozart, Haydn and Schubert are just a few of the composers who flocked to Vienna during the 18th and 19th centuries. Today, the visitor can attend a concert or an opera every night. And during the day, small groups of musicians play in cafés, parks and even in the streets. The internationally respected Vienna Boys' Choir was founded here almost 500 years ago.

BELOW, *the name of the Palace of Schönbrunn means 'beautiful fountain', seen here against the 'Gloriette' temple built in 1765*

PRAGUE AND THE CZECH REPUBLIC

Leaving Vienna and travelling north, Route 7 crosses the Danube (Donau) and heads for the Austro-Czech Republic border. The north-eastern part of what is now the Czech Republic was once called Bohemia, and was independent of the adjoining lands to the east that formed Moravia. The largest city is Brno, a busy metropolis in central Moravia that has expanded rapidly in the 20th century, mainly due to its heavy industry. Yet in the centre of this young city is an ancient core of history. The church is six centuries old, and in the Augustinian monastery next door, Johann Mendel worked on his laws of heredity. The monastery courtyards are open to visitors.

Just to the east of Brno lies a small town called Slavkov, better known by its historical name: Austerlitz. On 2 December 1805 Napoleon Bonaparte's 68,000 French troops faced the combined Russian and Austrian armies, totalling 90,000 men, and crushed them in one of his greatest victories. The carnage of the 'Battle of the Three Emperors' was horrifying, with more than 46,000 killed in a single day, three-quarters of them Russians and Austrians.

After leaving Brno, the Road of the Emperors continues north-west, passing the city of Jihlava and the Zelivka river. North of the river is the ancient town of Kutná Hora, the site of a 14th-

century mint, which manufactured silver groats at the height of Bohemia's power. The gothic cathedral of St Barbara was built by the wealthy silver mine owners, but the silver ore ran out before the splendid façade could be completed. Many years later, Kutná Hora is paying the price for the silver: unmapped tunnels are causing subsidence, and several 15th- and 16th-century buildings have been damaged or destroyed.

Continuing north-west towards Prague, it is well worth making a diversion south to visit Karlstejn, which ranks as one of the most impressive castles in Europe. Standing on a hill among thick green trees, its sturdy towers and thick walls dominate the little town. It was raised in the 14th century for Charles IV (1347–78), partly as a peaceful country seat where he could retreat from the affairs of state, and partly to hold his impressive collection of treasure. Visitors to the castle today are guided through room after room of gold and red furnishings, still looking just as grand as when Charles was in residence.

ABOVE, *the romantic castle of Karlstejn stands guard over the little town below in the valley*

INSET, *The mine owners of Kutná Hora financed the building of a cathedral dedicated to St Barbara, patron saint of miners and gunners*

BELOW, *dramatic silhouettes at sunset, looking along Charles Bridge in Prague to the Staré Mesto or Old Town*

INSET BELOW, *this astronomical clock can be seen at St Michael's Square in Prague*

PRAGUE: GOLDEN CITY OF A HUNDRED SPIRES

Prague is perhaps the most beautiful city in Europe. Less scarred by the two great wars that deprived other European capitals of so many of their finest buildings, Prague is a jewel of elegant architectural styles, cobbled streets, and attractive squares. Even more remarkable is that it survived 50 years of Communist rule and, although the inevitable characterless concrete high-rise buildings slouch around its suburbs, the centre of Prague is blissfully untouched. Prague has been called the 'Golden City' and the 'City of a Hundred Spires'. Its skyline is pierced by many towers and pinnacles of all manner of shapes and sizes, but is dominated by the magnificent St Vitus' cathedral, the building of which was started in 1344 at the instigation of Charles IV. At the very centre of Prague is Wenceslas Square, a long, wide street fringed with trees and some of the most elegant buildings in Europe. Dominating the square is a huge statue of King Wenceslas astride his horse, clad in chain mail and holding his banner aloft triumphantly. How Wenceslas, the scholarly chieftain of Bohemia a thousand years ago, came to be the subject of a Christmas carol is unknown. He was murdered by his younger brother in a church in AD929 when he was only 26 years old, despite the traditional picture of him as a wise Father Christmas-like figure.

In the 14th century, Charles IV, or 'Charles the Wise', made Prague the capital city of the Holy Roman Empire, over which he ruled. It was Bohemia's golden age, memories of which live on in Prague's Charles University, the oldest of the central European universities. Charles is also commemorated in the Charles Bridge, Prague's finest bridge across the River Vltava. It is guarded on either end by powerful towers, while the bridge itself is decorated with life-size carvings throughout its entire span. During the summer months, the bridge is a hive of activity, with buskers, offering a variety of musical styles from jazz to Janácek, vying for space with street artists and dancers.

Although Prague escaped the destruction of the 20th-century world wars, it has had its share of bloodshed. In 1621 many of the Czech nobility were executed in the 11th-century marketplace in front of the Old Town Hall by the Catholic Habsburgs. This was one of the acts precipitating the Thirty Years War, at the end of which the population had been decimated. Today, this fine old square is a lively place, with the sounds of street musicians, the smells of open-air cafés and, as yet, relatively little traffic.

Crooked medieval streets wind haphazardly through Prague, where fine baroque palaces, such as Malá Strana, rub shoulders intimately with sturdy Romanesque buildings. The streets wind upwards towards the elegant splendour of Hradcany, or Prague Castle, an exuberant collection of buildings spanning a thousand years of history. In these streets, with their mellow sandstone buildings, many composers were inspired. Mozart was commissioned to write *Don Giovanni* in Prague, while native musicians include Dvorák, Martinu and Janácek.

Twelve miles (19 km) north-west of Prague, there was once a small village with some 500 residents. In 1942 Czech resistance fighters flown in from England attempted to assassinate Reinhard Heydrich, the much-feared man who was the chief of the German police, the second-in-command of the SS, and head of the German 'Protectorate of Bohemia and Moravia'. A grenade exploded between Heydrich's legs, but he did not die immediately despite terrible injuries. However, shreds of his uniform were blown into his body, which caused fatal blood poisoning, and he died eight days later. At the instruction of Adolf Hitler, a terrible retribution was brought onto the small local village of Lidice. More than 200 men were shot, the women were deported to Ravensbruck concentration camp, and the children were sent to different institutions in Germany. The houses, school, church and other buildings were systematically obliterated and ploughed over so that there would be no trace of this once-thriving community. In 1947 a new village was established nearby. Where Lidice once stood is now a peaceful meadow with a monument and a rose garden.

In Prague the Road of the Emperors ends, having spanned some 350 miles (560 km) of central European countryside and many years of bloody history. The road is far different from that which might have been travelled 100 years ago or more . Four independent countries are now traversed as opposed to the single great empire that was once united, albeit uneasily, under the Habsburgs. Fast roads now link the capital cities, where once trackways, sometimes impassable after heavy rains had turned them to morasses, would have wound through the land. The cities that the road joined each have their own distinct character, yet are bound by history. All are beautiful, although in very different ways: Budapest with its abundance of baroque and neoclassical buildings, and humming with life; Bratislava combining the heart of its ancient city with its new status as capital city of an emerging nation; Vienna bursting with vitality, yet still retaining the elegance of the centre of one of Europe's most powerful empires; and Prague's medieval squares and soaring spires.

The 20th century has seen dramatic changes in this part of Europe: the fall of an empire, two world wars, Soviet domination and attempts for independence, first failed and then successful. Yet the cities have survived, and so has the route that connected them, even though it no longer bears the name 'Road of the Emperors'.

ABOVE, *the castle in Prague is set high on a hill overlooking the Vltava River*

PRACTICAL INFORMATION

- The Hungarian Tourist Board (called Tourinform) office in Budapest is at V Suto utca 2, Tel. (Budapest) 117 9800, Fax 117 9578.
- The Vienna Tourist Office is at Opere Augartenstrasse 40, 1025 Vienna, Tel. (Vienna) 211 140.
- The Bratislava Information Office is at Nedbalova Ulica, 81428 Bratislava, Tel. (Bratislava) 334 059. Further information can also be obtained from the Slovak Information Office at Bratislava on Tel. 333 715 or 334 370.
- The Tourist Information Office in Prague is at Panska 4, Prague 1, Tel. 54 44 44.
- Traffic drives on the right in Hungary, Austria and the Czech and Slovak republics.

The Grossglockner Highway from Lienz to Zell am See

RICHARD SALE

ABOVE, *the rare white-starred edelweiss grows along the road that bears its name*

BELOW, *magnificent views from the highway of a glacier, and flowering meadows*

There is something magical about mountain highways. Because they visit places that, under normal circumstances, would be inaccessible to the untrained, they have a special majesty. Of all the roads that reach up into the high alps of Europe, the Grossglockner Highway is the finest, both for its scenery and its audacity. At 12,553 feet (3797 m) the Grossglockner is Austria's highest peak, so the idea of deliberately creating a road along its eastern flank caused much surprise, which was followed by a remarkable find during excavation work. The nature of that find adds an intriguing historical note to a scenically magnificent route.

THE HUGE MOUNTAIN WALL of Austria's Eastern Alps has represented a barrier to trade throughout centuries of recorded history. In the early 20th century there was still no road between that which crossed the Brenner Pass and the one over the Radstädter Tauern. The Brenner road linked Innsbruck and Bolzano, both Austrian cities until a section of the Tirol was ceded to Italy in the aftermath of World War I; today it is the motorway that links Italy and Austria, while the Radstädter Tauern Pass carries Austria's A10 motorway, linking Spittal to Salzburg. Between those two roads the Eastern Alps stretched for over 100 miles (161 km), a barrier to trade and communication within Austria. This situation worsened after the loss of the South Tirol to Italy in 1918: the East Tirol was then separated from the rest of the province of Tirol by a jutting finger of foreign soil. To reach the Tirolean capital of Innsbruck the folk of East Tirol had to head east to Spittal, then north to Salzburg and back west again. It was a long, arduous journey, and seen as unacceptable by the Austrian government and East Tiroleans alike.

In the 1920s, the government decided to breach the wall and asked the engineer Franz Wallack to survey a new route. Construction of the highway started in 1930, the road rising in a series of hairpins to the top of Hochtor (8501 feet, 2576 m), just 7½ miles (12 km) to the east of the

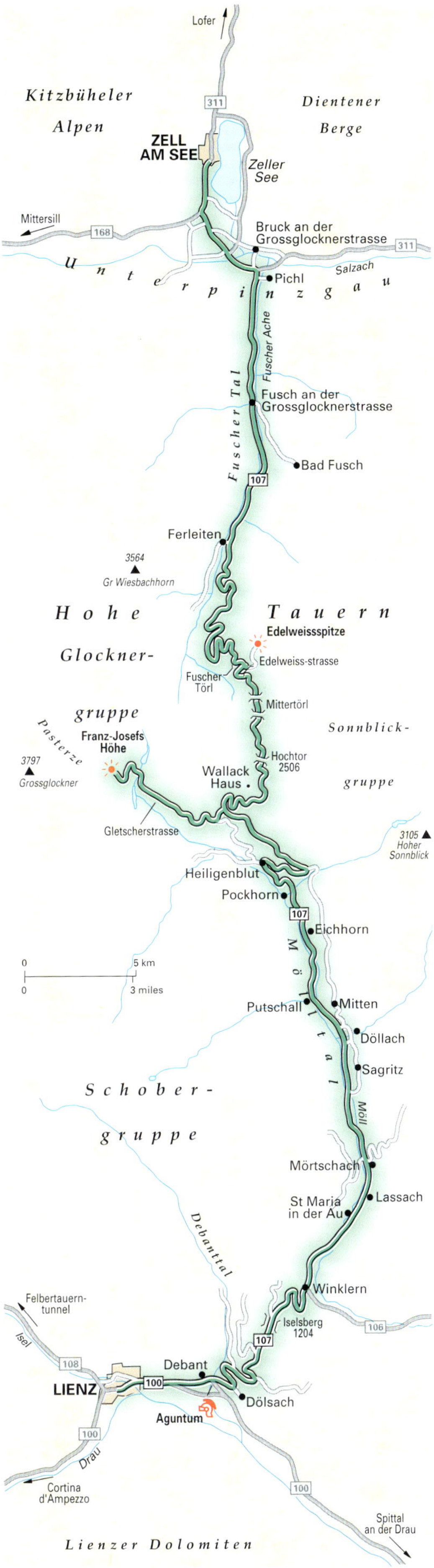

Technically this road, the Grossglockner-Hochalpenstrasse (Grossglockner High Alpine Road) to give it its correct title, covers only the 14 miles (22 km) between the toll gates on either side of the high point of Hochtor. This is a very narrow definition of the road, however, since it is necessary to drive from Winklern to Bruck an der Grossglocknerstrasse before reaching crossroads at either end of the highway.
Here the highway is expanded further, being defined by end points at Lienz and Zell am See, the two towns that lie, respectively, to the south and north of the Grossglockner.
Lienz lies in the East Tirol, in the Drau Valley beneath the peaks of the Lienzer Dolomites. Route 100, which follows the Drau westward from the town, crosses the Italian border just 20 miles (32 km) away; 35 miles (56 km) further on is Cortina d'Ampezzo, capital of the Italian Dolomites. From Lienz, Route 108 heads north-west to the Felbertauern Tunnel. Route 100 goes east towards Spittal, but turning left from it, Route 107 goes over the Iselsberg Pass, entering Carinthia at its summit and descending to reach Winklern and the start of the highway.
Heading north for the high Alps the road climbs through stunning scenery. The toll station is passed at Heiligenblut, after which the real climbing begins. The road's high point is in a tunnel, and the crossing into the province of Salzburg is in another, but the view is quickly restored for the long descent towards Bruck. Just before the village bear left on to Route 311 to reach the Zeller See and the pretty town of Zell am See, the terminus of our journey. Route 311 continues to Lofer, where a left turn leads to St Johann, Kitzbühel and the Inn Valley, while one to the right follows Route 312 over the Stein Pass and down into Salzburg.

ABOVE, *dramatic shadows darkening the mountain sides near the province of Salzburg*

Grossglockner's summit. There Wallack decided to bore a tunnel rather than attempting to traverse the actual top. Explosives were set for an initial charge and men retreated to cover. After the detonation they returned to discover, amongst the rubble, a Roman statue of Hercules.

The Romans placed statues of their gods at the summits of passes on the roads, a practice that was taken up by many who followed them; shrines, crosses and curious cairns abound on passes from Norway to Sicily. The Hercules statue certainly meant that the Romans had come this way – but was this a true road or merely an investigation of possibilities? Long research has not solved the mystery. Some see certain references as indicating that the Romans not only had a road over the Hochtor, but also managed to keep it open throughout the winter. Others are more sceptical, believing those references to refer to another pass altogether.

A chastened Wallack completed his road in 1935. It was a remarkable effort, for although the maximum gradient is only 12% (1 in 8), the climb is sustained and the carriageway is of adequate width for today's traffic – an amazing piece of foresight. In the course of the official Hochalpenstrasse's 14 miles (22 km) there are 26 hairpin bends, each one numbered (from the northern end). Drivers can therefore count up (or down), accompanied by dismay or disappointment depending on how the journey is going.

Beginning the Journey

Lienz, where our exploration of the Grossglockner Highway starts, is a charming place, the chief town of East Tirol. Historically, its position in the Drau Valley, at the confluence of the Drau and the Isel and close to the pass into the Möll Valley (Mölltal), had made the site one of great strategic importance. There was an Illyrian (pre-Celtic) settlement here as early as 1000BC, and the impressive Schloss Bruck (Bruck Castle, about a mile west of the town centre) was built in the 13th century by the Counts of Görz, who later ceded it to the Habsburgs. The castle is extremely well preserved – note especially the 15th-century frescoes in the chapel – and is very imposing, with its battlements, massive keep and hill-top site. Today it houses a museum which includes locally excavated Roman finds and a collection of artwork. The latter includes paintings by Albin Eggar-Lienz and Franz Defregger, local artists whose work depicts life in the area at the turn of the century. Both artists are buried in the Soldiers' Memorial Chapel, erected to commemorate those who died in World War I. The chapel has several fine murals by Eggar-Lienz (who died in 1926). It stands close to the town church, to the north of the Isel.

The centre of Lienz is the Hauptplatz, to the south of the Isel. The southern edge of the square is dominated by the Liebburg, a 16th-century *palazzo* topped by twin onion-domed towers that is now the Town Hall. From the mid 15th century to the early 19th century Lienz was periodically devastated by fire, with a total of six great fires, as well as smaller incidents. The Liebburg is, therefore, a happy survival, most of the earlier town centre houses having been destroyed. Another survival is the Franciscan church a short distance north-westward from Hauptplatz. Inside the church, which began life in the 14th century as a Carmelite monastery, there is a fine late 14th-century Pieta and some excellent 15th century frescoes.

From Lienz take Route 100/107 eastward, admiring the dark towers of the Lienzer Dolomites to the south. Route 100 heads south towards Italy, passing the excavated remains of Roman Aguntum. The site dates from the first century – did its inhabitants occasionally cross the Hochtor almost 2000 years ago? A visit requires a detour, our way bearing left on Route 107A to join Route 107 for the journey over the Iselsberg Pass. Although this is a low pass, just 3949 feet (1197 m), it offers marvellous views of the Drau and Möll valleys, and of the high peaks to the north and south. Ahead now is Winklern: turn left here to start the climb to Hochtor.

The Mölltal is broad and lush, but offers a fine view of the difficulties and dangers that confronted the Romans and Wallack's army of road builders. At Döllach the church is worth visiting for its fine baroque interior. The village was once a gold mining centre, the local peaks being called the Goldberge because of the lode seams, and because they filled their streams with a continuous (but tiny) supply of gold particles. The history of the industry is illustrated in a small museum. At Heiligenblut, another former gold mining centre, you can join the local gold panning society. Membership allows you access to several of the best panning sites, use of panning equipment and an evening campfire. Sadly it does not guarantee a find, but if you should strike lucky you can keep the gold.

The village church, with its tall, slender spire, has one of Austria's finest Gothic altars, huge and elaborately carved. It also houses a phial of True Blood brought to the area in the 10th century. Legend has it that a Dane called Briccius was returning north after fighting in the Holy Land, where he had acquired the phial. Some versions say it held True Blood from the Crucifixion, others that it held Sacred Blood that had miraculously run from the wounds on a painting of Christ. At Heiligenblut a blizzard blew up. For the phial's protection – though quite why he should have been more afraid of robbers during a snowstorm than he had been before is unknown – Briccius cut open his leg and inserted the phial. Days later locals noticed wheat shoots growing through the snow and when they dug down to find the source of this miracle they found Briccius' body. Briccius was buried in the village but the

ABOVE, *the Hautplatz, or town square, is a good starting point to explore the varied history of Lienz*

BELOW, *the Grossglockner highway climbs up into the mountains giving majestic views*

INSET, *the imposing altarpiece at Heilingenblut was carved in 1520, in veneration of a relic of the Holy Blood*

following day the leg had pushed its way to the surface revealing the phial. Given the gruesome nature of the discovery it is hardly surprising that Austrian monks rapidly came to the village and built a church to house the phial.

At Heiligenblut the toll must be paid before the climb can begin. To the right is the Hoher Sonnblick, on the summit of which is Austria's highest meteorological station, while to the left are the first peaks of the Grossglockner range. The closest approach to the high peak is made by taking a turn to the left about half-way to Hochtor. This steep, 5 mile (8 km) long side road – the Gletscherstrasse – rises round six hairpin

bends to reach Franz Josefs Höhe at 7770 feet (2354 m). Here there is a hotel, shop and toilets and a phenomenal view of the Grossglockner and its satellite peaks. Many claim this to be the finest mountain view in Europe. From the road's end a funicular descends to the edge of the Pasterze glacier, the largest in Austria. The glacier, which descends from the Grossglockner's north-eastern shoulder, is 5.5 miles (9 km) long, almost a mile wide and quite beautiful, despite the dirty lines of moraine. If you decide to venture on to its surface please be cautious. From the funicular's lower station you can also follow a footpath to the picturesque Winkel waterfall. If you do follow the path you may hear a sharp whistle: this is the warning call of the marmot, a large, cuddly alpine rodent that lives in burrows on the easier, grassier slopes. You may catch sight of one by waiting close to a burrow entrance.

Beyond the Gletscherstrasse turn-off, the highway ascends the hairpin bends to Hochtor. Close to Hairpin 19 the Wallack Haus, named after the highway's builder, is passed. Here too there is a chairlift. Although the Hochtor summit tunnel (which is 1020 feet, 311 m, long) goes under the very top, there is a parking place nearby, from where the view to the high peaks is exceptional.

The Descent

The Highway now descends, passing through the short Mittertörl tunnel and threading through wild screes that offer a close-up view of the true mountain environment, to reach the Fuscher Lacke. From here it climbs again to reach the top of Fuscher Törl, where there is a car park and restaurant and a view of the Grossglockner, an imposing great mountain, and of other, perhaps more beautiful, conical, snow covered peaks. Close to Fuscher Törl the short but very steep (14% or 1 in 7) Edelweiss-strasse goes around six hairpins to reach a car park and restaurant. From here 37 peaks of over 9840 feet (3000 m) and 19 glaciers can be seen. To the north, on clear days, the Dachstein and Berchtesgaden Alps are visible. The area around the top forms part of the Hohe Tauern National Park, protecting an alpine flora which includes the edelweiss.

Back on the Highway as you descend the hairpins, look out for the Walcherbach waterfall on the left, after which the valley opens out. Beyond the hamlet of Ferleiten the road crosses the river and passes through a delightful wooded gorge. Next, to the right, a road goes off to Bad Fusch, named for its thermal springs of mildly radioactive water. On the Highway the sister village of Fusch an der Grossglocknerstrasse is reached, a hamlet whose name is almost as long as the main street. The village church has an interesting and unusual stepped tower. On again and Bruck an der Grossglocknerstrasse is reached, but our route bears left, then right to reach the Zeller See and Zell am See, picturesquely sited on the lakeside.

The name of the town and lake derives from the cells of monks who came here from Salzburg in the eighth century. The town square, dominated by the 13th-century Constable's Tower, is pedestrianized, allowing the visitor to explore its delights and those of the side streets, in peace and safety. The Town Hall occupies the 16th-century Renaissance Schloss Rosenberg, and the church is worth visiting for its 16th century statues of St Hippolyte (to whom the Romanesque church is dedicated) and St Florian. But best of all is to wander along the lakeside, pausing occasionally to look south, back to the high hills.

Practical Information

■ The Grossglockner Highway is a toll road with a daily rate. As it is not the main thoroughfare crossing the eastern Alps, the highway is not kept open during the winter. As a rule it is open from May until October, but there may be days when it is blocked by early or late snows. Allow a full day or long half-day for the crossing.

■ There are tourist offices at both Lienz and Zell am See: Ost-Tirol Information, Postfach 800, Hauptplatz, A-9900 Lienz, Tel: (0485) 265265, Fax: 2652652; Kurverwaltung Zell am See, Brucker Bundsstrasse, A-5700 Zell am See, Tel: (065) 422600/422601, Fax: 422032.

LEFT, *the 15th century church in Heilingenblut is the guardian of an extraordinary legend*

RIGHT, *Zell am See is reflected in the waters of the beautiful Zeller Lake, ideal for boating and swimming after a long drive*

India's Spice Coast – from Mangalore to Kanniyakumari

MELISSA SHALES

Back in the mists of time, the great god Vishnu came to earth as the warrior Parasuma. He fought in many battles and slew many enemies, but towards the end of his life he repented of his violent ways, walked high up into the mountains and hurled his battle axe out to sea. Where the blade struck, the waters parted and the land rose to form Kerala.

ABOVE, *the Kathakali dancers of Kerala perform in heavy, ornate costumes*

BELOW, *coconut palms shade a village street in rural Kerala*

LUSCIOUS KERALA, a true gift of the gods, has never been in step with the rest of India, cut off and protected by the formidable mountains along its border. It has spawned different kingdoms and architecture, has its own language, Malayalam, and has traditionally looked across the Lakshadweep Sea to trade in ivory and pearls, timber and spices, with lands beyond. The Egyptians and Phoenicians, Romans and Arabs, Chinese and Europeans all visited over the years. In 1957 Kerala became the first state in the world willingly to elect a Communist government. On the whole, this has worked remarkably well. By Indian standards, most of the 30 million people here are positively well-kept and well-fed; the state is the first to claim 100% literacy (somewhat optimistically); and the birth and infant mortality rates are both under half the national average.

KERALA – LAND OF PLENTY

Kerala may be the most densely populated state in India, but it seems calm and peaceful, an enchanting respite from the chaos of the north.

The food is hot but the wiry, dark-skinned people are gentle, pouring their energies and creativity into spectacular dance and festivals. The land and waters are so fertile that the rice flows from the fields, fish leap willingly into the nets and the coconuts pile high on the quays. Elsewhere are the groves of cashew nuts and cloves, ginger, pepper, cardamom and cinnamon, betelnut and coffee which earned the area its name 'Spice Coast' from early travellers.

The journey begins just north of Kerala, in Mangalore, a somewhat uninspiring place which

ABOVE, *cultivating rice in paddy fields in Mangalore, Karnataka*

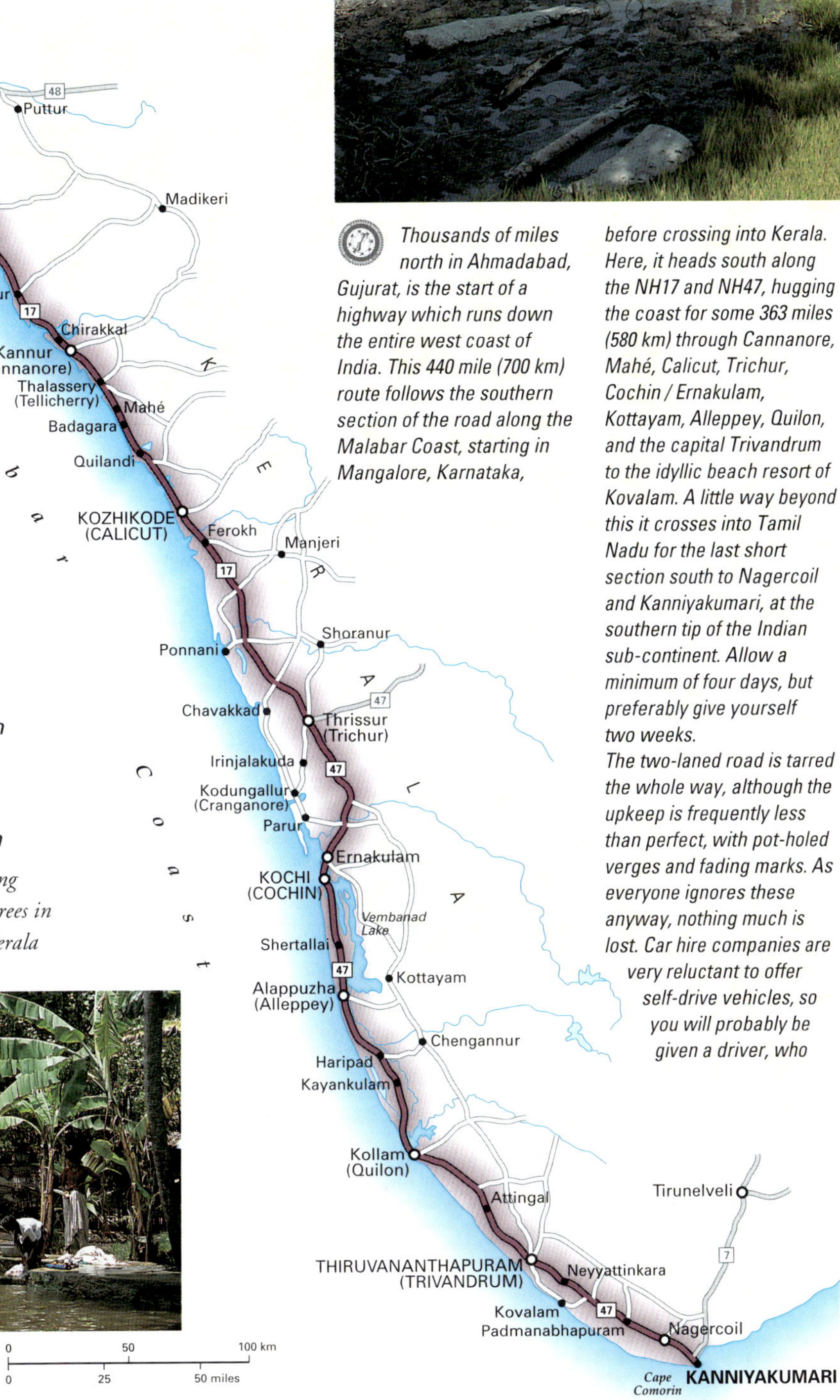

BELOW, *laundering clothes beneath the trees in the Backwaters of Kerala*

Thousands of miles north in Ahmadabad, Gujurat, is the start of a highway which runs down the entire west coast of India. This 440 mile (700 km) route follows the southern section of the road along the Malabar Coast, starting in Mangalore, Karnataka, before crossing into Kerala. Here, it heads south along the NH17 and NH47, hugging the coast for some 363 miles (580 km) through Cannanore, Mahé, Calicut, Trichur, Cochin / Ernakulam, Kottayam, Alleppey, Quilon, and the capital Trivandrum to the idyllic beach resort of Kovalam. A little way beyond this it crosses into Tamil Nadu for the last short section south to Nagercoil and Kanniyakumari, at the southern tip of the Indian sub-continent. Allow a minimum of four days, but preferably give yourself two weeks.

The two-laned road is tarred the whole way, although the upkeep is frequently less than perfect, with pot-holed verges and fading marks. As everyone ignores these anyway, nothing much is lost. Car hire companies are very reluctant to offer self-drive vehicles, so you will probably be given a driver, who will also double as tour guide and courier. It's a sensible precaution – the Indian approach to traffic is totally anarchic. Buying a motorbike locally is also possible for the adventurous and/or foolhardy. Otherwise, there are plenty of local buses and 'luxury' coaches, the railway follows the route most of the way, and you can also take to water buses for an enchanting journey through the Alleppey–Quilon backwaters.

Many towns have recently reverted to their original names – officially. In practice, few people use the new version and locals will probably look blank if you do. Amongst those to look out for are Alappuzha (Alleppey), Kozhikode (Calicut), Kodungallur (Cranganore), Kochi (Cochin), Kannur (Cannanore), Kollam (Quilon), Thrissur (Trichur), Thalassery (Tellicherry) and Thiruvananthapuram (Trivandrum).

ABOVE, *Chinese fishing nets silhouetted against the sunset at Kochi (Cochin)*

INSET, *threshing rice by hand near Mangalore*

has survived for the last 2,000 years by trading in coffee and cashew nuts. From here, the journey south hugs the coast, past enticing deep blue sea and sandy coves – although beware of swimming unless the beach is designated for tourists. (The others are usually the local lavatory.) Every bright green scrap of land is a patchwork of fields and rice paddies outlined by thin rows of coconut palms and banana trees, bending under the weight of pendulous fruit. The road itself is fringed with a ribbon of village houses with woven roofs, tiny stores piled high with old sacks and saucepans, and steamy *chai* stalls selling sweet milky tea and Thumbs Up cola.

Travelling along India's roads is an education, a sensory overload of colour, sight, sound and smell, and is also utterly terrifying. Brightly painted lorries belching thick black smoke hoot frenetically as they pass; people cling like barnacles to the sides of battered windowless buses; 'luxury' coaches with lace curtains and video screens screech by, blaring high-pitched Hindi pop songs. There are five to a motorbike, only the driver wearing a helmet; heavily laden ox-carts creak slowly down the centre line; fleets of ancient, black-framed bicycles prowl the verges; and a stately cream Ambassador, India's own car, based on the 1950s Morris Oxford, sails through the tangled throng. The villagers squat gossiping in the shade while their children play cricket under the lorries' wheels, and bristly black pigs snuffle and grunt as they hoover up the litter. A sacred cow lies on the warm tar, placidly chewing the cud, and the traffic builds to a mile-long tailback behind a wandering *sadhu* (holy man) and his disciples. No Indian would dream of asking them to move.

ABOVE, *the Basilica of Santa Cruz in Kochi (Cochin) dates from 1557; the interior walls and ceilings are decorated with bright paintings*

Colonial Influences

The history of this northern stretch of the coast is closely bound up with the European colonists. Cannanore, about 81 miles (130 km) south of Mangalore, was once capital of the northern kingdom of Kolatirri, but today it is a small city in Indian terms, with a massive fort built by the Portuguese in 1505 and later taken over by the British. Tellicherry, 12 miles (20 km) on, was founded as a trading post by the British East India Company in 1684, and still boasts a fort built by them in 1708. Today, the village has two main exports, fishing and circus performers. Six miles (10 km) south, the pleasant town of Mahé was founded as a French trading post and actually remained a French-owned enclave until independence. It is still officially ruled from Pondicherry on the east coast and is not part of Kerala.

Modern Kerala was formed only in 1956, along linguistic and cultural boundaries. During the first millenium AD the whole Malabar Coast was dominated by the Chera dynasty, whose name offers one explanation of the word Kerala (the other is that it is from *kera,* meaning crocodile, after its shape). Neighbouring Tamil Chola and Pandiyan kings did wrest power every now and then, but the area remained strongly Hindu throughout, with some distinctive local traditions. The Brahmans (priests), known locally as *Nambudiris,* managed to build up an extraordinary power base by declaring any land taken in battle as sacred and under their jurisdiction. The Kshatriya (warrior and ruling) caste, known as the *Nairs,* lived to a strict chivalric and military code, similar to that of the Japanese Samurai. Inheritance was through the female line, the property of the entire extended family was held communally, and the head of the family never married, with the eldest son of his eldest sister inheriting. Today most of this has changed but the Brahmans are still very powerful, it is virtually impossible for a non-Hindu to enter a temple, and women have more rights and freedom than in most other parts of India.

In the 10th century, Chera rule finally collapsed and the area split into three smaller kingdoms: Travancore in the south, Cochin in the centre, and to the north Calicut, 37 miles (60 km) south of Mahé, whose rulers took the title Zamorin (Lord of the Sea) and gradually gained ascendancy over the other two, largely thanks to their close ties with the Arabs.

It was in Calicut, which later gave its name to the cotton cloth *calico,* that Vasco da Gama first set foot on Indian soil during his epic voyage in 1498. He succeeded in persuading an extremely reluctant Zamorin to give him trading rights, and the Portuguese set about wresting control of the trade routes from the Arabs. Shortly afterwards the Dutch, English and French also arrived, and the battle for control was on. Nearly a century later, the Arabs were out of the picture and the Europeans reached a happy compromise. The English dealt with Travancore, the Dutch with Cochin, the French had their own territory in Mahé and Calicut dealt with the Portuguese.

In 1766 came a new threat, the terrifying arrival

ABOVE, *temple elephants line up in their finery at Alappuzha (Alleppey)*

of the great Muslim emperors, Hyder Ali and his son, Tipu Sultan, the first to cross the Western Ghats and threaten the independence of the Malabar states. It was enough to frighten the three Indian rulers into working together and they begged the powerful British military machine for help. In 1789 their combined forces drove Tipu Sultan back across the mountains, and in 1792 Lord Cornwallis forced him to give up all claim to the territory. Somehow, however, in the new order Calicut became a British territory and Travancore and Cochin both had puppet governments. It spelt the end of independence.

The main road turns inland a little way on its 72 mile (115 km) journey to Trichur, a small town with a magnificent temple (closed to non-Hindus), a small museum and zoo. For most of the year, the town is probably not worth a stop. In late April or early May, however, it hosts the festival of Pooram, the Malayalam New Year and one of the most colourful events in the whole Indian calendar. In Trichur the festival is dedicated to eight minor gods and two goddesses, Paramekkavu and Thiruvambady. Rivalry between their followers became so serious it was made official, and now the two groups huddle together in strictest secrecy for months on end, designing ever more splendid costumes for the great parade. On the day, each side fields 15 elephants lined up to attention in the square beside the Vadakkunathan Temple, the animals decked out in gold and jewels, silks and peacock feathers, their Brahman riders carrying an image of the deity shaded by a sumptuous parasol. An orchestra plays itself into a frenzy as the animals are inspected, the winners being proclaimed by the roar of the crowd, after which there is a splendid procession and a really good party.

From here it is only about 19 miles (30 km) to Cranganore, once the most important port on the Malabar coast. According to legend, after the events of Pentecost the apostles spread out across the world to deliver the message of Christ. Thomas (Doubting Tom) ended up in India, supposedly landing in Cranganore in AD52. A memorial stone is said to mark the spot where he landed, and the extravagantly designed local church claims to contain his relics. In the 4th century a colony of Syrian Christians also settled here; when crusading Portuguese missionaries arrived in the 16th century, they were astounded to find a thriving Christian population already *in*

CENTRE, *the Backwaters between Alleppey and Quilon are a highway for goods and passengers*

situ. Backed by the Inquisition, the Portuguese tried their hardest to convert the Syrians, even arresting the Patriarch, but they never really succeeded. They did manage to collect some other converts, however, as did later Anglican missionaries. Today some 20% of the population is Christian, and all three branches of the faith have strong followings.

Cranganore was also a regular port of call for Arab traders. Local Muslims claim, quite without foundation, that their mosque dates back to AD664, and is therefore the oldest in India by some 400 years. Even if this particular building is much later, it seems certain that Islam was introduced here peaceably in the 7th century, considerably before the rest of India was converted by the sword.

The most magical section of the route starts 31 miles (50 km) south in the twin cities of Cochin – Ernakulam. Ernakulam, on the mainland, is the modern town, the business and industrial centre, while the modern harbour, the airport and the enchanting old town of Cochin are sprawled across the Mattancheri Peninsula and several surrounding islands.

For most of its life a capital and the residence of kings, Cochin only lost its status in 1956. It still has one of the busiest harbours in India and is the Southern Command Headquarters of the Indian Navy. It also has an extraordinarily cosmopolitan history. Not only did the Hindus, Christians and Arabs work happily side by side, but the city was home to a thriving colony of Jews, who arrived in two separate waves of migration. The first 'black Jews' are said to have arrived in 587 BC, fleeing from the tyranny of Nebuchadnezzar. They were certainly well-integrated and inter-married by the time the earliest Christians arrived in the first century AD. A second wave of 'white Jews' who arrived in the late 10th century tended to keep to themselves, but lived harmoniously alongside all the other communities. It was the Portuguese who unsettled the status quo. Complaining about the quality of the pepper they were sold, they managed to whip up a storm of anti-Semitism which resulted in the massacre of several Jewish traders. The rest fled into Cochin to live under the protection of the Raja, where they continued to trade happily until the young emigrated *en masse* to Israel in 1948. It is fascinating to wander through the narrow streets and brightly painted spice warehouses of Jewtown, and to visit the current synagogue, dating from 1664. Even though the Jewish community now consists of only a tiny handful of old people, the synagogue is still a proud creation, with a floor of blue and white Chinese tiles, massive chandeliers and brocade wall-hangings.

The European enclaves, with Dutch gables, Portuguese villas and English cottages, cluster together in what would have been the lee of the now defunct 16th-century fort. In its grounds stands the rather shabby Church of St Francis, built in 1546 and the earliest European church in India. Vasco da Gama spent the last 14 years of his life as Portuguese Viceroy in Cochin, and on his death in 1524 was buried in an earlier church on this site. His body was taken back to Lisbon in 1538 but you can still see the grave. The church also has a splendid *punkah* fan in working order.

The Portuguese first built the beautiful little Mattancheri Palace in 1557, giving it to the Raja in exchange for trading rights. The Dutch later rebuilt most of it – for the same reason. The two-storey palace is built in traditional Keralan style around a courtyard containing a temple to Bhagavati. Many of its rooms are literally covered with superb 16–19th century murals, some religious, some highly sensual. The royal bedroom, off the Coronation Hall, has 45 pictures dating from the 16th century which tell the story of the Ramayana.

Cochin is also the best place in which to see a performance of the magnificent Keralan Kathakali dance-drama. Part religious, part theatre, it draws on the sacred epics for its stories and on tribal dance and Nair martial arts for its style, a graceful and hypnotic sequence of slight, deliberate movements with meanings so precise that those in the

BELOW, *loading bales of coir on to a lorry; the coir industry is one of Kerala's main sources of income*

ABOVE, *colourful snake boat races form part of the temple festival at Aranmula, near Chengannur*

BELOW, *there are three essential ingredients in the Keralan diet; fish, coconut and rice*

know can read the dance as we would read a book. It can take 20 years to train the all-male dancers, and nearly two hours for them to don their elaborate, mask-like make-up, heavy robes and towering headdresses. In many cases, these preparations have actually become part of the show.

As you leave Cochin, heading south for 35 miles (56 km) alongside huge Lake Vembanad, you will see rows of vast cantilevered Chinese fishing nets, introduced, some say, by a traveller from the court of Kublai Khan. Billowing gracefully against the sky, they duck their heads into the water like herons and are hauled back out, dripping with silver fish, by teams of sweating fishermen heaving together on a heavy rope.

Alleppey, a pleasant little market town which trades in coir, is the home of Kerala's second main festival, Onam, held in August–September to celebrate the end of the monsoon, the gathering of the harvest and the annual return from exile of the legendary Asura king, Mahabali, with processions and dance, music and flowers and, above all, hotly contested snake boat races, each narrow, brightly decorated canoe holding up to 100 oarsmen.

The Backwaters

Here you are on the edge of an emerald sea known as the Backwaters, 1250 square miles (3200 sq km) of paddy fields, dredged from the swamps by Tipu Sultan in the 17th century, broken only by narrow dykes and small canals. The road leads down the edge of the area, but you will never feel its real magic unless you take to the water. There are tourist boats, but for a fraction of the price and a great deal more enjoyment, take the local water bus to Quilon, another small town famous for its cashew nuts, but once so important that the Malayalam calendar is calculated from the date of its foundation in the 9th century AD. It is an eight-hour journey of sheer heaven, drifting through fields where women work patiently, up to their waists in water, while little dug-out canoes and heavily laden barges with sails of plaited palm creep through overhung canals, and every passenger, from pristine schoolgirls and businessmen to field hands and traders, wants to talk.

From Quilon, take to the road again for the 44 miles (71 km) to Trivandrum, the capital of modern Kerala, whose new–old name, Thiruvananthapuram, means 'home of Anantha', the sacred multi-headed serpent in whose coils Lord Vishnu takes his rest. The town is large and

bustling with a population addicted to noisy political demonstration and newspapers, with over 40 published locally. Every May people flock south to await the arrival of the monsoon, officially monitored and declared by the local observatory, gathering on the beach to welcome the solid line of heavy black cloud as it thunders ashore to renew the earth.

Most tourists choose to stay 10 miles (16 km) south at delightful Kovalam beach, once a little known outpost of the hippy trail. A series of small secluded coves punctuated by rocky promontories is lined with small hotels and tiny shacks glorying under names like Woodstock, Velvet Dawn and Giggling Sausage, serving superlative shark and chips, mango milkshakes and banana pancakes. Local women cruise the sand selling fresh pineapple and green coconuts, and the musselmen dive from their canoes within sight of the beach. But Kovalam is under threat because of its popularity. The beach has been widened by 330 feet (100 m), beach umbrellas are appearing, new five-star developments are underway and the area is being heavily promoted as a potential goldmine.

The Padmanabhapuram Palace, 26 miles (42 km) further south, is now in Tamil Nadu, but was for a long time located in the capital of Travancore. The low-slung decorative palace, dating from 1550, is the finest surviving example of traditional Keralan architecture. Because they were frequently built in wood, few great buildings have survived the ravages of time and termites.

Finally, after another 28 miles (45 km), you reach Kanniyakumari on the southern tip of Cape Comorin, at the end of the Indian sub-continent. It is one of the holiest places in South India and it was here that Gandhi chose to have his ashes scattered. Every day crowds of pilgrims visit his memorial, pray at the many temples and then gather to watch the sunset glowing over the multi-coloured sands of red, gold and black, at the point where three seas meet – the Arabian Sea, the Bay of Bengal and the Indian Ocean.

PRACTICAL INFORMATION

■ All foreigners require a visa, available from your nearest Indian embassy. There are regular flights to Cochin and Trivandrum from Bombay and Madras. For Mangalore, fly to Bangalore.

■ Driving is meant to be on the left; in practice you go through any available gap, deferring only to any vehicle larger or more powerful than your own. Petrol is available in all larger towns.

■ It is always hot; it is best to travel in November to February, avoiding monsoon rains in late May to July. The main festivals are in April–May and August–September.

■ Visitors will need various inoculations – consult a doctor before travelling.

ABOVE, *the Suchindram Temple near Kanniyakumari is dedicated to the Hindu Trinity of Brahma, Vishnu and Shiva*

BELOW, *a memorial to the Hindu philosopher Vivekananda, on the rock where he meditated at Kanniyakumari*

ABOVE, *brightly coloured prayer wheels and flags for sale in Lhasa's Bharkov market*

The Friendship Highway from Lhasa to Kathmandu

RICHARD SALE

In a list of the world's most exotic cities, whether compiled by a traveller in search of adventure, of the scenically breathtaking, or of the historically or artistically interesting, Lhasa would come close to the top, with Kathmandu close behind. Yet, even though these cities are only 600 miles (950 km) apart, the road that links the capital of Tibet to the capital of Nepal is only 20 years old. Fraught with difficulties, the road is not for the easily perturbed, but to compensate it offers stunning views and a glimpse of Shangri La.

FAR RIGHT, *the great Potala Palace, home of the Dalai Lamas, is reflected in the Dragon's Pool*

SO EFFECTIVE a barrier was the Himalayan mountain range that there was little interchange between the fledgling countries of Nepal and Tibet during the years following the birth of Siddhartha Gautama, the Buddha. The Buddha was born in Lumbini, in south-east Nepal about 540 BC, his message spreading through the country and southward through India during the following centuries . Only in the eighth century AD was Buddhism finally established in Tibet.

BELOW, *a smile of greeting from a young itinerant monk in Lhasa*

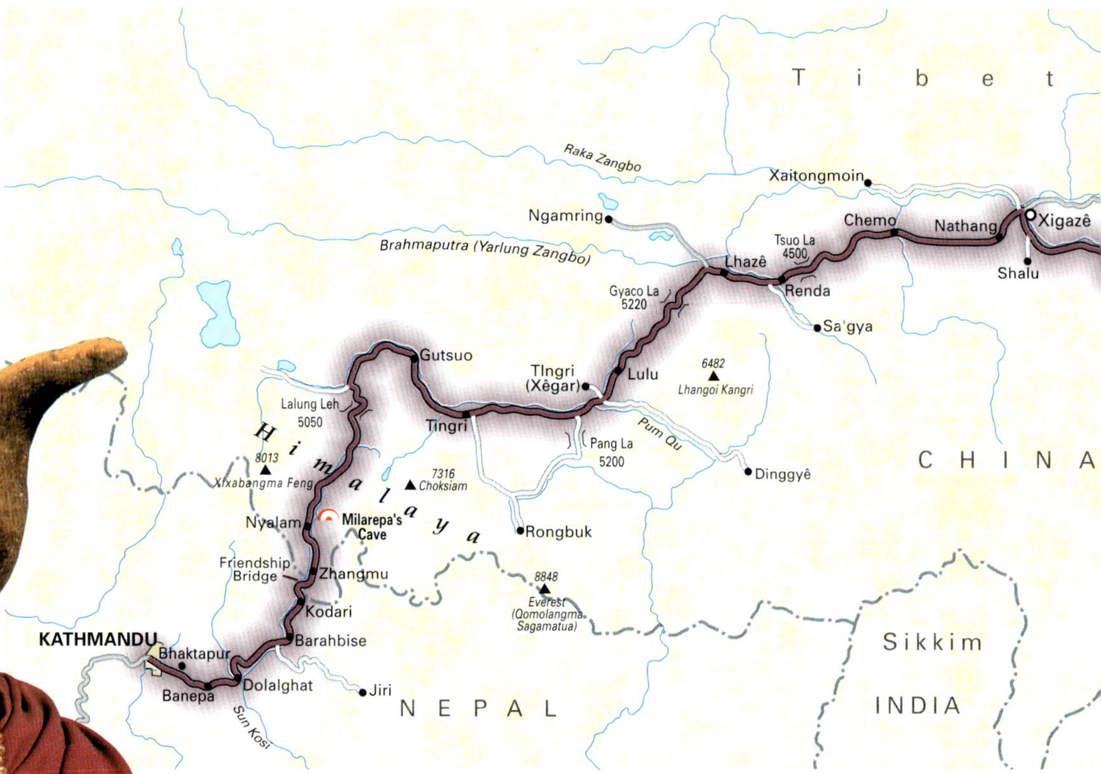

The city of Kathmandu stands at an altitude of about 4290 feet (about 1300 m). Since the Tibetan plateau, just 120 miles (192 km) away is over 13,200 feet (3900 m), travelling to Lhasa can cause problems with altitude sickness. These can be overcome, to a certain extent, by flying to Lhasa and travelling west to Kathmandu, especially if a day or two is spent in the Tibetan capital sight-seeing and acclimatising. The disadvantage of travelling in this direction is that it is a little more difficult to organise.

Assuming that the traveller does head west, the first few miles of road reverse the route from Lhasa to the Yarlung Zangbo bridge – Lhasa airport being at Gonggar. From the bridge the road climbs over two high passes (each at around 16,000 feet – about 5000 m) to reach Xigazê. This is mountainous terrain, with high, snow-topped peaks on each side. Beyond Xigazê is the real Tibet, a high plateau dusty with red and brown soil blown down from the barren hills. Between Lhazê and Xêgar the road crosses the Jia Tsuo La, its highest pass at 17,226 feet (5220 m). Further on, at Tingri, a road to the left leads to the Rongbuk Valley and the base camp for attempts on Everest's northern face. Everest itself is visible from the road at this point.

After one final pass, the Lalung Leh, the road falls to Zhangmu (Khasa), the final Tibetan village before Friendship Bridge (over the Bhote Kosi) is crossed into Nepal. The road on this last Tibetan section, and on the Nepalese side as far as Barabhise is prone to landslides during and immediately after the monsoon. Beyond Barabhise the road improves, finally traversing the beautiful Kathmandu valley and visiting Bhaktapur. Just a few miles further is Kathmandu.

The great trade routes from Tibet went eastwards into China and south through Sikkim into India: when the British army under Younghusband invaded Tibet in 1904 they entered along the Sikkim route. There would have been trade over the high passes, but the terrain and the climate limited it to a few hardy yak herders mostly dealing in silk. Then, in the early 1960s, the Chinese agreed to fund and construct the Friendship Highway between Lhasa and Kathmandu. By 1966 the Tibetan section of the road was complete. The Friendship Bridge, symbolically linking the two countries, was constructed and by the early 1970s the road to Kathmandu had been completed.

Palaces and Monasteries of Lhasa

The Potala Palace is the symbol of Tibet and will be on the itinerary of everyone travelling the Friendship Highway. It is a magnificent building, still dominating Lhasa despite the growth of the city since the Chinese annexed Tibet in 1950. The palace was started in 1645 by the Fifth Dalai Lama. The lower White Palace was completed during the Fifth's lifetime, but news of his death in 1682 was withheld from the populace until the Red Palace had been completed, twelve years later.

The Potala is an extraordinary place. The sheer scale of the engineering is breathtaking: the palace is built of stone, earth and wood only, there being no metalwork to support the building's fabric and no nails to secure the woodwork. The only exception is that molten copper was poured into the walls – which are up to 16 feet (5 m) thick – to give some protection against earthquakes.

ABOVE, *Lhasa, once the Forbidden City closed to foreigners, is dominated by the Potala Palace*

BELOW, *a massed ceremony of prayer at the Jokhang Temple, Tibet's centre of pilgrimage*

The Potala's rooms house the *chortens* – tombs – of many of Tibet's Dalai Lamas. The term Dalai means 'Ocean of Wisdom' and was conferred on the Chief Priest of the Tibetan Buddhists by a 16th-century Mongolian emperor. The Dalai Lama is the earthly incarnation of Chenrezi, the Buddhist Lord of Mercy and, upon his death, certain signs read by other lamas lead them to a child who is the new incarnation. The present Dalai Lama, living in exile in India, is the fourteenth. The tombs of earlier incarnations are astonishing: that of the Fifth Dalai Lama is covered with almost four tons of gold.

To the north of the palace is the Dragon's Pool, created, it is said, by the digging of earth to form the Potala. Legend has it that the dragon of the name was placated by an annual human sacrifice, this ceasing only when the strong lad chosen one year took on the beast, killing it after a seven-day struggle.

Near by is the Jokhang Temple, the spiritual centre of Tibet, home to a gold, coral and turquoise statue of the Buddha Sakyamuni, the country's most important religious image. The Jokhang was built in the 7th century on the filled-in site of a lake whose waters were said to reflect the future. There is still a pool of the lake below the main courtyard. The temple is Tibet's most important pilgrimage centre. The roof is a wonderful place, not only for the burnished statues and purple hangings, but also for the view of the Potala and of Barkhor Square below. The square is the centre of Lhasan life, with stalls selling to pilgrims and tourists alike. A walk around is a must, but remember to walk the circuit clockwise, as an anti-clockwise circuit is an affront to the Tibetans.

North of the Jokhang, the Sera Monastery is also worth visiting. From its roof the frames for huge *thangkas* – ceremonial silk or cotton squares with brightly painted illustrations of Buddhist texts – can be seen on the hillside beyond. To the east of the site, but hidden from view, is the sky burial site. Because of the country's shortage of wood and usable land, the Tibetans dispose of their dead by dissecting the corpses and laying them out on rocks for vultures and crows to consume. The bones, crushed and mixed with *tsampa* (a dough of roasted barley flour) are also eaten by the birds. At one time the Chinese allowed visitors to watch, and even to photograph these sky burials, but fortunately the site is now out of bounds.

Leaving Lhasa

After a day or so of acclimatization you will be ready to leave Lhasa. Bidding farewell to the coral and turquoise sellers you head west from the Potala, passing through the new Chinese Lhasa, passing, too, the Lhasa Holiday Inn Hotel. From the hotel you are travelling in the footsteps of pilgrims to the Drepung monastery, a town-like complex of buildings now sadly quiet after being depopulated of monks in 1959. Then there were over 7000 monks. Today there are just a few hundred, though pilgrims, grimy from days of travel and clutching their prayer wheels and chanting softly, still climb the path to the monastery's colleges of learning and holy places.

Ahead the road runs through the fertile valley of the Lhasa River. Here, and further on in the equally fertile Nyang Qu Valley, you may see folk working in the roadside fields. If your visit is in autumn you will see yak-drawn wooden ploughs tilling the soil. The yaks are driven by the farmer while his family follow, throwing out handfuls of barley seed. Look out for the young girls or boys with wicker baskets on their backs and curious long-handled, three-pronged sticks: they are collecting yak dung, which may be used as a plaster for house walls, or, when dried, to fuel the fire. If there is a fire in the fields – ready to provide tsampa and hot yak butter tea – look out for the long wooden cylinder in which the tea is made. (As an aside, if you are offered yak butter tea be sure to add lots of salt and to drink it hot, before the congealing fat globules rob you of your enthusiasm.)

Still within the Lhasa River valley, there are beautiful views eastwards over red-brown hills, and a fine close-up view of a painted, rock-carved relief of a seated Buddha. After 43 miles (68 km) the road crosses the Yarlung Zangpo, the legendary Brahmaputra River. Here, look out for Tibetans on the river in skin coracles. The coracles, made from yak skins stretched over sticks, are used, as they have been for centuries, to ferry people across the river (the bridges being far apart) and to move food and animals along it.

To the north, above the Yarlung Zangbo bridge, is Chuwori, one of the four sacred mountains of Tibet. The white ladders on the flanks of this 19,675 foot (5962 m) peak were painted by pilgrims. By using them the faithful are said to be able to reach heaven.

Beyond the bridge the main road goes eastwards to Lhasa's airport, but our road turns right, following the route of the old trade caravans from Tibet to Sikkim. Tiny villages here consist of a few mud-walled huts, sometimes nestling below the ruins of an old fort. Within them women and children in Tibetan dress will speak to you with a mixture of shyness and curiosity, while the

BELOW, *traditional ploughing with yaks in the craggy landscape near Zigazê*

menfolk play a game that looks like ludo and involves much laughter and slapping of hands on the table.

The road rises and falls to the first pass, the Kamba La at 15,820 feet (4794 m), just 43 feet (13 m) lower than Mont Blanc's summit. Over the pass is the huge Yamdrok Tso lake, bright blue or blue-green depending on the weather, and backed by red-brown peaks studded, on their lower shores, by bright green fields. Two villages are passed, Nagarzê and Langla, before the road crosses the Karo La. Despite its height (16,533 feet, 5010 m) the pass is identified only by the prayer flags and *mani* stones, and by the sight of a glacier falling from Nozin Kang sa, a 23,835 foot (7223 m) peak to the north (right). The Karo La was the scene of the world's highest battle when, in 1904, Younghusband's British force defeated the rag-tag Tibetan army during its march along the road towards Lhasa. From the pass the road drops into the fertile Nyang Qu Valley to reach Gyangzê.

The town's chief attraction is the Kumbum, the centrepiece of the Palkhor Chöde monastery. This incredible *stupa* temple consists of four blocks of multi-walled chapels topped by a cylindrical tower. On top of this is a square tower decorated with Nepalese-style all-seeing eyes, and this is topped by a gilded cone constructed of thirteen rings. Even that is not the end, the cone being finished with a final parasol of intricate golden metalwork and finials.

At Gyangzê the old trade route to Sikkim turned south, but our road continues along the

BELOW, *the journey provides several chances to view Mount Everest at Xêgar or Tingri*

INSET, *the Kumbum at the Palkhor Chöde monastery, a stupa constructed of layers of intricate decorations*

valley. In the farms old women, too old to work the fields, can be seen winnowing barley, while younger folk fork barley straw into piles.

Xigazê, close to where the Nyang Chu reaches the Yarlung Zangbo, is Tibet's second city, with its sprawl of modern Chinese buildings. Its highlight is the great monastery of Tashilhunpo (Heap of Glory), the seat of the Panchen Lamas. The Fifth Dalai Lama recognized his tutor as an incarnation of the Buddha of Boundless Light (Amitabha, or Opome, in Tibetan) and gave him the title Panchen Lama (Panchen means Great Scholar). Since that time the Panchen Lamas have been reincarnated, the new manifestation being found in the same way as that of the Dalai Lama. The monastery of the Panchens is magnificent and houses the world's largest bronze Buddha, an 86 foot (26 m) statue created in 1911. The statue is made of 150 tons of bronze and almost a quarter of a ton of gold; the third eye is a huge diamond.

Westwards from Xigazê the road crosses the Tibetan plateau, a virtual desert through which the road cuts a dusty route. Across the desert, red-brown peaks are striped in shades of grey and blue. About 10 miles (16 km) from the town the ruins of the Nathang Monastery, destroyed in 1966, are passed. Beyond, the road hovers around the 13,200 foot (4000m) contour before crossing over the Tsuo La.

Soon after this, a road to the left leads to the Sa'gya monastery. In the 13th century the monastery was the capital of Tibet, its abbot having been so great a teacher that he was employed by Genghis Khan to tutor his son. The great Khan's grandson, Kublai Khan, capital status to the monastery. But with the fading of the Mongolian empire, Sa'gya's influence waned.

Apart from the odd truck and tourist bus the road is empty now. It passes through Lhazê which, of all unlikely things, is a spa, then goes through a wild, rocky gorge to reach its highest point at the summit of the Jia Tsuo La, at 17,226 feet (5220m), again marked by little more than a collection of prayer flags. To the south here the highest Himalayan peaks can be seen for the first time, though it is not for another 6 miles (10 km) or so that Everest itself may be seen. The next town is Xêgar, nestling below a conical mountain up which march the walls of an old fort. If you have acclimatised well you should climb up the fortressed hill for a view of Everest.

Beyond the turn off to Xêgar is the turning for the Rongbuk monastery and the northern Everest base camp. For those with time this is an exciting detour, the ruins of the monastery (now being restored) and the view of Everest's huge north face recalling the visits, and the exploits, of the between-wars expeditions. Mallory and Irvine came this way.

ABOVE, *one of the many monasteries passed on the way – Tashilhunpo, in Tibet's second city of Xigazê*

For those without the time, Everest can be seen again – the huge pyramidal peak to the left – at Tingri, where another turn to the left offers an alternative route to Rongbuk. Further on again, at Gutsuo, there is another fine view of the world's highest peak. On again, at the Lalung Leh, the road's final pass, there is a magnificent view of the high Himalaya, dominated by the huge peak of Xixabangma Feng, the world's fourteenth highest mountain and the highest to lie wholly within Tibet. The road now descends in a gradient that is only halted 14,800 feet (about 4500 m) below in Nepal, as Kathmandu is approached.

But there are still places of interest in Tibet. About 30 miles (48 km) beyond the Lalung Leh, near a tiny village called Zhonggang, a path leads to Milarepa's Cave. Milarepa lived from 1040 to 1123 and is renowned as Tibet's most important mystical poet. He lived here as an ascetic (his name means 'cotton-clad Mila' from the light-weight robe he wore, even in winter). His poetry is collected into a book ambitiously titled *The Hundred Thousand Songs of Milarepa.* Close to the cave is a recently restored monastery.

The road now drops through Nyalam, a small market town, to reach a gorge with the imposing name of the Gates of Hell. The road in this section is prone to landslides, the lush green of the gorge telling you that you have reached the country of the real monsoon. The gorge is traversed by a raging stream – a combination of the monsoon stream and winter's snows. If a landslip has occurred you may be delayed, or even have to walk around it to reach alternative transport. Finally Zhangmu (known as Khasa by the Nepalese) is reached. It is an enclosed place, set in a forest, a remarkable change from the plateau villages of the last few days.

ABOVE, *Durbar Square in Bhaktapur is the meeting point for a cluster of medieval streets*

CROSSING INTO NEPAL

The road goes through Zhangmu on a series of hairpin bends to reach the Chinese customs post. Your documents will be checked here, although it is a further 5 miles (8 km) – and a drop of 1750 feet (530 m) – to the actual border on Friendship Bridge. The road through this last piece of Tibet is often washed away and you may well have to walk to the Nepalese frontier post at Kodari.

The Kathmandu valley is lushly green with waters from the Langtang National Park, but the villages, while interesting, have little to hold the visitor's attention.

Legend has it that Kathmandu valley was once a lake which was emptied when a single sword thrust (by a Hindu or a Buddhist hero depending upon which version of the legend you choose) breached the valley wall and drained it.

Within the valley most visitors head straight for Bhaktapur. Bhaktapur is the best of the three Royal cities of the valley, a near-perfect medieval Nepalese town with a series of delightful streets radiating out from the impressive Durbar Square with its array of temples. Close to the square is the Nyatapola Temple, five storeys high and, at 100 feet (30 m), the tallest temple in the Kathmandu valley. The stairway to the temple is flanked by superb carved figures, a pair of legendary wrestlers, elephants, lions, griffins and two goddesses in the forms of a lion and a tiger. Behind the Nyatapola is the splendid triple-footed Bhairabnath Temple.

From Durbar Square it is a short step to Potters' Square, one of the main centres for pot making in Nepal. Here thousands of vessels stand drying in the sun, while the smell of wood smoke from the pot kilns hangs in the clear air. Dotted around the square's edges, in the shady corners, potters can be seen at work.

KATHMANDU

The final stretch of the road takes you close to Tribhuvan Airport and then into Kathmandu. After Lhasa and the Tibetan Plateau, even after Bhaktapur, Kathmandu is an assault on the senses: smells from the street markets, the incessant din of car horns, thousands of people moving all ways at once. Unlike Lhasa, which has a relatively small number of defined palaces and temples, Kathmandu is alive with interest and can be wandered at will. Certain places should not, however, be missed, and chief of these is Durbar Square (Durbar means palace in Nepalese, explaining why each of the three royal cities – Kathmandu, Pathan and Durbar – has one). At the south-west corner of the square is the Kasthamandrop, a 12th-century wooden building from which the city derives its name. Near by – where Durbar Square meets Basantapur Square – is the Kumari Bahal, the House of the Living Goddess. The goddess is the Kumari Devi, a pre-pubescent girl chosen from among a select band of Nepalese craft families at the age of four or five.

From then until she reaches puberty the girl lives in the house, appearing only for half-a-dozen festivals annually. At that time she rejoins her family and a new goddess is chosen. You can enter the Kumari Bahal and, for a consideration, the goddess's attendants will even get her to put in an appearance. But do not take photographs.

From Basantapur Square, Freak Street runs into the old city. The street's real name is Jochne, the new name deriving from its having been the meeting place of hippies in the 1960s. Time has now passed the street by, the centre of vigorous tourist buying and selling now being Thamel, to the north of Durbar Square, but it should be visited for sheer nostalgia value.

The Royal Palace lies east of Thamel and is worth visiting for the incongruous view of cows gently wandering past ceremonial guards.

Those with more time should visit Pathan, where the Durbar Square has another fine range of temples and the street entertainment includes snake charmers. But all visitors should try to reach Swayambhunath, the magnificent site on a hilltop to the west of the city. Legend has it that the hilltop was an island in the lake that once filled the Kathmandu valley and that, as the valley's waters receded, a flame ignited on the hill. Certainly the hill has been a sacred site for at least 2000 years. Prayer flags and countless steps greet the visitor.

At the top of the steps is one of Nepal's finest *stupas*, the all-seeing eye looking out across the lush Kathmandu valley.

PRACTICAL INFORMATION

■ The China National Tourist Office in Britain is at 4 Glentworth Street, London NW1 5PG, Tel: 0171 935 9427, Fax: 0171 487 5842. The best source of travel information is the myriad of travel agencies in Kathmandu, or the notice board in the Lhasa Holiday Inn.

■ It is best to travel in March to mid-May or mid-September to mid-November. The driving time from Lhasa to Kathmandu is 24–30 hours depending upon conditions.

■ Acute mountain sickness (AMS) will be a problem for almost anyone travelling this route. You would be well-advised to consult a doctor before travelling to the region.

ABOVE, *all-seeing eyes are a traditional Nepalse motif; they stare out from the Bodnath stupa at Kathmandu*

LEFT, *Kathmandu, seen here from the hills, was once the capital of the Gurkhas*

ABOVE, *with every available space set with jewels, the Grand Palace at Bangkok gleams in the tropical sunshine*

BELOW RIGHT, *swirling dust surrounds travellers on the road between Phang-nga and Krabi*

BELOW, *the serene features of the Golden Buddha in the temple of Wat Traimit*

The Asian Highway from Bangkok to Singapore

BEN DAVIES

From the seething chaos of Bangkok, the Asian Highway snakes its way down the lush Malay Peninsula through rice fields and rubber plantations to the island nation of Singapore. A century ago, the journey would have taken several months on a bullock cart and involved fording rivers and swamp-infested jungle. These days, it's a three day drive on the superhighway with hotels, magnificent scenery and traffic jams beyond compare.

IT WOULD undoubtedly have been quicker leaving Bangkok on an elephant – and more pleasant. In the 19th century when these lumbering animals were the most common form of transport, Bangkok, city of angels, had no traffic jams, nor for that matter highways. King Mongkut, best known for his 35 wives and 83 children, soon changed that. In 1862 he ordered the first road to be constructed alongside one of the city's many canals.

Since then, Bangkok and its drivers have never looked back. The average Bangkokean spends 52 days a year in a traffic jam, wasting US$560 million in fuel bills and leaving 50% of traffic police with respiratory infections.

Of course that leaves plenty of time to see the sights. As you cross the Chao Phraya river, keep your eyes open for two of the city's best known landmarks. On the east bank is the Grand Palace, constructed by nine successive kings and made up of almost one square mile of glittering jewel-encrusted pavilions and spires, and on the west bank is Siriraj Hospital, where Thailand's most notorious murderer See-ouey is preserved in a large glass jar, pickled in formaldehyde.

Near by there are other monuments too: the famous 19th-century Wat Arun, temple of dawn, with its 284 feet (85m)central spire covered in fragments of multi-coloured porcelain; Wat Traimit, containing a 5.6 ton Buddha made of gold; the fantastically ornamented Royal Barges; and Wat Thong Noppakhun, which until the mid 19th century contained murals of urinating angels.

From Taksin Bridge, the Asian Highway heads down Krung Thonburi Road and across Wongwiang Yai in a great arc towards Thailand's lush peninsula. Office blocks and factories give way to Chinese shop-fronted houses and at length

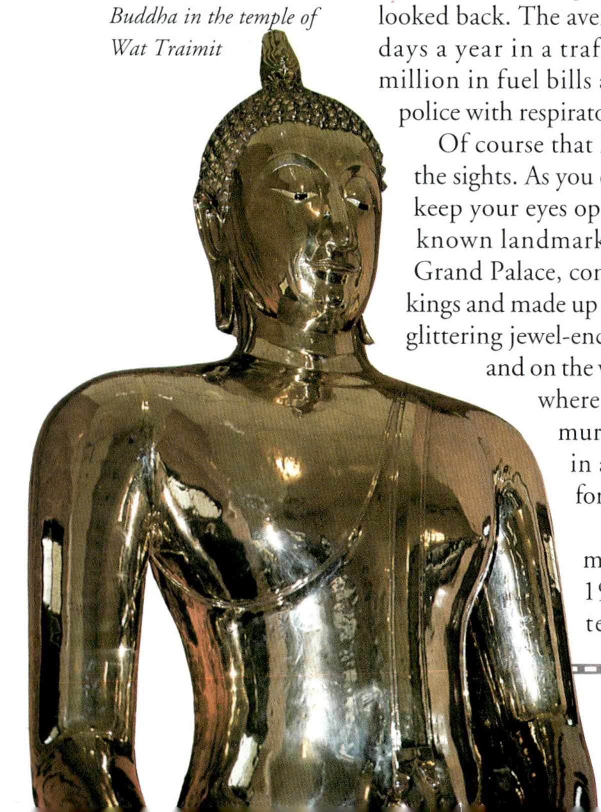

From Sathorn Road in Bangkok's business district, cross over Taksin Bridge to Thon Buri and join Highway 4, signposted to Nakhon Pathom. Before leaving the city, nobody should miss the Grand Palace at Sanam Luang, Wat Po on Maharat Road and a boat trip around Klong Yai and Klong Mon. From Bangkok, it's 37 miles (59 km) to Nakhon Pathom, home to one of the biggest pagodas in the East. A short distance beyond Nakhon Pathom, Highway 4 branches south towards the towns of Phet Buri and the old royal beach resort at Hua Hin. At Chumphon, the major route splits. Highway 401 continues along the east coast to Surat Thani and Highway 4 along the west coast to the beach resorts at Phuket and Krabi. For fantastic scenery, catch a boat from Krabi to the idyllic Phi Phi islands. Crossing back over the isthmus, visit the famous Thale Noi bird park at Phattalung and further south the sprawling city of Hat Yai. At the Malaysian border, arrive before 5 pm, and don't drive after dark.

From Bukit Kayu Hitam, you have the pick of the brand new North–South Highway or a smaller network of roads which run almost parallel. Most people will take the left turning at Tapah to Tanah Rata and the cool of the Cameron Highlands. At Kuala Lumpur, inspect Chinatown, the national mosque and the nearby Batu Caves. Melaka is a popular historic town with sights including the Cheng Hoon Teng temple ('the abode of green clouds') and the Porto de Santiago. From here it's a 125 mile (200 km) drive to Singapore and the border crossing at the town of Johor Baharu.

Finally remember, anyone driving will need considerable experience, an abundance of courage and lots of luck. Those lacking in such attributes would do better to take a bus.

ABOVE, *a jetty leads towards the sunset at Ranong, where there is one of Thailand's few hot springs*

MAIN PICTURE, *this* prasat *at Phet Buri has a typically needle-like spire*

to the rice fields and salt plains of Nakhon Pathom. After a short distance, you must turn left onto Highway 4, which veers south, snaking its way down towards the Malaysian border some 750 miles (1200 km) further.

That there is a highway at all is a major achievement. Until the early 20th century, bullock carts and elephants were the most common overland conveyance in Thailand, with villagers travelling in organized caravans to guard against wild animals and thieves. During the day, they would ford rivers and canals. At night, they would camp in the forest under the watchful eye of the *phedchaluukam*, or the god of the cart.

In 1936, the first real stretch of highway made its way into Thailand's history books, a narrow strip extending from Bangkok all the way to Petkasem and Nakhon Pathom, which was later continued to Chumphon and a few years later to Takua Pa.

Foreigners arriving in the 1950s were as captivated by the gravel surfaces of the road and the precarious wooden bridges as by the bemused look of the inhabitants they passed along the route. 'We bumped along at 40 miles an hour most of the time amidst clouds of dust,' wrote one W T Blake in 1953 as he motored from Chumphon to Prachuap Khiri Khan.

Completing the link to the Malaysian border posed more exacting problems. To the challenges of marshes, mosquitoes and malaria was added the danger of landslides and tigers, as well as attacks by Communist rebels and Muslim separatists. The stretch of road to Ranong on the west coast was not completed until 1962. Now Highway 4, known as the Asian Highway, runs all the way down the peninsula. However, with Thailand's delightful enthusiasm for inconsistency, parts of the highway have been turned into showpiece motorways, whilst others languish as a single lane.

Still one of the great pleasures of travel in Thailand is the opportunity to stop off along the way. At Phet Buri, one of the first major towns on the Asian Highway, the summer palace known as the Phra Nakhon Khiri is perched on the hill, built by King Mongkut and containing an observatory as well as several fine temples. Near by you will also find the Khao Luang caves where more than 100 years ago King Mongkut would come to make offerings to the Buddha. An hour's drive south of Phet Buri down a road lined with pineapple plantations will bring you to the 300 jagged hills where Mongkut, who was a noted astrologer, led an expedition of European dignitaries to witness an eclipse of the sun on 18 August 1886. The eclipse took place just four minutes earlier than Mongkut had predicted. But the king's triumph was to prove short lived, and two months later he died of malaria.

Beyond Sam Roi Yot, the road passes inland from Prachuap Khiri Khan and beautiful Ao Manao Bay past a sprinkling of beaches to busy Chumphon, where you must take the right fork towards Ban Takua Pa and the west coast.

As Highway 4 snakes its way through the hills down to Ranong and the Burmese border, watch out for the diminutive spirit houses perched on the most dangerous corners. Thais believe that, so long as the spirits are appeased with rice wine and joss-sticks and occasionally even pornographic pictures, they will ensure the safety of drivers. Upside-down cars however are by no means an uncommon feature along the highway. The locals put it down to Karma, but the passive observer might be tempted to blame Mekong whisky.

From Ranong, it's a pleasant five-hour drive to the turn off for Phuket (pronounced Poo-ket), Thailand's best known international beach resort.

INSET ABOVE, *traditional headgear gives protection from the sun in the island province of Phuket*

INSET BELOW LEFT, *the summer palace of Phra Nakhon Kiri provides spectacular views*

During the 18th and 19th centuries, the island's biggest commodity was tin, mined in abundant quantities and exported as far afield as Britain and Portugal. Since the early 1980s, however, Phuket's beaches, hotels and beer bars have transformed the province into the richest in the kingdom.

Some 30 miles (50 km) further down the road at the sleepy village of Phang-nga, turn off the main highway and park beside the pier. From here, it's easy to join one of the many tour groups that leave daily for Ko Tapu or Nail Island, featured in the film *The Man with the Golden Gun.*

South of Phang-nga is one of the most idyllic stretches of road in the whole of Thailand. For mile after mile, Highway 4 cuts through rubber and coffee plantations bordered by magnificent towering limestone cliffs and rich tropical vegetation stretching as far as the eye can see.

Passing Krabi, Highway 4 turns east, skirting Khao Chong wildlife preserve and the Thale Noi bird park to Phatthalung. During the 17th century, the inhabitants of this region were said to be a boisterous lot, much given to cohabitation and wife swapping. 'They take great delight in the eating of beetle and opium and love Areck [a strong liquor] exceedingly,' wrote one Thomas Herbert in the 17th century. These days the far south has a more measured feel to it. The people are predominantly Muslim, and Buddhist spires are replaced for the most part by towering mosques.

INTO MALAYSIA

From Hat Yai, the last major town in southern Thailand, you have the choice of two routes. The most scenic route to the Malaysian border is a four-hour drive through Chana and Pattani to Yala, from where Highway 410 curves spectacularly through limestone cliffs to the wild border crossing at Betong. The shorter and more frequently travelled Highway 4 follows close upon the railway line to the border town of Baan Klong Praun and then down Malaysia's densely populated west coast.

Of course you could take the modern North–South Highway from Bukit Kayu Hitam all the way south to Johor Baharu. Opened in 1994 by Malaysian prime minister Datuk Seri Mahathir bin Mohamad, it is Malaysia's most ambitious engineering project. In total it took more than 15 years to build, covers 529 miles (847 km) and contains 60 toll stations. Plans are now well under way so that the Asian Highway will one day extend all the way through Burma, India and Pakistan to the Central Asian Republics

BELOW, *'Nail Island' appears in a James Bond film, but is also famous for its bright corals and submarine caves*

and ultimately to Europe, connected via Turkey – a network of roads stretching 40,500 miles (65,000 km). This grand vision was originally conceived as far back as 1959, but suffered countless setbacks with the war in Cambodia, political turmoil in Burma and tensions between India and Pakistan. Now that Burma and Cambodia have once again become a party to the project, the Economic and Social Commission for Asia and the Pacific (ESCAP), which is acting as coordinator, is busily planning the next superhighway step.

What grand highways gain in speed, they lose in local colour, and drivers wanting to see the little towns and villages and experience the mood of the Malay countryside with its invisible rhythms would do better to avoid the Asian Highway or North–South Highway as much as possible. A better alternative is the older Route 1, which runs almost parallel through the towns of Butterworth, Taiping, Ipoh and Tapah, and down Malaysia's heavily populated west coast.

The first major town after crossing the border is Alur Setar with its fine state mosque known as the Masjid Zahir, and nearby the sultan's Thai-style audience hall known as the Balai Besar. The provincial capital of Kedah state has two other claims to fame. It is the gateway to Malaysia's biggest rice-producing region – and it is also home to prime minister Dr Mahathir Mohamad.

The hills east of Alur Setar have a different notoriety. During the turbulent 1960s and 1970s, the mountainous terrain and dense jungle that ran along the border were controlled by Communist insurgents seeking to undermine central government control. At one stage during the emergency period, and even during construction of the road, this was the scene of frequent hit-and-run attacks. Since 1989, however, a truce has been declared, although even now at night traffic is light.

From Alur Setar, it's a two-hour drive south through a coastal plain criss-crossed with paddies to Butterworth and the departure point for Pinang Island (Betel Nut Island). Captain Francis Light, working on behalf of the East India Company founded the island's pleasant capital at George Town in 1786. These days, the city has become a prosperous, cosmopolitan centre which has still preserved a flavour of the past in its crowded

ABOVE, *panoramic views of Pinang Island from the town of Butterworth*

BELOW, *Malaysian temple decoration differs from Thai style, but both are equally ornate*

ABOVE, *the highway sweeps through green city parklands at Kuala Lumpur*

streets, its vast Kek Lok Si Temple complex and hawker stalls selling *mee goreng* (fried noodles) and delicious squid.

South of Butterworth, Highway 1 cuts inland, passing rubber and oil palm plantations and further afield, the distant outlines of open-cast tin mines. When Ambrose Rathborne, a hardy Victorian prospector, travelled the same route in 1880, he found only a narrow track cut through the jungle. After floundering in swamps waist deep and climbing hills in 'tigerish localities', the local means of transport brought little relief. 'Elephant-travelling in this country is a slow method of progression,' noted the great man, 'for the animal's pace rarely exceeds one and a half miles an hour.'

Building roads in those early days was no easy matter. First the line of the road had to be staked out with numbered pegs, then undergrowth cut down and trees uprooted. Finally charcoal burners would be used to burn away the roots. Conditions were appalling. Many of the Malays, Chinese and Tamils collapsed from fever or dysentery. Other labourers fled into the jungle at night. The Chinese workers were considered the most reliable, but only when money was owed to them.

Passing Taiping, a short distance inland from the coast, Highway 1 bears east to Ipoh, a straggling town that sprung into notoriety for its rich finds of tin. During the early 1900s, this became known as the city of millionaires, after the Chinese immigrants who made their fortunes. Today the town, which is divided by the Kinta river, still boasts more than its fair share of opulent town houses as well as a thriving Chinatown.

From Ipoh, it's a two-hour drive south through spectacular limestone outcrops and jungle-clad hills to Tapah, where a side road leads east to the Cameron Highlands. Here, during the late 19th century, a Scottish surveyor named William Cameron discovered 'a plateau with gentle slopes shut in by loftier mountains'. In the early 1920s, the British constructed a tortuous road to their new hill station, building Surrey-style mansions

RIGHT, *the Batu caves, twelve kilometres north of Kuala Lumpur, are approached by a stairway of 245 steps*

FAR RIGHT, *one of Singapore's tourist attractions is the Tiger Balm Gardens, now an international theme park renamed Haw Par Villa*

and planting tea bushes, cabbages and strawberries to remind them of home.

The Cameron Highlands are remembered for another reason. It was here in March 1967 that Thai silk king, eccentric American and reputed CIA agent Jim Thompson mysteriously disappeared whilst on holiday. Despite extensive searches by local trackers, journalists and the military, no trace was ever found. Some speculated that Thompson had been kidnapped, others that he had been spirited away by the CIA, or even eaten by a tiger.

From the highlands down to the sea, the coastal plains are dominated by endless rows of rubber and palm oil trees. After crossing Perak, the centre of tin mining in Malaysia and one of the oldest states on the peninsula, Highway 1 enters the state of Selangor, home to the gigantic Batu Caves and to Kuala Lumpur, Malaysia's cosmopolitan capital. When the Rajah Abdullah, the Bugis chief of the state capital of Kelang came here in 1857 with members of the Selangor Royal Family, he discovered little more than a jungle swamp on the confluence of the Kelang and Gombok rivers. Now five star hotels, towering office blocks and traffic jams are more in evidence.

Despite its unprepossessing appearance, 'KL', as it is known to its expatriate residents, does have some redeeming features. In Chinatown, a swathe of crumbling shop houses and market stalls glares out surreptitiously at the high-rises beyond – an unlikely mix of east and west. Two other sights are of note: the magnificent railway station on Jalan Sultan Hishamuddin, and the Sri Mahamariaman temple on Jalan Tun H S Lee which is the oldest Hindu temple in the city.

The route south from Kuala Lumpur through Kajang, Seremban and Melaka is a pleasant enough drive through rubber and oil palm plantations formerly owned by the British. In 1883, the intrepid Rathborne and his gang of 'coolies' followed the same route, struggling through jungle infested with flying squirrels, lizards, leeches, ticks and snakes. 'The road was villainously bad, scarcely passable for carts and utterly unfit for any description of buggy,' declared the explorer. Today, the old road runs almost parallel to the North–South Highway, passing the town of Kajang, which is reputed to have the best *satay* (kebabs) in Malaysia.

At Seremban, an old tin-mining centre, turn off the main Highway 1 and follow the slip road west for 25 miles (40 km) to the seaside resort of Port Dickson, with its condominiums and its long sandy beach extending south to Cape Rachado lighthouse. From here, follow the coastal road via the beachside *kampungs* at Tanjong Bidara and Tanjong Keling to the ancient town of Melaka, situated at the mouth of the Melaka River.

Founded by a Hindu nobleman in 1400, Melaka's history is as diverse as its legacy of relics and monuments. Initially it received protection from the Chinese under Admiral Cheng Ho, but on 25 July 1511, General d'Albuquerque successfully attacked the Malays on elephants and took the city. Over the next 450 years the Dutch, the British and the Portuguese all at different times controlled the thriving seaport. Today there's a smorgasbord of different architectural styles, from the old Dutch red brick buildings on the east bank of the river and the Stadthuys on St Paul's Hill – reputedly the oldest-surviving Dutch building in the east – to the remains of the great Portuguese fort known as Porto Santiago.

Beyond Melaka, Route 5 follows the outline of the coast for 56 miles (90 km) before turning inland through rubber plantations towards Ayer Hitam, where you must rejoin Route 1. Nearing the end of the peninsula, the lush landscape gradually gives way to housing estates and to the vast industrial parks and condominiums of booming Johor Baharu, Malaysia's latest economic success story and the border town with Singapore.

SINGAPORE

From Johor Baharu, it's an easy 90-minute drive over the old causeway to Singapore, then along the spacious Bukit Timah Expressway to Tanjong Pagar and the southernmost tip of the island. When Sir Stamford Raffles arrived here in 1819, the place was inhabited by some 150 pirates and fishermen and almost wholly covered by mosquito-infested swampland. Today there are 2.7 million people, glistening skyscrapers, modern shopping centres, clean air and rules for absolutely everything – the perfect antithesis to Bangkok and a fitting place to end your journey.

PRACTICAL INFORMATION

■ Drivers in Thailand, Malaysia or Singapore must have an international driving licence, a vehicle registration book and special import and export papers, which can be obtained from the various embassies and travel authorities. You will want to spend at least 10 days driving from Bangkok to Singapore. For anything faster, take the train or bus.

■ Best months for travel are December to June. At other times expect heavy monsoons.

■ International rules are generally accepted. Vehicles are driven on the left-hand side of the road (mostly). Right of way given to cows, buffaloes and any vehicle that is bigger.

■ For information about the route, contact the Automobile Association of Singapore, the Tourism Authority of Thailand, the Tourist Development Corporation of Malaysia and the various embassies.

The Klondike Highway – Whitehorse to Dawson

BEAU RIFFENBURGH AND ELIZABETH CRUWYS

On 17 August 1896, three prospectors discovered a thumb-sized nugget of gold in the Klondike River. Once word of the find leaked out, thousands raced over the rugged landscape to the goldfields in a frenzied migration that became known as the Klondike Stampede. Some travelled by gruelling overland trails, while others braved the great North American rivers. Today a road winds through the Yukon Territory, from the little town of Whitehorse in the south, to Dawson City, the gold-hunters' capital, in the north. Although the thousands of hopeful prospectors have long since gone, evidence of this remarkable episode in Canada's history lingers on.

ABOVE, *the excitement of panning for gold in this Yukon creek is real, though today's tourists are no longer driven by necessity*

BELOW, *the Yukon is one of the world's last genuine frontier regions, but it is far from being bleak*

SKOOKUM JIM, Klondike Kate, Soapy Smith and Diamond Tooth Gertie were just a few of the people who played a part in one of the biggest gold rushes in history. Skookum Jim, along with his friends Tagish Charley and George Washington Carmack (also known as 'Lying George') discovered the nugget of gold that started the Klondike Stampede. Soapy Smith was a trickster whose fortune came from gullible prospectors, and Diamond Tooth Gertie and Klondike Kate were just two of the dance-hall girls who relieved many a lonely gold-digger of his hard-won wealth in return for company during the long cold winter nights.

The Klondike Gold Rush was an extraordinary event in North American history. Thousands upon thousands of would-be prospectors left their homes, jobs and loved ones to pursue a dream, a dream that would end in tragedy for some, financial ruin for others, and fame and fortune for only a very few. The Klondike story began on 17 August 1896, when the first gold was panned from a boggy stretch of river called Rabbit Creek. The name was quickly changed to Bonanza Creek, and within a few weeks, hopeful gold-seekers were flocking to lay claim to sections of Bonanza and neighbouring Eldorado Creeks. News of the strike did not reach the outside world until steamers carrying the lucky prospectors chugged into San Francisco in July 1897. Open-mouthed onlookers stared as the passengers disembarked, staggering under the weight of their finds. Someone uttered the phrase 'a ton of gold', and the Stampede was on. At least a million people made plans to make the hazardous journey north, although only about 100,000 actually set off. Among these were bank clerks and boxers, prostitutes and ministers, and laundrymen and poets. Anyone with money to buy a ton of food and equipment, and a desire to 'strike it lucky' could go.

There were several ways to reach this remote area of Canada. Some prospectors chose the 'All Canadian' route through Edmonton; others travelled by ship across the Bering Sea, and followed the Yukon from its mouth to Dawson City; but the quickest was to go by boat to Skagway or Dyea in Alaska, and hike across the White or Chilkoot Passes to the lakes that formed the headwaters of the mighty Yukon River. When many prospectors set off, they had little idea where they were going, or of the hardships that faced them: bitter winters with several feet of powdery snow and biting winds; high taxes to pay on transporting their goods across the US–Canadian border; gruelling climbs up mountainsides of packed ice; extortionate prices for anything from used boots to fresh bread; and miles of trudging along busy trails, hauling a ton of supplies through wind, snow, sleet and rain.

During the summer of 1897, when the first stampeders began to invade the Yukon, there were no roads, only crude trails through the barren landscape. Later, steamboats puffed up and down the Yukon from Whitehorse to Dawson, and a railway was built. In the 1940s, work began on the Alaska Highway and a supporting network of smaller roads that linked northern towns with the outside world. The 330 mile (528 km) Klondike Highway from Whitehorse to Dawson was one such road. It takes about 7½ hours to travel by bus; the same journey via the Yukon River is 460 miles (736 km) and can take anything from 10 to 16 days in a boat.

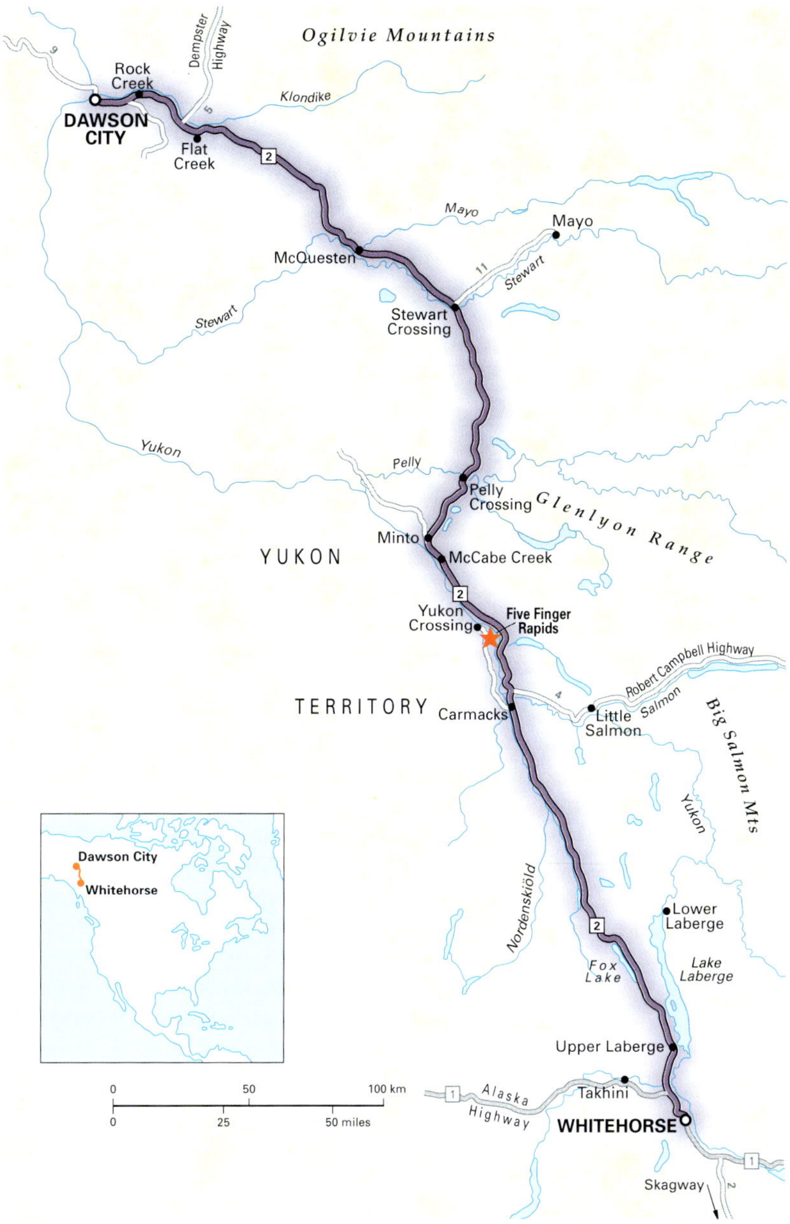

The 330 mile (528 km) Klondike Highway begins in Whitehorse, in southern Yukon Territory. Whitehorse, although small, has a large number of organized heritage walks and an informative museum. There are a number of cosy hotels, but campsites tend to be clustered around the Alaska Highway to the south of the town.
The Klondike Highway runs north-west along the western shore of Lake Laberge, before branching away to follow the path of the Yukon River. Settlements in this wild countryside are few, and running out of fuel can be a problem. The road is paved in parts, but comprises mainly a gravel surface that is, nevertheless, well-maintained. The first main town is Carmacks, a settlement that grew up where the Salmon River flows into the Yukon.
After Carmacks, the Klondike Highway, still hugging the east bank of the Yukon River, passes through Yukon Crossing and Minto. At Minto, the Yukon River meanders north-west, while the road travels north to Pelly Crossing, where a bridge spans the Pelly River. Some 37 miles (60 km) further on is Stewart Crossing, where the highway crosses the Stewart River.
Following the east bank of the Stewart River, the road continues north-west into McQuesten, and then cuts through the rugged land towards the Klondike River. The road follows the Klondike River for some 30 miles (48 km) before reaching Dawson City. On the road towards Dawson, the Dempster Highway swings away to the north, heading for the Arctic Circle.
Dawson City, a tiny settlement the population of which was swollen to 30,000 during the Gold Rush of 1896–99, now has only around 600 residents. Among the recently restored buildings dating back to the Klondike Stampede is the Palace Grand Theatre, which shows the 'Gaslight Follies', a vaudeville that is a major tourist attraction.

ABOVE, *Whitehorse offers botanical gardens, the* SS Klondike *and some three-storey log cabin apartments*

BELOW, *Indian prospectors are part of the Gold Rush story – a burial ground serves as a reminder*

The trip along the Klondike Highway is loaded with history and atmosphere. Abandoned ships lie in the shallows of the Yukon River, and small derelict shacks poke out from alder thickets along the way. The Klondike Stampede lasted only until 1899, when most prospectors left in the hope of richer pickings at Nome (1899) and Tanana (1903) in Alaska. In their wake, companies moved in, creating great tailings that lie like giant worms in the Klondike Valley. Prospectors still pan for gold in the Klondike today, and it still yields its treasure. It is estimated that it has produced $300 million worth of gold, a third of this during the Gold Rush years. All along the Klondike Highway, the epic age of gold-hunters never seems far away, and it needs little imagination to believe oneself back in those extraordinary, wild days when a Thanksgiving turkey cost $100, when fortunes were won and lost in a night in Dawson's gambling tents, and when ladies with names like Dog-faced Kitty, the Oregon Mare, and Lime Juice Lil ruled the pleasure palaces in 'Paradise Alley' and 'Hell's Half Acre'.

WHITEHORSE: THE BEGINNING OF THE RIVER JOURNEY

Whitehorse, the capital of the Yukon Territory since 1951, lies at the upper limits of steamboat navigation on the Yukon River, the main reason for its development after 1900. The origin of its name is uncertain, but local legend has it that the foaming rapids on the river (now tamed by a dam) looked like the white manes of a herd of galloping horses. It was at Whitehorse that the exhausted stampeders rested before beginning the journey up the Yukon River to the gold fields.

By the time Whitehorse was reached, the worst of the journey was over. The stampeders had made the ocean voyage from Seattle, San Francisco and Vancouver on cramped and unseaworthy vessels; had dragged their supplies across the wet sands at Dyea and Skagway, and hauled them many miles along the mud-filled, miserable trails to Chilkoot Pass where horses and cattle died in their hundreds; had endured the attentions of tricksters and conmen, such as Soapy Smith, the unofficial dictator of Skagway who was killed in a gunfight in 1898; had made 30 or 40 gruelling trips ferrying their gear up icy mountain slopes too steep for pack animals; and had built crude boats on the shores of the Yukon's headlakes that would bear them and all their provisions down the Yukon River.

The Royal Canadian Mounted Police (RCMP), knowing that there was little food in the Yukon, would not allow prospectors across the border unless they had enough food to last for a year. As well as food, the prospectors needed shovels, pans, dredges, guns, ammunition and warm clothing. In all, the supplies weighed about a ton, and those not rich enough to buy a pack animal, or pay someone else to carry it for them, had to carry every ounce themselves. While winds screamed through the mountain passes, and avalanches threatened and grumbled, the Mounties policed the borders, sending back any who were inadequately provisioned.

Following the Yukon River

As the road takes the traveller away from Whitehorse, the Yukon River broadens to about 1320 feet (400 m), as it meanders through low, rounded hills of limestone and granite, and scrubby trees and shrubs line its banks. The river slows as it nears Lake Laberge and myriad mudflats glisten above the surface. Lake Laberge was named after a telegraph explorer in 1870, although it is likely that he never actually saw the lake himself but had heard it described by Indians. The lake was deserving of such praise. Surrounded by gently rolling hills that dip down to wide expanses of beach, its shores are home to many wild flowers during the short summer, including purple lupine, creeping snowberry and fireweed.

At the head of the lake stands Upper Laberge, an old RCMP post. A few cabins still survive, occasionally used by local Indians. At the far end of the lake a diversion leads to Lower Laberge, also an old police barracks, where the sunken steamboat *Casca* can be seen poking above the water. The road follows the path of the river, passing the point where the Nordenskiöld (pronounced 'Norden-shelt') River flows into the Yukon, named after the great Swedish explorer Baron Adolf Erik Nordenskiöld in 1883.

After the lake, the road hugs the banks of the Yukon, winding its way through the vast, unchanging countryside. The length of the Yukon River is hotly debated, since the location of its true source and mouth are contentious. However, it is at least 1980 miles (3186 km), and possibly even 2300 miles (3680 km) long, a great silver thread that sweeps its way grandly through the vast wilderness of the Territory named after it. It is the fifth largest river in North America, and drains 330,000 square miles (845,000 square km) of land.

About 200 miles (320 km) downstream from Whitehorse, where the Salmon River flows into the Yukon, is Carmacks, a tiny town named after George Carmack, who helped set the Stampede in motion. Carmack was not much interested in gold when he first went to the Yukon from Illinois. He found a coal seam and built himself a cabin on the banks of the Yukon River, near Five Finger Rapids, in 1883. Carmack was an educated man, despite his tendencies towards exaggerated story-telling. He made friends with the local Tagish Indians, and took the daughter of a chief for his wife. When he found gold, his co-discoverers were Skookum Jim and Tagish Charley, both Indians. Carmack's discovery was no accident: he had been pointed in the direction of Rabbit Creek by a

BELOW, *Lake Laberge is a good place to stop and watch the abundant wildlife – the lake teems with fish, and eagles and peregrine falcons soar above*

ABOVE, *visitors can enjoy the breathtaking scenery of the Yukon River on a river cruise, or even paddle a hired canoe*

fellow prospector named Robert Henderson. Henderson, however, detested Indians, and the three friends neglected to tell Henderson of their find until all the best claims had been staked. The village of Carmacks grew rapidly during the Gold Rush, and continued to grow as a stopping place for steamers. Its importance dwindled when the Klondike Highway was built with its new bridge.

Twenty miles (32 km) from Carmacks is Five Finger Rapids, named because four islands in the river drive the water into five channels. The scenery here is spectacular, with high canyon walls encasing the river, and tree-cloaked hills rolling off into the distance. A small parking area has been provided to allow drivers to admire the view, watch small boats skipping across the racing water of the rapids, and observe the swallows dipping and weaving around their cliffside nests. The next settlement is Yukon Crossing, another ghost town that faded away when the new road was built. During the summer a ferry operated here, carrying stagecoaches across the shallow waters. Little more than the old roadhouse and a barn is left now, both standing in a field of long grass, their log walls crumbling and unsafe, and their roofs leaking and moss-covered.

After Yukon Crossing is Minto, an Indian settlement, the name of which means 'Place Between Two Hills'. Like Yukon Crossing, Minto is a ghost town; it consists of a police post, a church and a cemetery. This small community had the dubious distinction of being the scene of some unsolved murders in the 1950s, after which it was abandoned.

INLAND TO THE PELLY AND STEWART RIVERS

Leaving Minto, the Klondike Highway veers away from the Yukon River towards Pelly Crossing. The Pelly River was one of the first streams to be panned for gold in 1883, and was once a thriving trading post and ferry station. Despite the loss of ferry business, Pelly Crossing has survived, and a small community still lives there. Travelling through the rugged countryside, the road next encounters Stewart Crossing, a stopping point where prospectors could buy hay for horse-powered transport at Maisy May Ranch. Some cabins remain from the Gold Rush period and are protected by the territorial government. Stewart River did not escape the attentions of the gold-seekers. It was first prospected in 1884 and yielded small quantities of gold that paled into insignificance when compared with the fabulous finds in the Klondike.

Leroy Napoleon ('Jack') McQuesten was one of the first to discover gold in the Stewart River, and today the tiny settlement that remains bears his name. It was abandoned in the 1950s. The highway leaves McQuesten and heads towards the Klondike River. 'Klondike' derives from the Indian 'Thron-Duick' or 'Tron Deg', but the intricacies of Indian pronounciation eluded the pioneers, and they settled for 'Klondike'. It means Hammer Water, and referred to the Indian practice of hammering stakes into river beds to catch fish. The Klondike is still rich in salmon. Six miles (10 km) further along the road, the Dempster Highway swings off north, the only public road in North America to cross the Arctic Circle.

ABOVE, *negotiating Five Finger Rapids led to tragedy for many early prospectors trying to reach Dawson City by river*

LEFT, *travelling the Klondike Highway by campervan is rewarding provided safety rules are observed*

RIGHT, *Dawson City, seen here from the Dome, has been restored as an authentic Gold Rush town*

BELOW RIGHT, *the Palace Grand Theatre in Dawson City has a Hollywood-style false front*

BELOW, *the Venus Mine can be seen from the Klondike Highway*

DAWSON CITY: GOLD CAPITAL OF THE NORTH

Another 26 miles (42 km) and the road enters Dawson City, the Klondike Stampede capital, and capital of the Yukon Territory until replaced by Whitehorse in 1951. It was named after George Mercer Dawson, known principally as a government geologist, but also an outstanding naturalist and ethnographer.

Dawson was founded in 1896 by Joseph Ladue, an enterprising businessman who moved his sawmill here at the first whisper of gold. His gamble paid off, and by the time of the Klondike Stampede, his sawmill was operating 24 hours a day to cope with the demand for new buildings. Dawson began to grow at a fantastic rate. By the summer of 1897, it was no longer a few log cabins and Ladue's sawmill and saloon, but a burgeoning muddle of roughly built stores, bars and hotels to serve the 30,000 prospectors who poured into the city. It became the largest Canadian city west of Winnipeg virtually overnight, and thousands of tents were hastily thrown up on the shores of the river to accommodate the exhausted travellers. In the wake of the hopeful prospectors came a variety of people who saw the prospectors themselves as their ticket to fabulous wealth.

Among these was Swiftwater Bill, an early owner of the notorious Monte Carlo Palace of Pleasure, a sleazy gaming room and theatre that nevertheless drew enormous crowds. Swiftwater Bill took a fancy to Gussie LaMore, a 19-year-old strumpet who loved eggs, an expensive commodity in Dawson. Legend has it that he bought every egg in Dawson for Gussie, but then was later jailed for bigamy for marrying two other women. Another Klondike prince was Arizona Charlie, the owner of the exclusive Palace Grand. On its opening night, Arizona Charlie threw a sumptuous banquet for 40 people, and placed a $100 dollar bill under every plate. Arizona Charlie was a sharpshooter who claimed he had personally fought with Geronimo. He could shoot the spots off playing cards at 30 feet (9 m), and shot marbles from between the fingers of his wife, a party piece that came to an abrupt halt when he relieved her of a thumb.

In the dance-halls, saloons and bawdy houses, the Klondike prospectors faced another drain on their hard-won gold. Cad Wilson wore a belt of enormous nuggets around her waist presented by admirers, while at least one other girl was sold for her weight in gold (including the several pounds of birdshot in her corsets). Others sold their services more cheaply in Paradise Alley, or in the filthy runnels of Dawson's suburb Klondike City, more commonly called Lousetown. Here the Oregon Mare, Nellie the Pig, and the Grizzly Bear (a 170-pound woman with one eye) plied their trade, fleecing the miners mercilessly.

Overseeing all this activity was 'the Lion of the Yukon', Sam Steele of the Mounted Police. Largely due to his iron but fair justice, murders

PRACTICAL INFORMATION

■ Parts of the Klondike Highway have a gravel surface. Norline Coaches Ltd make the journey between Whitehorse and Dawson two (winter) or three (summer) times a week. Tourist Radio (96.1FM) broadcasts information about weather and road conditions. It also gives details of local events.

■ The Visitor Reception Centre at Front Street and King Street in Dawson offers informative slide shows, films and information on local history. It is open from mid-May until mid-September.

■ The City of Whitehorse Information Centre is at 3rd Avenue and Wood Street, and offers free brochures and maps of the area. It is open May to September.

and thefts were few in Dawson. Steele oversaw the casinos, allowed no work on Sundays, and ensured that the dance-hall shows were not too risqué. Later, a book and a film were released called *Steele of the Mounted,* commemorating this giant of a man who so skilfully kept the peace in this uneasy town.

One astounding fact about the Klondike Stampede is that, although about 30,000 hopefuls managed to reach Dawson, only the merest handful actually bothered to look for gold. Perhaps this was because the best claims had already been staked, or because most felt that by reaching Dawson they had already fulfilled their ambition. Dawson's mud-filled streets teemed with thousands of men, milling around with nowhere to go, nothing to do, and no money to spend. Prices for everything rocketed, and fresh onions were so rare that they sold for $2 as a cure for scurvy. This crowded city of aimless men existed for two years, until news of other gold strikes came in. Dawson emptied in the summer of 1899, and its heydey was over.

In 1899 a fire swept through the town, destroying 117 buildings, many on famous Front Street. It was rebuilt within two months, grander and more glamorous than before. Some of these newer buildings still stand in modern Dawson, carefully restored by the Canadian government in an attempt to salvage relics from this fascinating period . Now, only 600 people live here, relying more often on the tourist trade than gold. Yet mines still operate, littering the Klondike Valley with their long snake-like tailings of earth. Visitors too can pan for gold on sites about 5 miles (8 km) out of Dawson. Old closed mines can be visited; some give the impression of having been abandoned overnight by miners who left behind machinery, shovels and picks, and personal belongings. In the silence of the Yukon wilderness, walking around these deserted rigs is eerie. Here the dreams of thousands were realized and shattered , and it seems almost possible to hear the voices of those who shaped the Klondike story – Soapy Smith, Skookum Jim, Swiftwater Bill, Diamond-tooth Gertie and Steele of the Mounted – whispering in the ghostly ruins.

The Trans-Canada Highway from St John's to Victoria

BEAU RIFFENBURGH AND ELIZABETH CRUWYS

ABOVE, *totem poles such as this one in Vancouver's Stanley Park were used to record social history*

Stretching 4800 miles (7680 km) across the second largest country in the world, the Trans-Canada Highway links the Atlantic and Pacific coasts, from St John's, Newfoundland, in the east to Vancouver, British Columbia, in the west. Along the route are picturesque fishing towns, flat plains stretching as far as the eye can see, huge silent forests, the shores of lakes so large they are like inland seas, and the white-capped summits of the Rocky Mountains.

FROM A GRASSY KNOLL overlooking the colourful fishing boats of the attractive port of St John's in Newfoundland, an unassuming road winds west away from the coast and into the rugged interior of the island province. This is the beginning of the great Trans-Canada Highway, a road that roams approximately 4800 miles (7680 km) across the southern part of

Much of the Trans-Canada road is designated as Highway 1, although the numbering system becomes complicated in eastern Canada. Beginning in St John's in Newfoundland, the Trans-Canada (as Highway 1) runs directly west across the Avalon Peninsula, and then northwards towards Gander. It then curves across the northern part of Newfoundland, and dips south towards the south-eastern end of the Long Range Mountains. Ferries leave from Channel-Port aux Basques for the 110 mile (176 km) journey across the Cabot Strait to Sydney in Nova Scotia. After this the Trans-Canada (as Highway 105 and then 104) heads south and then west to Moncton in New Brunswick (Highway 20), and then north-west to the St Lawrence Seaway and Québec. In Québec, the road becomes the 'Transcanadienne', and continues south-west to Montréal and then Ottawa in Ontario (Highway 20). After Ottawa, the highway divides, the Northern Route following the Ottawa River, and then rolling on towards Cochrane (Highway 11), and the older Southern Route moving west through Ontario to Peterborough and Toronto, and running along the shores of Lakes Huron and Superior (Highway 17). The two roads reunite in Nipigon, and run south to Thunder Bay. Leaving Lake Superior, the Trans-Canada heads west into Manitoba, towards Winnipeg (Highway 1). The route continues through the prairies of Manitoba, through Portage la Prairie, and into Saskatchewan and its capital city Regina. After Regina, the road passes through Swift Current and Medicine Hat, and into the province of Alberta. As Calgary is approached, the land begins to rise towards the Rocky Mountains. At Kamloops, the road continues west for about 60 miles (96 km) before turning to run directly south towards Hope (as Highway 1 and 97). At Hope, the road turns west again, and runs into the heart of the city of Vancouver in British Columbia.

Canada, linking the Atlantic Coast in the east with the Pacific Coast in the west. Meandering across a continent, through six time zones and nine provinces, this road visits vibrant cities as well as remote forests and plains. From the hilly coastal regions of New Brunswick, Nova Scotia and Newfoundland, it arrows across the great prairies of Manitoba, Saskatchewan and Alberta to the towering Rocky Mountains in British Columbia. It is the longest national highway in the world.

Canada is the second largest country in the world after Russia. It is about 3.9 million square miles (10 million square km) of land and water. Most of the population of 26.3 million people is concentrated in the southern part of Canada, and communications have always been important in this huge land. The first main road in Canada was the King's Way, which was completed in 1737, and covered the 200 miles (320 km) between Québec and Montréal, a journey that is now included in the

ABOVE, *the Trans-Canada highway provides a link between towns and villages in remote and beautiful areas*

LEFT, *Native Canadians belong to ten distinct linguistic groups, and are successfully conserving their cultures*

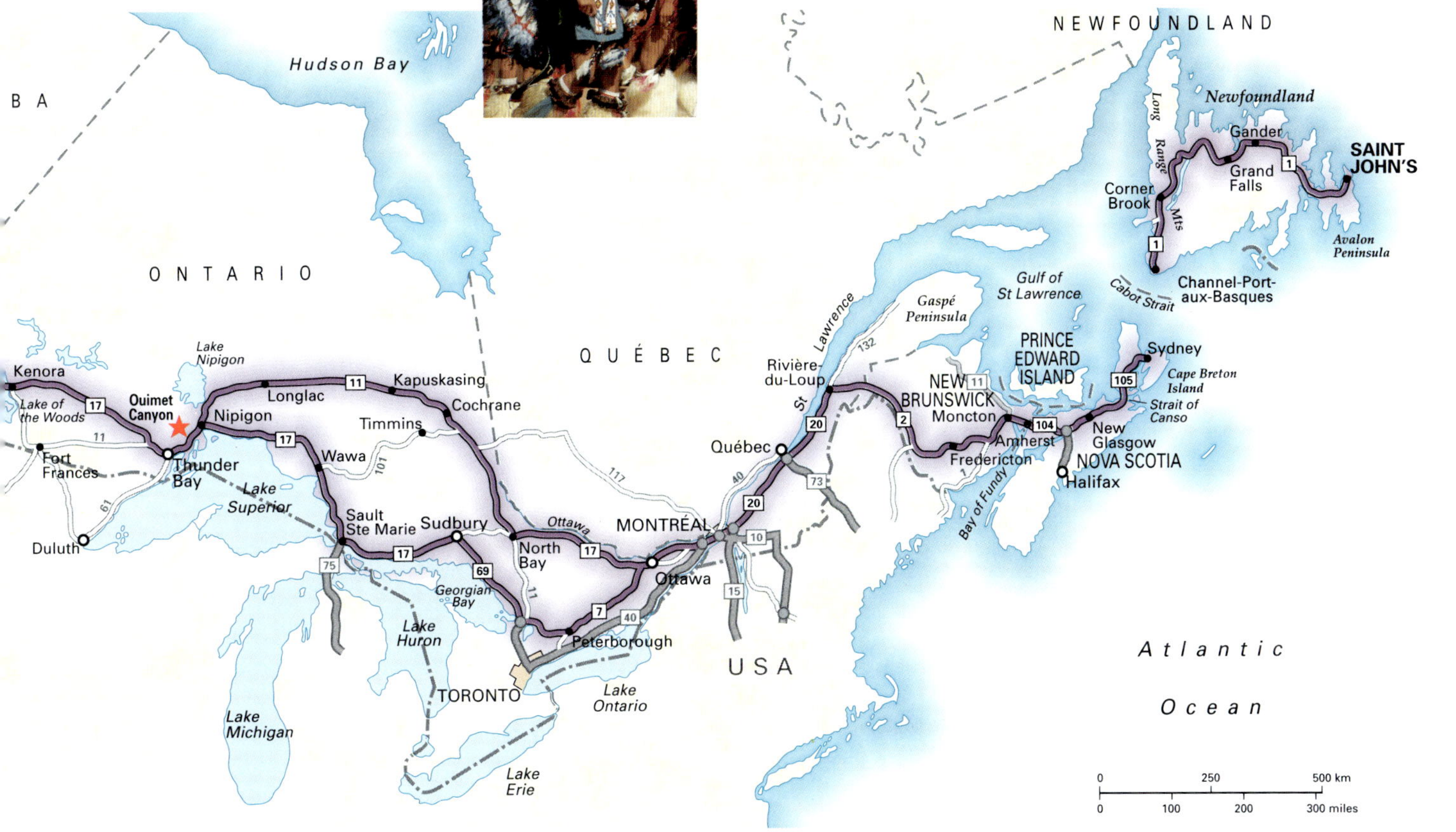

RIGHT, *the harbour at St John's in Newfoundland is a colourful sight, with ships flying the flags of all nations*

Trans-Canada. However, by 1920, Canada still only boasted 1000 miles (1600 km) of paved roads, while many others were little more than cattle tracks.

It was not until 1949 that the Canadian government passed the act for a road that ran from coast to coast, linking the major cities, and in 1950 work began on a project that was to cost $CAN 1.4 billion. Although the road was officially opened by Prime Minister John Diefenbaker on 3 September 1962, it was not actually completed until May 1971.

The Atlantic Provinces

From the castle-like structure on Signal Hill in St John's, where Guglielmo Marconi received the first transatlantic radio signal from England in 1901, the Trans-Canada curves around the city through the barren terrain of Newfoundland. Passing rocky outcrops and innumerable ponds and swamps, the road heads north to Gander, where, surprisingly, there is an international airport. On these lonely roads, the traveller is likely to see caribou wandering, while the tumbling creeks that cut deeply into the land are rich in Atlantic salmon. After Grand Falls and Corner Brook, the road runs south to Channel-Port aux Basques, a town that owes its origins to Basque whalers in the 16th century.

The stretch of water separating Newfoundland from Nova Scotia is called the Cabot Strait, commemorating John Cabot, who in 1497 became the first European to sight the coast of Newfoundland. Buffeted by the Atlantic rollers, it is often choked with loose ice during the winter months. Despite this, the ferry between Channel-Port aux Basques and Sydney on Cape Breton Island in Nova Scotia is open all year, linking the Newfoundland section of the Trans-Canada with the mainland.

Sydney is Nova Scotia's largest industrial city, becoming a major steel centre in the early 1900s using iron ore imported from Newfoundland. From Sydney, Highway 105 meanders south, through St Ann's, and on across the bridge that spans the Strait of Canso, a narrow strip of sea that separates Cape Breton Island from the rest of Nova Scotia. Seasonal European fishermen took advantage of the rich fishing grounds around the coasts of Nova Scotia from about 1500. In the mid-1600s, there was a migration of Acadian French, followed by Scots in the 18th century. It was the Scots who gave the province the name Nova Scotia: 'New Scotland'. There is still a strong Gaelic presence in Nova Scotia; Gaelic is still spoken in some areas, and there is a Gaelic College at St Ann's. At Baddeck, the museum recalls a summer spent here by the Scots inventor Alexander Graham Bell.

Once across the bridge, the Trans-Canada becomes Highway 104, heading west towards New Glasgow. Nearby is Pictou, where the arrival of a barque in 1773 heralded the beginning of a long period of migration of Scots highlanders to Nova Scotia. After New Glasgow, the road heads south-west past Salmon River, noted for its tidal bores. The Salmon River empties into an arm of the sea which is connected to the Bay of Fundy, which has the most extreme tidal ranges in the world, sometimes reaching 50 feet (15 m). In the spring huge volumes of muddy brown water surge up the Salmon River in a series of towering waves.

After Amherst, a city on the border between Nova Scotia and New Brunswick, the Trans-Canada becomes Highway 2, and heads through

Moncton. French Acadians came to Moncton in the 1750s, followed by a wave of Germans from Pennsylvania. It became an important railway centre, and it offers the only major French language university outside Québec. Continuing west, the road winds and curves through hilly country watered by lakes and rivers shimmering bright blue among the trees.

After Fredericton, the capital of New Brunswick and a lively town with a blossoming arts scene, the Trans-Canada heads north along the Canada–US border through the drier, flatter and more fertile lands farmed in the 1870s by settlers from France. French is still spoken in these border lands, and Acadian culture thrives in music, festivals, and a growing awareness of the unique history of the area. This celebration of European ancestry is continued as the road moves from New Brunswick to the province of Québec.

QUÉBEC: CANADA'S LARGEST PROVINCE

At Rivière-du-Loup, the Trans-Canada becomes Highway 20, heading south-west into Québec. It also meets the great St Lawrence River, a huge body of water that moves slowly, but powerfully, from the Great Lakes to the Atlantic Ocean. As early as 1783, the Government saw the advantage of making this route navigable by ships, and began to construct a system of lochs, canals and channels that was not completed until 1959.

The first attempts by the French to settle along the St Lawrence River were not successful, and it was not until 1608 that Québec City was founded by Samuel de Champlain. Even so, the settlement was little more than a fur trading post when the British seized it in 1629. Modern Québec is a city where the old has been carefully preserved among the new. The Château Frontenac raises its elegant spire-bedecked towers to the sky, while in the distance are modern suburbs.

After Québec City, Highway 20 leads the way south-west to Montréal, where it passes under the St Lawrence River via a tunnel. The busy city, whose skyline bristles with tall buildings, sprawls along the banks of the river. Viewed from Mount Royal, Montréal spreads out in a patchwork of trees and buildings, with the vast flow of the river glittering in the distance. Montréal is unquestionably French, and buildings such as the city hall in Place Jacques Cartier are modelled very much on Parisian architecture. Old Montréal itself comprises cobbled streets and squares lined with elegant 19th-century buildings, with cafés that spill out onto the pavements in the summer, giving the city its Continental atmosphere. The city's oldest surviving building is a seminary built in 1685, an attractive building dwarfed by the twin towers of the early 19th-century Notre Dame Church. In turn, Notre Dame is overshadowed by the vast glass towers of the city's finance and business sector.

Montréal owes its growth and prosperity to its status as a port. Many handsome harbour warehouses and offices have survived from the last century, and have been renovated during the past 20 years. Where tall ships once docked to load and unload cargoes from Europe and the US, small pleasure boats now bob against the 19th-century jetties. After an afternoon absorbing the lively atmosphere of Old Montréal, you can take an evening cruise up the mighty St Lawrence seaway to watch the sun set over the broad waters, or travel south to shoot the foaming white-water Rapides de Lachine in aluminium boats.

ONTARIO: PROVINCE OF LAKES AND WATERWAYS

Leaving Montréal behind, the Trans-Canada follows the Ottawa River before cutting south and then west towards Ottawa in the province of Ontario. This is Canada's capital city, selected by Queen Victoria in 1867 as the leading city for the

BELOW, *the Château Frontenac in Québec opened a new wing to celebrate its centenary in 1993*

RIGHT, *dark trees lining the route contrast with the snow-covered peaks of the Hermit Range*

RIGHT INSET, *the highway passes close to Castle Mountain in Banff National Park*

'Province of Canada', then made up of Ontario and Québec. Ottawa remained the capital when the Confederation, which added New Brunswick and Nova Scotia, was formed 10 years later. Modern Ottawa is a city based on finance, business and government, reflected in its smart buildings and clean streets. As Montréal's character is French, so Ottawa is essentially English, and guards in elaborate uniforms march in a daily display of the 'changing of the guard' outside the splendid government buildings on Parliament Hill.

After Ottawa, the Trans-Canada offers a choice of routes. The older route, now Highway 7, travels west towards Peterborough and Toronto, Canada's largest city. 'Toronto' is an Indian word meaning 'meeting place', and in many ways it is the centre of English Canada. The oldest part of the city is the area around Yonge and Bay Streets, which today are bustling thoroughfares flanked by high-rise buildings and shops. As in Montréal, the harbour area has been developed as a recreational area, and row upon row of small pleasure craft sway on the lake shore in Downtown Toronto. Turning north again, the road hugs the shore of Lake Huron's Georgian Bay, before curving north and then west to meet the shore of Lake Superior at Nipigon, where the two routes reunite and push south to Thunder Bay.

The newer route, Highway 17, follows the Ottawa River north-west towards North Bay and Cochrane. Ontario is often called 'the lake province', and both the northern and southern Trans-Canada routes pass hundreds of silent silver lakes, fringed with trees. Slender ribbons of water twist through wooded valleys that are best seen in autumn, when the leaves turn all shades of red, gold, orange and brown.

Twenty-six miles (42 km) east of Thunder Bay, a town that sits on the shores of Lake Superior, is Ouimet Canyon, a narrow gorge two miles long and 495 feet (150 m) deep. The sheer sides of the cliffs are broken by patches of green, as small trees and plants maintain a tenuous hold on the rocks. After Thunder Bay, Highway 17 curves away from the Great Lakes towards the vast rolling prairies of Manitoba, Saskatchewan and Alberta.

THE PRAIRIE PROVINCES: MANITOBA

After Kenora, the Trans-Canada becomes Highway 1, which continues to Kamloops in British Columbia. The road crosses the Lake of the Woods, and slices through the south-east corner of the Whiteshell Provincial Park, a region of beautiful jewel-like lakes and wooded slopes that is a popular recreational area for the residents of Winnipeg and nearby towns.

Winnipeg, the capital city of Manitoba, sits astride the Trans-Canada Highway, and is home to about half the population of the province. This attractive city has come a long way from the fur-trading post sited on the confluence of the Red and Assiniboine Rivers, and hosts some internationally renowned events, such as the Festival du Voyageur, a celebration of Canada's old-time trappers and traders, which takes place in the bitterly cold month of February. For those nervous of braving a ferocious Manitoba winter, Folklorama Week is in mid-August, when visitors can view ethnic dances and handicrafts, listen to music, and try the national dishes of the 30 or so cultural groups that have made Manitoba their home. About 30 miles (50 km) north of Winnipeg is Lake Winnipeg, a vast, dark blue body of water fringed with purple hills.

The road cuts straight across the vast prairies, which stretch in all directions, an endless blanket of uniformly coloured fields. The plains have a special beauty of their own, partly because of their sheer size, but also because they give an exhilarating sense of freedom. There are no fences, hedges, buildings or walls for mile after mile, a far cry from the crowded bustle of Montréal,

BELOW, *the prairie province of Saskatchewan produces about 60% of Canada's wheat*

Ottawa and Toronto. The skies appear vast under the prairies, and distant storms can be seen from miles away as slanting pearl-grey clouds, with occasional rainbows arching down to touch the ground. Rapeseed oil is grown in the area around Portage la Prairie, 50 miles (80 km) west of Winnipeg on the Trans-Canada, and in summer nothing but this blazing yellow crop waving in the breeze can be seen for many miles.

Spruce Woods Heritage Provincial Park, about 10 miles (16km) south of the road, includes the curious Bald Head Hills, 15 square miles (39 square km) of shifting sand dunes that early homesteaders tried, unsuccessfully, to farm in the last century.

After Sioux Valley, through which the Assiniboine River flows, Highway 1 turns north-west towards Elkhorn, where the Manitoba Automobile Museum is situated. Crossing the border into Saskatchewan, the traveller is presented with yet more prairie, once roamed by buffalo and the nomadic Indian tribes who hunted them. Mass slaughter wiped out the herds, and pioneer farmers changed the prairie wilderness that supported them into agricultural land. Today, Saskatchewan grows about two-thirds of

RIGHT, *the expressway curves across the Bow River at Calgary, famed for its friendliness to visitors*

OPPOSITE, *reflections of Vancouver where ferries cross the harbour from Canada Place*

BELOW, *glacial lakes lie close to the highway in Banff National Park, where cable cars climb high above the panoramic mountain views*

the country's wheat, and is sometimes called 'Canada's breadbasket'.

In the 1880s, descendants of the Indians objected to the flood of settlers, and, led by Louis Riel, fought Canada's militia at Batoche. Riel lost, and was tried and executed in Regina, on the site where the training academy of the Royal Canadian Mounted Police (RCMP) now stands. There is an RCMP museum in Regina, which includes a chapel built in 1883 (Regina's oldest building). The museum includes displays of weapons, uniforms, and a stuffed horse. Moving west again through towns with names such as Moose Jaw and Swift Current, the Trans-Canada crosses the border into Alberta, heading for Medicine Hat.

MOUNTAINS AND THE PACIFIC: BRITISH COLUMBIA

After Medicine Hat, Highway 1 moves north-west, eventually taking you through the centre of Calgary. An influx of settlers occurred after 1883 when the Canadian Pacific Railway was completed, and Calgary grew up as a trading centre for

surrounding farms and ranches. Oil and gas were discovered in 1914, further contributing to the city's wealth. Calgary is the venue for the Calgary Stampede, a rodeo and parade in the summer, and offers 'Prehistoric' and Heritage Parks.

Once the outskirts of Calgary have been left behind, Highway 1 begins to climb towards the snow-capped Rocky Mountains and some of Canada's most spectacular scenery. Four National Parks – Jasper, Kootenay, Banff and Yoho – straddle the Rockies, and the Trans-Canada bisects three of them. First, Highway 1 curves upward to the city of Banff, set in the oldest (established in 1887) and most publicised of Canada's national parks. Its huge areas offer excellent winter sports, as well as towering mountains sweeping down into wide green valleys. Lake Louise, a short distance from Highway 1, is a beautiful tree-ringed lake nestling in the Rockies at an altitude of 5700 feet (1727m), fed by the icy waters from a glacier.

Adjoining Banff is Yoho National Park. Yoho is a Cree word that signifies wonder (often translated into North American English as 'Wow!'), and describes a region of cascading water, silent valleys and glittering lakes. After Yoho comes Glacier National Park, once home to great herds of buffalo and the warlike Blackfoot Indians. Glacier is characterized by snow-dusted mountain peaks, thick pine forests and thundering waterfalls, many reflected in mirror-calm lakes.

The section of the Trans-Canada between Golden and Revelstoke was one of the most difficult and expensive parts of the road to build. It was necessary to take the route through Rogers Pass, where snowfall can reach 76 feet (23 m) per year. Not only did heavy falls block the road, meaning that snow-ploughs needed to be available throughout the winter, but there was also a serious danger of avalanches. A huge system of snowsheds, earth mounds and other avalanche-preventing measures was devised in order to make the road safe.

The road continues to descend, passing Revelstoke with its impressive dam, and Kamloops, before turning to run directly south to Hope. After Hope, the road runs west towards the Pacific coast and Vancouver. Vancouver is an expanding city that has developed around one of the world's finest natural deepwater harbours. It has grown rapidly and recently, and even today many older Indians recall their fathers and grandfathers talking about hunting in the woods now covered by houses and roads. There are still two Indian Reservations in Vancouver, belonging to the Musqueam and Capilano. Meanwhile, Stanley Park is a spit of land projecting into the sea that has been designated a recreational area for Vancouver's citizens. It offers large areas of unspoiled land, a zoo and aquarium, beaches, a lagoon and a fine collection of totem poles.

But the Trans-Canada ends not in Vancouver but in Victoria, at the southern tip of Vancouver Island. It is necessary to make another ferry journey, and drive the last few miles to Beacon Hill Park, where the mighty highway ends.

PRACTICAL INFORMATION

- The Canadian AAA provide motoring information for those wishing to travel the Trans-Canada Highway. The road is in excellent condition, but is single-laned in parts. Snow-ploughs keep the road clear in winter, but there can still be problems, especially in the Rockies.
- At 60 miles per hour (96 kph), the Trans-Canada takes about 80 hours of driving. Since there are sections where there are no buildings (including fuel stations) for many miles, any journey should be planned carefully.
- For a detailed account, the National Geographic book *Travelling the Trans-Canada: From Newfoundland to British Columbia* by William Howarth (1987) is very informative.

Highway 1
South to Los Angeles

BEAU RIFFENBURGH AND ELIZABETH CRUWYS

Snaking along the California coast between two of North America's most famous cities, California State Highway 1 passes through some of the most spectacular coastal scenery in the world. It starts 150 miles (240 km) north of San Francisco and ends in the myriad small cities which form the Los Angeles metropolitan area. This is a land of contrasts, where rugged mountains plunge into foaming seas, but where gentle waves lap at beaches of pale golden sand. 'Wonderful One' hugs the coast almost the entire way, flanked by majestic mountains on one side, and the heaving Pacific Ocean on the other.

ABOVE, *the cable car has become a symbol of San Francisco – invented in 1873, it even has its own museum*

TOP RIGHT, *reaching Los Angeles the road widens to become a six-lane freeway slicing through the city*

BELOW, *Highway 1 runs close to the coast in San Mateo County, south of San Francisco*

HEMMED IN by the restless Pacific Ocean to the west, and hazy mountains to the east, California State Highway 1 meanders its way southwards, passing rugged cliffs, golden beaches, gentle valleys and lush woodland. Twisting and turning to follow the line of the coast, this historic route almost feels a part of the land, far more so than the multi-laned Interstate 5, which provides a quicker route from Los Angeles to northern California and beyond.

Highway 1's 550 miles (885 km) offer the visitor an outstanding variety of things to do and see. For those seeking spectacular scenery, it travels past wild and lonely coasts, silent green forests, purple-blue mountains and parched scrubland. For those wanting to sample city life, the bustling and charismatic Los Angeles and San Francisco may be explored. Historic sites include the opulent Hearst Castle, a monument to the wealthy newspaper magnate, William Randolph Hearst, while the simple, serene mission at Carmel was founded in 1770 by the Franciscans. For those interested in wildlife, sealions and the spumes of whales can often be seen from Highway 1, while short stops and detours are often richly rewarded with bright carpets of flowers and glimpses of exotic birds.

State 1 begins about 150 miles (240 km) north of San Francisco, at Leggett, crossing the scenic south fork of the River Eel, and heading west to the coast. It zig-zags south, following the rims of the deep gulches that slice into the land from the sea. In places, the road seems to cling precariously to the sides of the cliffs that tumble down into the frothing sea. The San Andreas Fault runs very close to the road between Point Arena and San

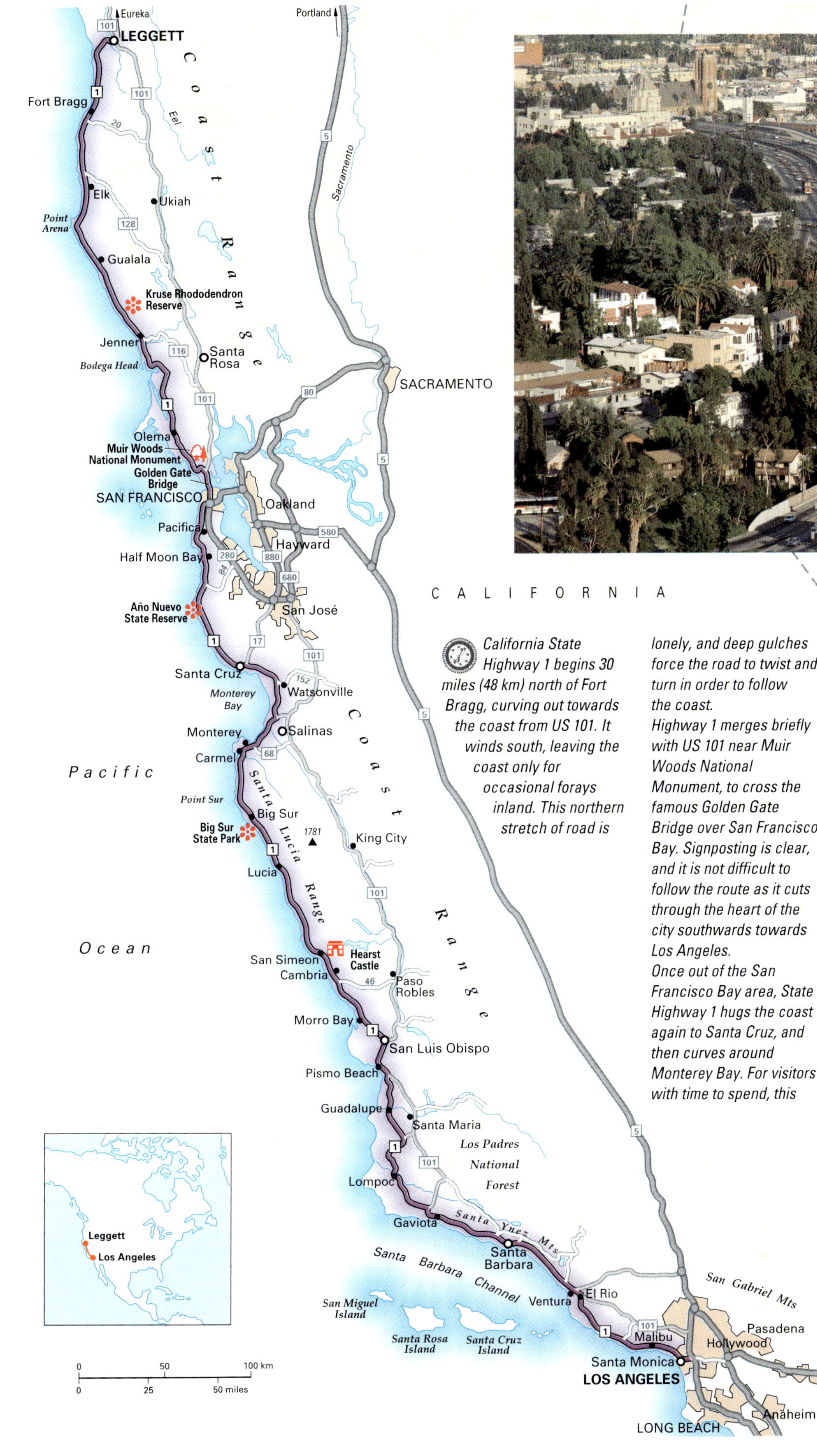

California State Highway 1 begins 30 miles (48 km) north of Fort Bragg, curving out towards the coast from US 101. It winds south, leaving the coast only for occasional forays inland. This northern stretch of road is lonely, and deep gulches force the road to twist and turn in order to follow the coast.

Highway 1 merges briefly with US 101 near Muir Woods National Monument, to cross the famous Golden Gate Bridge over San Francisco Bay. Signposting is clear, and it is not difficult to follow the route as it cuts through the heart of the city southwards towards Los Angeles.

Once out of the San Francisco Bay area, State Highway 1 hugs the coast again to Santa Cruz, and then curves around Monterey Bay. For visitors with time to spend, this beautiful bay has much to offer, including an impressive aquarium, clean beaches and an abundance of wildlife. South of Monterey is the breathtaking Pfeiffer Big Sur State Park, a strip of coast noted for its outstanding beauty, and Los Padres National Forest.

With the Santa Lucia Range to the east, Highway 1 continues its southwards route down the coast. On a hill in the distance can be seen the gleaming white towers of Hearst Castle at San Simeon, the fairy-tale home of the fabulously wealthy newspaper magnate William Randolph Hearst, now a State Historic Monument open to the public.

The towering rock at Morro Bay marks the point where Highway 1 turns inland briefly, towards San Luis Obispo. Returning briefly to the coast at Pismo Beach, it meanders inland through the pleasant valleys around Lompoc, before running along the Santa Ynez Mountains, through Santa Barbara, and into the outskirts of the sprawling conurbation that makes up the Los Angeles metropolitan area.

ABOVE, *at 4200 feet (1280 m) the Golden Gate Bridge is one of the longest suspension bridges in the world*

Francisco. Near Bodega Head, a spur of land that juts out into the Pacific, Highway 1 reaches its highest altitude – about 600 feet (182 m) – affording magnificent views across spray-shrouded headlands and mountains crowned with clouds.

Point Arena lighthouse is a dramatic landmark, and warns ships away from the treacherous coast. The first lighthouse here toppled into the sea during the 1906 earthquake, and it is said that the wrecks of at least three ships lie beneath the waves that gnaw at the ragged coast. The Kruse Rhododendron Reserve, about 18 miles (29 km) south of Point Arena, is best visited in May or June, when the 30 foot (9 m) high shrubs blossom.

The Golden Gate Bridge

North of San Francisco is the Muir Woods National Monument, a park of towering redwood trees that were already growing when the Battle of Hastings was fought in 1066. When the Golden Gate Bridge was built in 1937, access to these magnificent trees became so easy that the feet of millions of tourists began to wear the woodland paths down to the roots of the redwoods, while the vibrations and fumes from passing traffic on the highway also threatened to damage them.

State 1 is absorbed by US 101 to form the Golden Gate Freeway, which runs down to the famous bridge. Deep red, and rising 750 feet (227m), the majestic twin towers of the Golden Gate Bridge are one of America's most famous landmarks. From all directions the freeway affords splendid views, no matter what the weather, for San Francisco is as memorable basking in bright sunlight as it is cloaked in the fog that so often hangs low over the city.

It is commonly believed that Los Angeles is eternally swathed in smog, while San Francisco's atmosphere is clear and clean. The reality is that both coastal cities, and their surrounding areas, are prone to palls of airborne pollution, because both are surrounded by mountains that prevent the smog from blowing away.

In the 1830s San Francisco was little more than a small town, but the California Goldrush of the 1840s transformed it into a thriving commercial centre. It is the fourth largest metropolitan area in America – a 1990 census put its population at more than 6 million people in the San Francisco, Oakland, and San Jose area. Its population is a melting pot of many ethnic groups – Africans, Europeans, Latin Americans and Asians, and many areas have a distinctive ethnic character, such as the famous Chinatown. The scene of many dramatic car chases in movies and television programmes, many of San Francisco's smaller streets plunge up and down hills that seem impossibly steep. Standing at the top looking down at what is said to be the city's steepest road makes one realize that descending it without reliable brakes is not a good idea.

Highway 1 splits again from US 101, and proceeds south, travelling through pleasant residential areas such as Richmond, Sunset, and Ingleside, before turning west to hug the coast once more. Between Half Moon Bay and Año Nuevo State Reserve lie several State Beaches, long strips of sand that have

been designated areas of outstanding natural beauty, or regions that possess unusual wildlife. It is on these beaches, and some further south, that Californian sealions and northern elephant seals haul out to breed, moult or simply to bask in the sun. Californian sealions are attractive creatures, and are the species most often seen performing tricks in zoos and circuses. Northern elephant seals are perhaps less appealing in terms of their looks and habits (they like to wallow in smelly puddles of mud, and the dirtier and smellier the wallow, the happier the elephant seal), but colonies of them lying on shore roaring and snorting is a sight not to be missed.

Still clinging to the coast, the route rolls further southward, to the famous Monterey Bay area. This is a much sought-after area in which to live, with its warm-climate architecture and tree-lined streets. Attracting millions of visitors per year is the ultra-modern Monterey Bay Aquarium, opened in 1984. It is built on the site of a sardine cannery, which closed after World War II because of overfishing. The Aquarium houses tanks 30 feet (9 m) deep, with walls of transparent acrylic that allow visitors to see the fish in near-natural environments. One display even houses a shoal of small sharks, and visitors can watch them being fed by divers.

The beaches of Monterey Bay are not the only areas of interest. A vast area of coast, from San Francisco in the north to the small town of Cambria in the south, has been designated as the Monterey National Marine Sanctuary. The futures of an enormous range of marine species are being protected in this pocket of sea, including jellyfish, sea anemones, corals, sponges, Pacific sleeper sharks and seals .

Looking at the calm waters of Monterey Bay, it is difficult to imagine that underneath it lies a gorge as impressively deep as the Grand Canyon. At Moss Landing, the site of some marine laboratories destroyed in the 1989 earthquake, a small gorge winds out to sea, becoming progressively deeper. It meanders 110 miles (176 km) out to sea before it flattens out, reaching depths of up to 1.8 miles (3 km), forming the largest underwater chasm along any continental American coast.

Continuing south, Highway 1 curves around Monterey Bay towards Carmel-by-the-Sea. The settlement of Carmel dates back to the 1770s,

ABOVE, *among Carmel's claims to fame is its 18th century mission; it has attracted many fine photographers, and Clint Eastwood as its mayor*

BELOW, *the highway sweeps high above the Pacific coast at Big Sur, south of Monterey*

ABOVE, *Monterey and Carmel are separated by the private estate of Del Monte Forest; a lone cypress stands on a crag along the famous Seventeen Mile Drive*

when a Franciscan friar, Father Junipero Serra, built a mission here with a fine church. This mission served as Serra's headquarters for founding a series of Franciscan outposts along the coast. Less than 100 years later, Carmel's mission church was in disrepair, but it was restored in the 1870s by another priest, Father Angelo Casanova. The church, with its classically Spanish architecture, may be visited by tourists, and its cool interior offers a welcome respite from the bright Californian sun.

The road continues ever southwards, now passing the great rock at Point Sur, and travelling down the stretch of coastline known as Pfeiffer Big Sur State Park. The Big Sur River waters the lush wooded valley, and cool green pillars of coastal redwoods arch over the highway like the nave of some great cathedral. Tumbling streams from the Santa Lucia Range plunge into the sea, and flowers blossom in an explosion of colour. Here, looking out across the shifting blue-grey surface of the Pacific Ocean you might see vertical spouts of water, blown by migrating whales that move up and down the coast.

Hearst Castle

At San Simeon, glittering white towers and terracotta roofs stand starkly atop a low hill. This is Hearst Castle, the fantasy house built by the fabulously rich newspaper magnate, William Randolph Hearst. Hearst's heirs bequeathed his 'castle' to the State of California in 1958, and it is open to the public. The Hearst family has secured itself a place in American history. Orson Welles' film *Citizen Kane* was loosely based on William Randolph, one of the most powerful and influential figures in popular journalism for more than 50 years. Patty Hearst, William Randolph's granddaughter, was the victim of a widely publicised kidnapping in the early 1970s.

Hearst Castle is definitely worth a visit, and is one of California's most famous tourist attractions. A number of different tours can be taken, which explore different parts of the house and estate. Buses collect visitors from the huge car park and take them up to the castle on the hill

RIGHT, *no expense was spared in the design and furnishing of the extraordinary Hearst Castle at San Simeon*

OPPOSITE, *exotic tropical palms in the grounds of the Beverley Hills Hotel, home of the famous Polo Lounge*

with its sprawl of associated buildings, swimming pools, intimate bowers and rolling ranchland. Hearst was wealthy enough to afford whatever he wanted, and employed buyers to travel all over the world purchasing articles as diverse as carved stone fireplaces from European castles, wooden confessionals (that Hearst used as an elevator) from churches, paintings, porcelain and beautiful medieval illustrated manuscripts.

The castle's interior is literally stuffed with these treasures and priceless works of art. For example, the refectory is like a room taken directly from a medieval castle. A handsome carved wooden ceiling was brought from a 400-year-old palace in Italy to adorn the roof, while silken banners from medieval Siena hang on the walls. Hearst had his own cinema too, with plush deep-red seats, where he entertained his guests. He also built swimming pools – one indoor and one outdoor – to ensure he catered to all tastes.

After a while, the staggering number of treasures jostling and cramping each other in room after room in this curious American stately home becomes too much to absorb. Art and furnishings from the ancient world of the Greeks and Romans, from Africa, and from medieval and modern Europe are hurled together randomly in a manner that verges on the tasteless.

Back on Highway 1, the road leaves the coast at the towering rock in Morro Bay, and travels inland to the mission at San Luis Obispo. The road becomes double-laned until it touches the coast again briefly at Pismo Beach. Thereafter, it winds through the attractive valleys around Lompoc, before joining US 101 again to run down the side of the Santa Ynez Mountains between Gaviota and Ventura. The small islands of San Miguel, Santa Rosa and Santa Cruz can be seen hazily across the Santa Barbara Channel, past the oil rigs that litter this part of the coast.

Los Angeles – City of Angels

State 1 separates from US 101 at El Rio, and travels along the coast to the vast city of Los Angeles. With a population of over 3.5 million people, LA is America's second largest city after New York. However, LA City is only one city of many that form a continuously built up area that stretches for more than 60 miles (96 km) along the coast from Malibu in the north to San Clemente in the south. The total population of this area is a staggering 14.5 million people.

Los Angeles teems with life. It is the centre of the movie business, and many film stars live in the smart, bright mansions scattered in the wealthy areas of the megalopolis, like Brentwood and Bellaire. Although there is a public bus service, getting around this vast, freeway-covered sprawl is not easy without a car, and the region's tourist attractions are far flung – from Disneyland, which is in Anaheim in Orange County; to the Rose Bowl, the nation's largest sports stadium, in Pasadena; to Universal Studios, located north of Hollywood.

Los Angeles is surrounded by a rim of purple mountains. In the winter, these peaks glitter white with snow, and Los Angeles County is one of the few places in the world where you can ski in sparkling white snow in the morning, and bask in the sun on a golden beach in the afternoon. Walking along one of the trendy beaches – such as Venice Beach or Santa Monica – or driving on the freeways that are at points six lanes wide in each direction, it is difficult to believe that LA is actually part of the baking Mojave Desert that houses Death Valley, one of the hottest and driest places on Earth. Finding enough water to serve its vast population is often a problem, and droughts can sometimes last for years.

At Los Angeles, Highway 1 comes to an end, having wound its way along some of the most varied and spectacular scenery in America. It serves two of America's largest cities, and some of California's most remote and desolate beaches. It passes golden beaches fringed with scallop-shaped waves, rocky peninsulas battered by heaving surf, 18th-century Spanish missions and 20th-century bridges. There can be few roads in the world that encompass such a variety of natural and man-made attractions.

Practical Information

■ The California State Highway covers a distance of about 550 miles (880 km). A section of Interstate 5 also runs north from Los Angeles and, being a more direct route, takes much of the traffic away from Highway 1, which is single-laned in parts.

■ Southern California is on the San Andreas fault and is subject to earthquakes. This occasionally affects traffic. The best information about road conditions can be obtained from any AAA office, which will also provide free maps to members.

Route 66 – Chicago to Los Angeles

BEAU RIFFENBURGH AND ELIZABETH CRUWYS

Perhaps more than any other road, Route 66 has a place in America's history. Although it officially ceased to exist in 1985, it has not been forgotten. Route 66 carried farmers and businessmen west during the Great Depression, and it was a vital supply route to the army bases and armaments factories in World War II. After the war, it took people west again, seeking their fortunes in the promised land of California. Passing through farmland, deserts and over mountains between Chicago and Los Angeles, Route 66 was more than a highway; it was a unique and vital part of America's heritage.

If you ever plan to motor west,
Travel my way, take the Highway that is best.
Get your kicks on Route 66...

ABOVE, *the Saguaro is the largest of the cacti, and grows to 70 feet (21m) in the Arizona desert*

ABOVE RIGHT, *the skyline of Chicago, where skyscrapers were invented; in the background is the Sears Tower*

RIGHT, *the Route passes close to the fascinating colours and rock formations of the Painted Desert in Arizona*

AFTER MAKING the gruelling journey along the narrow, crowded Route 66 from Chicago to Los Angeles after World War II, Bobby Troup wrote a song about it. He showed it to Nat King Cole, who immediately turned it into one of the most popular blues classics of the time.

After the war, people began moving from the east to the promising golden lands that beckoned 'out west'. In the post-war years, 3.5 million people moved across the country and settled in California alone. Many of these migrating people took Route 66, and Bobby Troup's song appealed to them: they had made the journey in the song.

It was not the countryside through which Route 66 travelled that made it famous: it was what the Route embodied for the millions of people who drove along it in search of a better life. This was not the first time people had moved *en masse* along these roads. The 'Great Diagonal Highway' had carried the 'Okies' and 'Arkies'

Because Route 66 no longer officially exists, it is difficult to follow the precise path of this great American highway. No single road has replaced Route 66: parts of five interstate highways now cover the 2200 mile (3540 km) journey from Chicago in the north-east to Los Angeles in the south-west. The interstates that replaced Route 66 are: Interstate 55 – between Chicago and St Louis; Interstate 44 – between St Louis and Oklahoma City; Interstate 40 – between Oklahoma City and Barstow; Interstate 15 – between Barstow and San Bernardino; and Interstate 10 – between San Bernardino and Los Angeles. The old path of Route 66 cut through eight states. It began in Grant Park, Chicago, on the shores of Lake Michigan, continuing through the city and heading south-west towards St Louis on the Illinois–Missouri border. Continuing south-west, it headed for Springfield and Joplin, before cutting across a small corner of Kansas and crossing the state border into the flat countryside of Oklahoma. After Oklahoma, Route 66 travelled west towards Amarillo, crossing the dusty hot desert of the 'panhandle' of Texas. Continuing through the desert of America's southern states, the route entered the dry plains of New Mexico, through Albuquerque and Gallup, and crossed the border into Arizona at Box Canyon. Through the Petrified Forest National Park and the Painted Desert, it continued west to Flagstaff. After Flagstaff, Route 66 meandered through Indian territories and over the Black Mountains to Needles on the Arizona–California border. At Barstow, lying in the Mojave Desert, it plunged south for about 60 miles (96 km) to San Bernardino, before turning west again towards Los Angeles. After Los Angeles, it continued to the coast and a small park at Santa Monica, where a plaque designated Route 66 as the 'Will Rogers Highway'.

ABOVE, *Lake Shore Drive is a fast route through Chicago following the edge of Lake Michigan*

from the Dust Bowl states of the Midwest to California in the 1930s, a trip immortalized by John Steinbeck in his classic American novel *The Grapes of Wrath*. During previous years, great dust storms had raged, removing millions of tons of fertile soil from Texas, Oklahoma, Arkansas, Kansas and Colorado. Their farms destroyed and the Depression at its height, displaced families went west as labourers, travelling with everything they owned in ramshackle trucks and wheezing cars.

Route 66 was born in 1926, mainly by the efforts of one man: Cyrus Stevens Avery, a Tulsa businessman who saw that a major road between Chicago and Los Angeles would bring immense trading advantages to Oklahoma. In 1927 he founded the US 66 Highway Association to urge the government into action. This association was not disbanded until 1976.

At first, Route 66 was little more than a set of connecting trackways, some dirt and some planked, and it was not fully paved until 1938. Many people can still recall the road being almost impossible to travel, and cars and buses being bogged down in clay and mud when it rained. But despite its sometimes appalling conditions, people used the route in ever increasing numbers. All these people on the move needed fuel for their vehicles, they needed somewhere to sleep after an exhausting drive, and they needed places where they could stop for something to eat and drink. Roadside business along Route 66 began to boom. As more and more cafés, motels, gas stations and shops sprang up, competition between them became intense. Traders began to use all manner of gimmicks to persuade travellers to stop. Advertising signs grew larger and more inventive, and Indian traders near Gallup even had a tethered buffalo to attract customers.

However, in 1965 the Highway Beautification Act was passed (due in part to the efforts of the wife of President Lyndon Johnson) which limited the number of signs that could be displayed. Traders on Route 66 complained bitterly about loss of business; the damage was compounded by the effects of the 1956 Interstate Highway Act. The Act aimed to replace the single-laned Route 66 with newer, bigger, safer and faster roads, fenced along the sides, that bypassed all the small towns along the route. It took more than 30 years before all of the route was finally replaced, but in 1985 a ceremonial ribbon-cutting closed the last part of this historic road in a blaze of publicity.

It winds from Chicago to LA,
More than 2000 miles all the way...

In a small park in the heart of what is now America's third largest city, looking out across the shimmering waters of Lake Michigan, lay the beginning of Route 66. Chicago today is a very different city from the one that Route 66 first linked with the west coast, when Prohibition was in force, and Chicago was notorious for its warring gangsters. The modern city speaks of success and wealth. The Sears Tower, at 1454 feet (441 m), or 1707 feet (520 m) including the TV antenna, is the tallest office building in the world, rising

LEFT, *a stately Mississippi paddle steamer moored at St Louis*

majestically to dominate Chicago's skyline. Chicago is also known for its culture, and for being the home of some of the best pizza in the world, thanks to its Italian immigrants.

The old road west went past the soaring skyscrapers, out into the sprawling suburbs towards Cicero. This was the centre of Al Capone's bloody empire until his arrest in 1931 for tax evasion. Moving south-west towards Joliet and Bloomington, the road crossed areas once cloaked in tall-grass prairie all the way to St Louis. Little can be seen of the tall-grass prairie as Interstate 55 follows the path of Route 66 towards St Louis, by-passing small towns like Pontiac, Lincoln, Divernon and Edwardsville, for which Route 66 was once a lifeline.

Small pockets of tall-grass prairie can still be found among the flat farmland that rolls endlessly in all directions. Just outside Chicago, the Gensberg-Markham Prairie is a fragment of the grasslands that once covered 400,000 square miles (1,024,000 square km) of the Midwest. Long grasses wave in the wind, and are home to horned larks, prairie chickens and migrating Swainson's hawks. Flowers abound here, too, and in spring the prairie is a rich carpet of plants of all colours.

Now you go through St Louis,
Joplin, Missouri...

The border between Illinois and Missouri is formed by the great meandering Mississippi River. The route of US 66 is taken from Interstate 55 by Interstate 44 at the river. It is worth pausing to watch the Mississippi flow past, since the lumbering old steamboats immortalized by Mark Twain still paddle past carrying tourists, and are an impressive sight.

Although the Mississippi is mostly a lazy river, winding slowly along its meandering course, seasonal rains can turn it into a torrent of swirling brown mud, and, despite attempts by the US Corps of Engineers to control it, 'Old Muddy' remains as wild and unpredictable as in the days of Mark Twain. Fifteen miles (25 km) north of downtown St Louis, the Mississippi meets the Missouri River, and the two appear to run side by side, because their colours do not blend together for at least 30 miles (48 km). The explorers Lewis and Clark camped here on their epic journey across America in 1804-6, and a monument to their achievement is located here.

St Louis, named by a French fur trader in 1764 after the canonised King Louis IX, is one of the busiest ports on the Mississippi-Missouri river system, along with New Orleans 1000 miles (1610 km) south. Its most famous monument is the soaring 630 foot (191 m) stainless steel arch, symbolizing the 'Gateway to the West', that stands in the Jefferson National Expansion Memorial. An observation room at the apex of this testament to western settlement offers breathtaking views down the river and across the historic town itself. St Louis is packed with history. Daniel Boone's cabin, once in the depths of the wilderness, stands in part of the St Louis Metropolis, and Charles A Lindbergh named the aircraft in which he made the first solo crossing of the Atlantic *The Spirit of St Louis*, because it was in this city that he obtained sponsorship for the venture.

Continuing south-west, Route 66 aimed for Springfield. (Route 66 visited two Springfields on its way to the Pacific: Springfield, Illinois, and Springfield, Missouri.) Interstate 44 follows the same route across the ridges of the Missouri Ozarks in America's 'Show Me State'. Southern Missouri is dotted with forests and national parks, many named after Mark Twain. The state also abounds with scenic lakes and romantic stretches

BELOW, *the Gateway Arch in St Louis stands on the banks of the Mississippi, framing the Old Courthouse*

MAIN PICTURE, *the hills of Arizona turn blue in the distance, viewed from the seemingly endless dusty highway*

ABOVE INSET, *Buffalo Bill Cody is just one of the real-life and screen heroes honoured at the National Cowboy Hall of Fame in Oklahoma City*

of tree-lined river.

Between Rolla and Lebanon, Route 66 wound through the picturesque Clark National Forest with its slow rivers and lush vegetation. The notorious Devil's Elbow is located here, a stretch of Route 66 that followed a treacherous bend in a nearby river. This part of Missouri is especially hilly, and the engineers simply followed the easiest route when building the new paved two-lane Route 66. After the war, when it began to take heavier traffic, a new route was taken that by-passed that dog-leg of the road and the little fishing community located there, but by then Route 66 had a reputation for being dangerous, to the point where it was called 'Bloody 66' because of the number of accidents there. Another accident black spot was at Groom, Texas, which was known locally as 'Death Alley' or 'Blood Alley', because its surface became slippery in the rain, causing drivers to lose control. These gruesome nicknames were not entirely unjustified – highway statistics for 1956 show that one in every six traffic deaths in Arizona occurred on Route 66. Drivers today, however, can be assured that no such design flaws mar the new Interstates.

Interstate 44 continues in the footsteps of its predecessor through Missouri, passing lead and zinc mines until it reaches Joplin, birthplace of the eminent botanist George Washington Carver. Carver, born into a black slave family, attained national repute for his innovative farming methods, which included introducing peanut and sweet potato plants to restore fertility to soil that had been farmed under one crop for too long.

After Joplin, Route 66 dipped briefly into Kansas, staying in the 'Jayhawk State' for less than 10 miles (16 km), before plunging south into Oklahoma at Picher. Interstate 44 omits this slight bend, arrowing directly from Missouri into Oklahoma towards Tulsa.

..and Oklahoma city is mighty pretty...

Oklahoma is cattle country, with rolling hills and winding rivers. Many pioneers crossed Oklahoma in search of new lands in the 19th century, long before Route 66 existed. First explored by the Spanish, it became part of the United States in 1803 as part of the Louisiana Purchase, and was, at first, reserved as Indian land. However, with its herds of buffalo and fine fertile land, Oklahoma posed too great an attraction, and white settlement began after the Civil War. Less than a century later, many of these settlers found

themselves unable to scratch out a living from the soil after all. The Depression of the 1930s, combined with a series of ferocious dust storms and droughts, drove the people away from their farms to the promise of the west.

Interstate 44 by-passes Vinita, Tulsa and Arcadia as it heads for Oklahoma City. Parts of the old Route 66 can still be seen, some still in use as the main street for small settlements, and others barely visible beneath weeds and gourd vines. Fifty miles (80 km) south-east of Tulsa lies Muskogee, made famous by Merle Haggard's song *Okie from Muskogee.*

Oil was discovered near Tulsa in 1901, making it the centre of a scramble for the wealth to be had in 'black gold'. It was developed as a river port linking Oklahoma with the Gulf of Mexico, and today it is a rich city. Oklahoma City also owes its development to the oil industry. While Route 66 visited the heart of this thriving city, the Interstate system skirts around it. Interstate 44 curves south, and the route of US Highway 66 is taken up by Interstate 40 coming from Little Rock, Arkansas.

After Oklahoma City, Route 66 travelled west, running flat and straight across land battered by the prevailing winds from the south. Few trees grow here, and those that do lean northwards, forced to grow that way by the ever-present wind. It was this wind that caused the great dust storms of the 1930s.

From Oklahoma, Route 66 passed through the northern part of the Texas Panhandle, an arid, dusty region where even the sparse trees of eastern Oklahoma do not grow. Shamrock, just inside the Texas border, is a small town where the air is dry and gritty with blown dust. It is one of the many

ABOVE, *the road about to enter Arizona, driving west towards Springerville*

ABOVE INSET, *Oklahoma City began as a tent town; today it is a prosperous city, mainly thanks to oil*

RIGHT, *children outside a pueblo; Route 66 passed through large areas of Indian country*

OPPOSITE, *the multi-laned Santa Monica Freeway speeds travellers through western Los Angeles*

towns that owed their growth to Route 66. By the time this section was paved, Shamrock had several motels, and one of the most memorable gas station/cafés in the country. The Tower Station, or Nunn's Café as it was later called, had two towers that rose impressively from its white-washed walls. It was built in April 1934, perfectly timed to take advantage of the 1930s migration to the west. When Interstate 40 by-passed Shamrock, the café lost much of its casual trade, and the people of Shamrock protested vociferously in the 1960s about what the loss of Route 66 might mean, not only for trade, but also as part of American transport history.

You see Amarillo, Gallup, New Mexico...

It was the arrival of the railway in 1887 that spurred the growth of Amarillo, now a thriving industrial town. Route 66 ran straight through its centre. After Amarillo, Route 66 continued west towards Tucumcari in New Mexico, a small town where giant concrete teepees offered passing drivers food and an imaginative array of souvenirs. Like Shamrock, the advent of Interstate 40 deprived it of passing customers, and today it is a quiet backwater set in the mountains of eastern New Mexico. Between Tucumcari and Albuquerque, a short diversion leads you away from Old 66 to the glittering lights of Las Vegas – no, not *that* Las Vegas!

BELOW, *logs in Arizona's Petrified Forest, transformed into fossils by the gradual infiltration of mineral-rich water*

After peaceful Tucumcari, Albuquerque is a surprise, a high-tech town offering the National Atomic Museum and several other museums dedicated to native Indian cultures. The Isleta Indian Reserve lies to the south, and the Laguna and Acoma Reserves to the west. Route 66 travelled through these reserves, flanked on both sides by eroded *mesas* and *buttes*. Gallup, lying just south of the vast Navajo Indian Reservation, is home to the Museum of Indian Arts and Culture, and holds the Inter-Tribal Indian Ceremonial, designed not only to attract tourists, but to educate them about Indian history and ways of life. Indian *pueblos* or settlements are plentiful in New Mexico, such as Ancona Pueblo, a village on the plateau of a 300 foot (91 m) *mesa* that has been inhabited since the 12th century.

After Gallup, Route 66 dipped south-west again, heading through the high deserts of Arizona to the Petrified Forest National Park and the Painted Desert. Millions of years ago, logs floated down rivers long since turned into a swampy basin, where they became covered in sediment. Over time, the logs became quartz fossils, containing deposits of amethyst and other gemstones. Theodore Roosevelt declared the Petrified Forest a national monument in 1906, and it became a national park in 1962. During the heydey of Route 66, fragments of the petrified wood could be bought at the roadside cafés and stores. The Painted Desert to the north is an area of dry rock, with a rich variety of delicate shades ranging from rose-pink to deep blue. Like the Grand Canyon, the Painted Desert changes by the hour, depending on the light, so that it never appears to be quite the same colours twice.

Flagstaff, Arizona, don't forget Winona. Kingman, Barstow, San Bernardino.

Moving west again, Route 66 continued through the desert, passing the cliff dwellings at Walnut Canyon National Monument, to Flagstaff, situated in the Coconino National Forest. The San Francisco Mountains just north of Flagstaff offer excellent skiing, while south of Flagstaff are more cliff dwellings and Indian *pueblos* tucked

into secluded valleys and bluffs. Grand Canyon National Park is about 60 miles (96 km) north of Flagstaff.

Route 66 then ran through more towns and villages towards Kingman, after which it swung south-west towards Oatman, high in the Black Mountains, in an impressive series of snaking hairpin bends. Many of the 1930s migrants were forced to walk this part of Route 66 to try to relieve the strain on the engines. The descent from Oatman was just as precarious, zig-zagging down towards the Colorado River and the town of Needles in California. Interstate 40 cuts further south to avoid the mountains, and doubles north again at Needles.

Needles heralds the beginning of the baking Mojave Desert, a vast area of land that runs into Nevada in the north and the Sonoran Desert in the south. After Needles, Route 66 ran west across the desert, passing some of the most desolate scenery of its 2200 mile (3540 km) journey. The traveller is greeted by mile after mile of bleached rock, heaps of gravel and chalk-dry clay burned by the blistering heat of the sun, interspersed with cactus, Joshua trees and desert flowers.

Interstate 40 is superseded by Interstate 15 at Barstow, following Route 66's path south and up, heading for the Cajon Pass in the San Gabriel Mountains. Death Valley, so named by migrants taking a shortcut to the gold mines in 1849, lies north of Barstow and is well worth a diversion. After the run down to San Bernardino, the scenery changes as you approach the sprawling metropolis of Los Angeles. Route 66 (which now becomes Interstate 10) skirted the feet of the San Gabriel Mountains through Fontana, Cucamonga and Pasadena, and cut through Los Angeles to Santa Monica, the location of some of California's most famous beaches. There, in a small park, is a plaque designating the end (or beginning) of Route 66.

Won't you get hip to this timely tip:
When you make that California trip.
Get your kicks on Route 66...

Route 66 is not merely a highway that was superseded by better, faster roads, but a fascinating part of America's history. It carried millions of Americans to new lives during the Depression and after World War II, and the constant stream of travellers from east to west provided livelihoods for thousands more. In many ways, Route 66 became a national symbol of the promise of a better future for American citizens. Route 66 may be gone, but it will never be forgotten.

PRACTICAL INFORMATION

- The AAA offers the best practical information about travelling by road in North America. Because the old Route 66 catered to the needs of travellers, accommodation and restaurants can usually be found by turning off the interstates into the small towns that have been bypassed.
- A good history of the road can be found in *Route 66: the Highway and its People*, by Susan Croce Kelly, University of Oklahoma Press, (1989).
- The speed limit on interstate highways is between 55 and 65 miles per hour (88-100 kmph). The 2200 mile (3540 km) journey can be travelled comfortably in five days.

BELOW, *the road hugs the coast at Santa Monica, the 'Bay City' of Raymond Chandler's novels*

The Inca Road from Quito to Santiago

ELIZABETH CRUWYS AND BEAU RIFFENBURGH

High up in the snow-dusted Andes, a great road once ran, linking the cities of a great empire, running from the Ecuador–Colombia border to Santiago in Chile. Today this great royal road has fallen into disrepair, its paved surface crumbling. Yet its route can still be travelled, some 3125 miles (5000 km) through rugged mountains, dense jungle, and freezing, tumbling streams. And at every step the traveller is reminded of the great empire of the Incas, for the ruins of their houses, bridges, settlements and temples are still standing, more than 400 years after the death of the last emperor.

ABOVE, *original Inca stonework, tapering upwards, in Cuzco's streets*

BELOW, *cloud clings to the foothills of the Andes Mountains near Loja, on the Ecuador–Peru border*

THE ANDEAN MOUNTAINS curve like a spine down the western part of South America, created by great pressures as land masses were forced together. It was here, in these beautiful, snow-crested mountains that the Incas began to establish their empire and to build roads.

The Inca story began in the 13th century, when the ancestors of these Quechua-speaking Indians were little more than local chieftains based in Cuzco, a city in southern Peru that stands 11,200 feet (3394 m) above sea level. Only the rulers called themselves Incas, although the Spanish later referred to all subjects of the empire as Incas. In 1438 the ninth Inca, Pachacuti, became leader, and determined to establish an empire that would be one of the greatest the world had ever seen.

There were two royal highways: one that meandered through the coastal region, and another that passed along the Andes. The second route is better known today, perhaps because it passes Machupicchu, the most famous of the Inca ruins. Although both roads were paved, most parts are inaccessible by motor vehicles and the Inca Road can only truly be travelled on foot.

The old Royal Highway started at the northern tip of the great Inca empire at what is today the Ecuador–Colombia border. It dipped south towards Quito, the present capital of Ecuador. There is much to detain the traveller in Quito, including fine museums, Spanish-style buildings with white walls and terracotta roofs, palaces, monasteries and churches.

After Quito, the Inca Road began to climb up into the Andes, heading for the Peruvian border. The first major Inca settlement was Cajamarca, set in a beautiful fertile valley and worth visiting for its colonial monasteries, cathedral and the strange pre-Inca designs cut into the rocky outcrops above the town.

Winding south and upwards through Peru, the Inca Road passed Chavin and ran on to the fantastic settlement at Machupicchu, clinging precariously to the side of an Andean mountain. Houses, stairways and narrow streets can still be seen in one of the most stunning archaeological finds of the century. About 50 miles (80 km) from Machupicchu lies Cuzco, the capital of the Inca empire. Great blocks of cut stone still form parts of the city walls, and the foundations of the great cathedral once held a mighty Inca temple. The road then travelled south-east towards the glittering lake of Titicaca, lying 12,505 feet (3790 m) above sea level. After Titicaca, it swung out into modern Bolivia, and then ran south into Argentina, ending at Santiago in Chile.

With his son, Topa Inca, he began to conquer nearby Indians, forging an imperial dominion that stretched from Colombia to Chile. Pachacuti and Topa Inca did not merely conquer, but introduced a system of political and social reform that still has repercussions today. They united their empire by imposing the highland language of Quechua, and by establishing an impressive network of roads linking major cities and settlements. The Incas had no written language, and a complex system of knotted strings (called *quipus*) was developed, enabling messages to be sent to distant parts of the kingdom by specially trained runners.

Because the roads were important to maintain the stability of the Inca empire, special permission was needed to travel along them. The responsibility of maintaining the roads fell to nearby towns and villages as a form of taxation. These people repaired the swaying suspension bridges that hung at dizzying heights across canyons, kept the inns (or *tambos*) placed every 15 miles (24 km) or so in which travellers rested and ate, and maintained the paved or cobbled road surfaces. By the time of the Spanish conquest there were about 10,000 miles (16,000 km) of roads in the Inca empire, some built by the Incas, others dating from earlier cultures. The two main roads, one through the Andes and the other along the coastal plain, were linked at regular intervals by smaller roads.

ABOVE, *Cotopaxi in Ecuador , with its unmistakable volcanic cone, is the centre of a national park where llamas are bred*

ABOVE, *the Plaza de la Independencia in the centre of Quito is dominated by the cathedral with its green tiled cupolas*

The road that ran across the Andes was around 3125 miles (5000 km) long. Where the terrain was flat, the road was up to 19 feet (6 m) wide, and paved with cut stones. Where the road was forced up or down mountains, the track narrowed to about three feet (1 m), and comprised tiring arrays of switchbacks and, where the mountainside was especially steep, stairs hewn into the rock. The horse was unknown in South America until introduced by the Spanish in the 16th century, and the roads were built for those travelling on foot. Llamas were used as pack animals, and when the Spanish used the royal roads to aid their defeat of the Inca empire, they found the steep steps, narrow tunnels and frail bridges were difficult for horses to travel. But this did not save the Inca empire from Europeans greedy for gold and new lands, and within 20 years of Pizarro's first expedition south from Panama in 1524 the Incas had been thoroughly defeated and were ruled by Spain.

QUITO: CITY ON THE EQUATOR

The ancient Inca Road began in southern Colombia, winding its way upwards towards Mount Cayambe, a towering peak of 19,107 feet (5758 m), perpetually caped in snow. The road twisted and turned in a series of violent zig-zags as it attempted to cut a direct route to Quito, originally the capital of the northern part of the Inca empire. Fourteen miles (22 km) north of Quito the road crossed the equator, at a point called La Mitad del Mundo ('the Middle of the World'), now marked by an attractive monument and some small shops.

Today, little remains of the Inca civilization in Quito. In 1534 it was seized by the Spanish, and many charming buildings date from the time of Spanish occupation. Standing in a pleasant valley, Quito has a comfortable climate, with clean, fresh air sweeping in from the mountains, but without the chill of some of the cities at higher altitudes. Elegant Spanish-style buildings give the town a colonial air, particularly the splendid baroque church of La Compañía, which was started in 1605 but not completed until the 18th century.

Towering 15,820 feet (4762 m) above Quito is 'the boiling mountain', Mount Pichincha, an active volcano that oozes dark smoke from its snowy summit. The Inca Road continued southwards, passing Cotopaxi, which at 19,347 feet (5897 m) is the highest active volcano in the world. Cotopaxi's base is 12 miles (22 km) across, and evil yellow wisps of sulphur constantly drift from it. It is possible to climb to Cotopaxi's summit, an excursion that takes about three days.

Continuing south, the Inca Road passed Ambato and Cuenca, once Inca settlements but now featuring predominantly Spanish architecture. Two hours from Cuenca by car is Ingapirca, one of Ecuador's most important Inca sites. It contains a ruined fortress and was probably an administrative centre.

Clinging precariously to impossibly steep mountainsides, the Inca Road travelled on, moving across what is now the Ecuador–Peru border to the ancient city of Cajamarca.

THE GREAT INCA CITIES OF THE PERUVIAN ANDES

Set in a narrow but fertile valley, the Cajamarca of the Incas is long gone. Today cows graze among eucalyptus trees and the older buildings are in the white-walled, red-roofed style of classic Spanish architecture, including the fine cathedral that dominates the town. Pizarro reached Cajamarca on 15 November 1532, and it was near here that he first encountered Atahualpa, the ruling Inca emperor. Pizarro was lucky in that the Inca empire was deeply embroiled in a civil war in which Atahualpa, a usurper, had captured the legitimate heir to the throne, his half-brother Huascar; Pizarro was able to take advantage of this political instability. He arranged a meeting with Atahualpa, at which the Spanish slaughtered the emperor's guards and took Atahualpa prisoner. Atahualpa offered to pay a ransom for his freedom: a room filled with gold and two rooms filled with silver.

Atahualpa paid his ransom, but was a danger to Spanish dominance as long as he was allowed to live. In 1533 he was executed by being strangled. With Atahualpa's death, the Inca empire began to crumble. Some of the Inca royal family managed to escape, possibly fleeing to the great fortress at Machupicchu, a city high in the Andean mountains. The last Inca emperor, Tupac Amaru, surrendered to the Spanish in 1572, but was quickly executed along with his family. Machupicchu was deserted, its walls left to decay and crumble, until it was rediscovered in 1911 by the American archaeologist Hiram Bingham.

MACHUPICCHU: LOST CITY IN THE ANDES

Machupicchu is easily the best known of the Inca ruins. Set 7860 feet (2373 m) high on a tree-cloaked mountain and swathed in wispy clouds, the hidden city of the Incas is an awesome array of shrines, houses, stairways and narrow cobbled streets. Two sturdy sets of walls and a dry moat faced would-be invaders on one side, while the precipitous sides of the mountain and the churning brown waters of the Urubamba River that sweep around their base further protected the other three. The most imposing building in this magical city is the Temple of the Sun, in ruins now, its creamy yellow stones providing a glimpse of the splendour and elegance of this ancient culture. The city itself formed two distinct parts, the layout of which can easily be seen by the visitor. The peasants and soldiers lived in the smaller, less grand houses on the outskirts, while the fine granite residences in the centre were the homes of the nobility.

The Inca Road between Machupicchu and Cuzco is the most travelled part, and the walker will not encounter the solitude and peace of earlier sections. Zig-zagging up and down mountainsides, this section of the road is quite

BELOW, *the Inca ruins of Machupicchu form a dramatic picture against the dark mountainsides*

INSET, *the ruins remained well-preserved while buried in jungle, until Hiram Bingham rediscovered them in 1911*

FAR RIGHT, *Uros women and children make use of a traditional* balsa *or reed boat on Lake Titicaca*

impressive, despite being in ruins. Often sheathed in fog, but also often stretching far into the distance under bright, clear sunlight, the mountains around which the road travels are constantly changing, sometimes dark green, sometimes bathed in golden light, sometimes misty grey.

Near Cuzco, the Inca Road had to cross the boiling waters of the Apurimac River. This was achieved by a slender straw bridge slung from one side of the gorge to the other. Amazed accounts of this bridge swaying in the wind high above the river were written by the Spaniards. Such bridges could be used for defence: it was easy to slash the great cables that held them, or set them alight. After the brutal execution of Atahualpa, groups of Inca warriors burned bridges behind them as they fled from Pizarro and his small force. But the local people were easily cajoled or browbeaten into repairing them, and the Incas' burn and destroy policy could not prevent Pizarro's relentless advance to Cuzco, the mighty Inca capital.

Along this stretch of paved highway, the traveller encounters the remains of several *tambos*, or travellers' inns. Tambo Machay, near Cuzco, was such an inn. It is in excellent repair, and water still runs into baths designed to refresh the weary traveller. Sturdy blocks of dusty yellow stone form the main part of the *tambo*, which also has an enclosure for animals at the back.

Nearing Cuzco there is a series of fortress-cities at 10 mile (16 km) intervals, designed to repel invaders intent on the royal city itself. Pisac, 21 miles (34 km) from Cuzco, is perched precariously on a pinnacle of rock. This fortress is a fine example of Inca buildings, with their inward-slanting mortar-less walls. The fortress of Sacsahuamán actually overlooks Cuzco, and was built on three terraces, with walls about 60 feet (18 m) high. Parts of these vast walls still stand, but most are ruined, and topped by grass and flowers. Other fortresses have names like Ollantaytambo, Huamanmarca, Patallacta and Wiñaywayna, all cunningly designed with secret tunnels, rooms for soldiers, storehouses and watertanks that would allow a garrison to resist a siege for many weeks.

CUZCO: CAPITAL OF THE INCAS

Passing through ancient terraces on which the Inca peasants grew their staple crops of potatoes and corn, the city of Cuzco comes into view. The modern city is a red-brown huddle of houses lying on the rich green slopes of surrounding mountains, but unlike many cities on the Inca Road, Cuzco has retained a great deal of its Inca heritage. Cobbled streets, the cleanliness of which once impressed the Spaniards, are now dirty but still functional, and will remain so as long as motor vehicles are prevented from damaging them. High walls tower on either side of narrow, noisy streets, so that the sky appears as little more than a slender strip of blue high above. Crowning all this was the magnificent Golden Enclosure of the Temple of the Sun, a vast walled structure in which sacrifices were offered to the Sun god.

One of the most outstanding features of Inca buildings is the huge blocks of stone, expertly hewn to match their neighbours so perfectly that no mortar was needed to bind them. Cuzco offers many examples of this skilful building technique. Often the edges of the stones were bevelled

BELOW, *Cuzco was the capital of the highly developed Inca empire, which was united by worship of the Sun god*

PRACTICAL INFORMATION

- There is a Ministry of Tourism branch at Quito airport, which will supply maps and information.
- Machupicchu may be reached by train or bus, but both may be unreliable in the rainy season. The higher parts of the trail may cause altitude sickness. It might be necessary to allow a day or so for the body to acclimatize to the reduced oxygen in the air.
- The Peruvian communist group the Shining Path has been causing problems to tourists travelling the Inca Road. It is advisable to check with the relevant embassy to ascertain which parts are and are not safe to travel.

slightly, so that the joins between them were accentuated. This not only served to decorate the buildings, but also highlighted the great skill of the masons in matching these great blocks of stone so precisely that even the most slender of blades cannot pass between them.

The Incas called their empire the 'Four Quarters of the World' and it was in Cuzco's city square that the royal roads from all over the empire met.

THE ROAD SOUTH AND THE LAKE IN THE MOUNTAINS

One of these roads led south, towards Lake Titicaca, a glittering blue sea 12,505 feet (3790m) above sea level. Inca legend tells of how the first emperors were created on Isla del Sol in Titicaca by the Sun god. This beautiful island can be visited by hiring a boat from Copacabana, and it is worth spending a night to fully appreciate the tranquility and grandeur of the many Inca ruins. Around the shores of Titicaca people still occasionally use the traditional *balsas*, or reed boats. The boats are a dusty beige, but the clothes of the people are bright splashes of colour, still woven in the traditional designs worn by their Inca ancestors.

At Tiahuanaco in Bolivia are the remains of the Temple of the Moon, a great stone building with a flight of worn stairs leading majestically to an imposing square entrance. Great carved slabs of stone stand sentinel to these silent ruins and their beautifully carved walls and statues.

Finally, the Inca Road travelled to Santiago, lying at the southernmost point of the Inca empire. Santiago today is a bustling modern city, full of noise and cars, but the sight of the Andes gleaming white in the distance reminds the visitor that the peace and solitude of the Inca Road lie not too far away.

THE END OF THE INCAS

The Inca empire lasted only 100 years before it was crushed by the Spanish in their frantic quest for gold, but its many fine buildings bear testament to its greatness. When earthquakes shook South America in 1986, the Inca ruins shrugged them off with disdain, such was the skill and durability of the builders' handiwork. The Inca Road offers a great deal to the traveller, from the lonely and deserted stretches of moss-strewn causeway, interspersed with dangerously ill-maintained suspension and foot bridges, to the busy section from Cuzco to Machupicchu. Yet, wherever you walk on these ancient pathways, it is easy to imagine a time more than 450 years ago when the roads teemed with people herding llamas, or hurrying to do the empire's business. Looking up at the clean, bright snow on the summits of the lofty Andes and down into deep green valleys, lush with vegetation, one can also imagine these roads carrying the emperors of the Incas, aloof and majestic in their golden litters.

BELOW, *the Ponce monolith in the ruins of Tiahuanaco, at the southern end of Lake Titicaca*

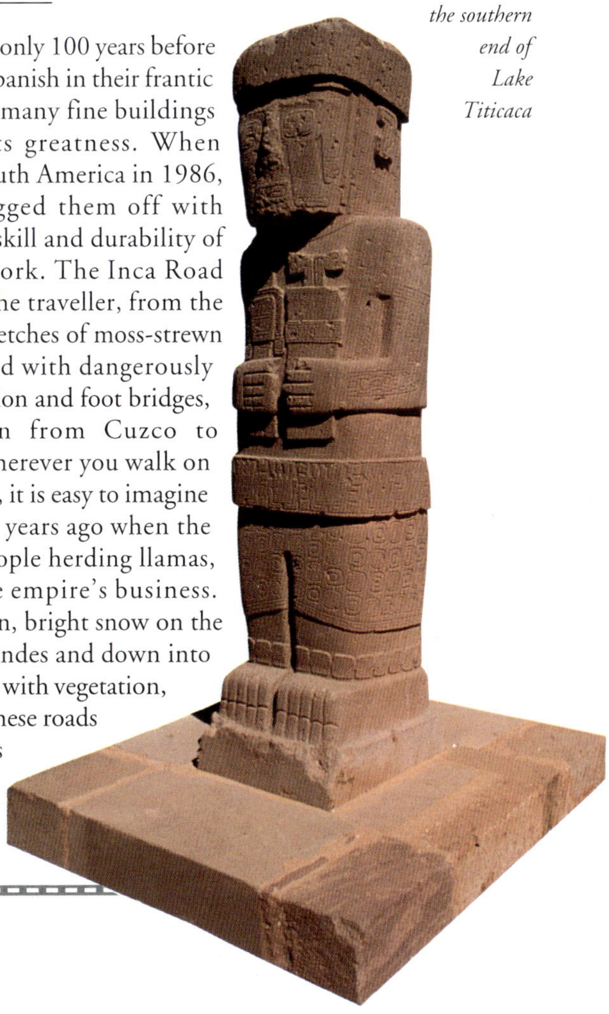

The Odessa Highway – St Petersburg to Odessa

RICHARD SALE

The collapse of Soviet socialism has, in principle, opened up the world's largest country to the traveller. In practice it has replaced one set of problems with another; but the problems are becoming less intractable, and road travel is now becoming possible again. The Odessa Highway is one such journey, linking the old Russian capital of St Petersburg with the Soviet (and now Russian) capital of Moscow and the Black Sea port of Odessa, now in the emerging nation of Ukraine.

ABOVE, *the Church of the Resurrection in St Petersburg is extensively decorated with mosaics*

BELOW, *the magnificent Hermitage complex, seen from the River Neva*

BY THE END of the 13th century, with virtually the whole of Central Asia under the control of the Mongol Khans, Moscow was a small town under Mongol rule. Free Russia, in as much as it existed, was centred on Novgorod, which lay outside the borders of the Mongol Empire. As the power of the Khans waned, the influence of the princes of Muscovy began to rise. Within 100 years their fiefdom had expanded enormously, but was still small in comparison to the area controlled by Novgorod. A century later the power struggle between the two cities had been won by Moscow. From then on the expansion of Russia was remorseless; by the end of the 18th century it extended westward to include Ukraine and all of what is now European Russia.

THE FOUNDING OF ST PETERSBURG

Until 1703 the capital of this vast Empire was Moscow, but in that year Peter the Great decided to move it to a site in newly acquired territory to the west. The marshy site was occupied by a few Finnish farmers, but Peter's engineers laboured to create a new city which the Russian Tsar named for his patron saint. With its access to the seas of Europe, St Petersburg rapidly rose to become Russia's most important port as well as its capital, and the road between it and the old capital of Moscow was improved. Later, in 1789, the

ABOVE, *Dolls in national costume are widely available for visitors to purchase*

St Petersburg lies on the eastern extremity of the Gulf of Finland, as far north as Alaska's southern shores, its rivers and canals freezing in winter. Odessa is on the same latitude as central France and lies on the shores of the Black Sea, renowned for its summer resorts. This gives some idea of the great areas covered by the old Russian and Soviet empires, and an immediate hint of the distance covered by the road that links the two cities which, with Moscow, were once the largest in the Russian empire. The road – which also passes through Kiev (Kiyev), capital of the new state of Ukraine – is 1300 miles (about 2100 km) long. It varies from excellent, with dual carriageways and a good surface, to mediocre, with a single carriageway, poor surface and poorly-defined edges. But with care even its worst sections are comfortably negotiated, and those who travel it gain a fascinating glimpse both of the countryside of European Russia and of its history.

From St Petersburg the road heads south to Novgorod through a land of forests and cultivated fields, studded with marshland. From Novgorod, famed for its historical centre, the road turns south-east to Tver, once the capital of a small state that vied with Moscow for control of Russia, and on to Moscow itself.

From Moscow the road heads south again, crossing vast areas of rolling steppe to reach Orel. From there it heads south towards Kharkov, but then turns south-west and heads for the Ukrainian border and on to Kiyev. From there the road turns south again, passing through Uman to reach Odessa and the shores of the Black Sea.

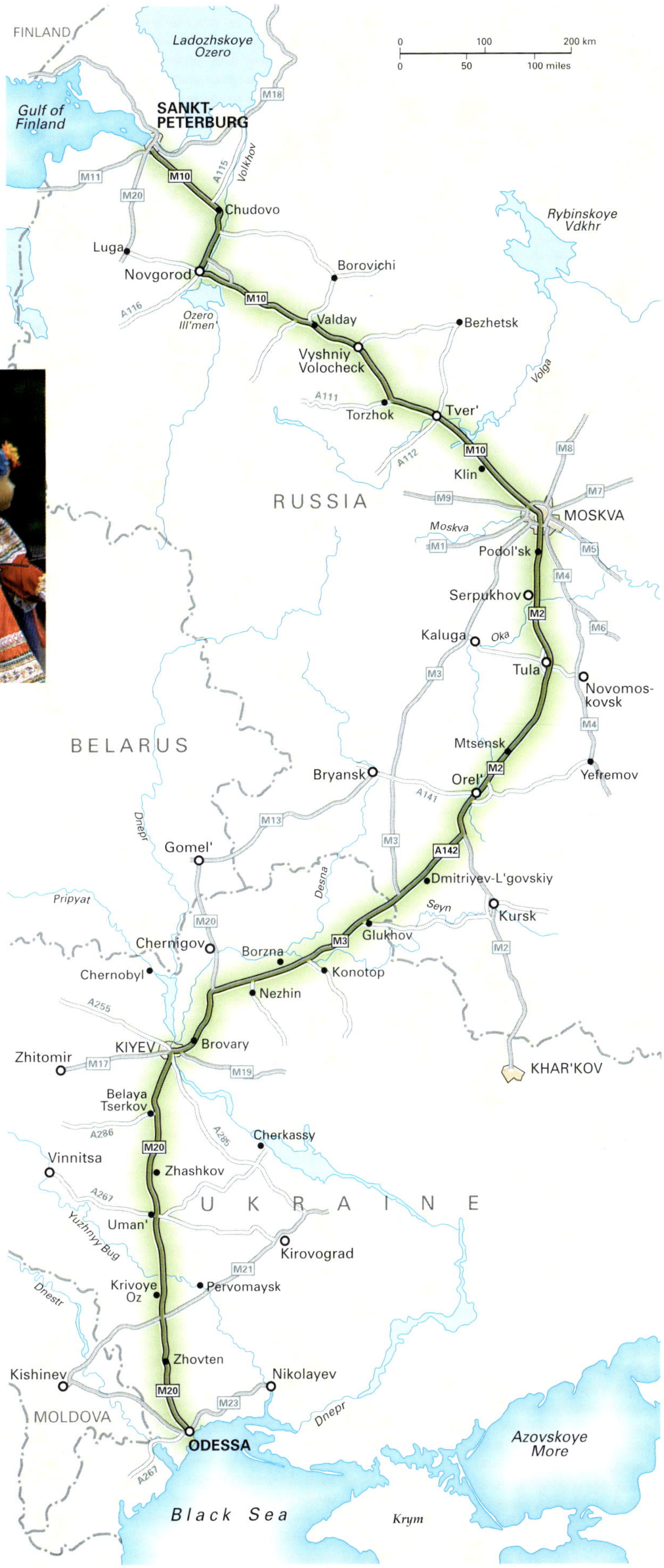

ABOVE, *the first Winter Palace was built by Peter the Great in 1711; the present palace, elegant in green and white stone, is the seventh version*

capture of the old Ottoman port of Odessa gave Russia access to the Black Sea. A new naval base was constructed, giving rise to fears of Russian expansionism and eventually leading to the Crimean War. The new port was linked to the centres of Russian power, but though a route north to Kiyev (Kiev) was straightforward, the road builders favoured a turn towards Moscow. Later, the arrival of railways made road building a secondary occupation, as the vast size of Russia made rail travel more attractive than days spent on muddy or dusty roads. Only with the advent of the car and truck were the roads consolidated. From then on the three great cities were linked inextricably with the evolution of Russia, the Soviet Union and with the fall of Communism.

Having the advantage of a barren site at St Petersburg, the European architects employed by Peter the Great could work in unlimited space. Nor was there any control on their expenditure. The result was a city that within half a century of the laying of the first stone could stand comparison with the finest cities in Europe. The magnificence of the buildings is matched by that of the site, a view of the Winter Palace from across the River Neva matching any view in Paris or Vienna.

The Winter Palace forms part of the Hermitage complex. The name 'Hermitage' was the normal Russian nomenclature for the cluster of small buildings around a Royal palace and does not imply that the site was ever a monastery. At the heart of the complex is the Palace, built in Russian baroque style, in attractive green and white stone. It forms a square around a large inner courtyard. Beside it stand the Old and New Hermitages and the Hermitage Theatre. Today the complex is one of the world's great museums, famous for its art collection housed in lavishly decorated rooms. Beside the Hermitage is the Admiralty building, famed for its gilded spire, and beyond that a statue of Peter the Great known as 'The Bronze Horseman'. This superb equestrian statue (named from a poem by Pushkin) stands in Decembrists Square. The name of the square was changed in 1925 to commemorate the 100th anniversary of the uprising against Tsar Nicholas I in December 1825, which was brutally crushed in hours.

Also close to the Hermitage are two of the city's cathedrals. The Kazan Cathedral is now a museum of the history of religion and atheism. St Isaac's Cathedral is one of the world's largest domed structures, and was extensively rebuilt following damage in World War II. It is modelled on St Peter's in Rome. Across the Neva from the Hermitage stands the Peter and Paul Fortress, the first building of the new city to have been started. The fortress, which has served successive governments as a prison, houses another cathedral.

As Russia's capital, St Petersburg saw the start of the Revolution. In 1905 the sailors of the battleship *Potemkin* mutinied at Odessa, at the other end of our road, and an uprising led to Bloody Sunday, with hundreds of demonstrators being shot dead by the Tsar's troops. The October Revolution began in St Petersburg in 1917 with Lenin's Bolsheviks seizing power, and the rebellion of the naval base of Kronstadt in 1921 – and its subsequent crushing – effectively ended opposition to one-party rule. In the course of these events the city's name changed – to Petrograd in 1914 and to Leningrad after Lenin's death in 1924. In a referendum in June 1991 the city folk voted for the name to be changed back to St Petersburg. The majority in favour was small, but sufficient for the change to become official in September of that year.

HEADING SOUTH TOWARDS MOSCOW

South from St Petersburg, a journey of 120 miles (192 km) leads to Novgorod. Although the name means 'new town' the site has been occupied since the 9th century, and for several hundred years was the centre of a Russian state that existed outside the borders of the Mongol Empire. Beside the River Volkhov stands the city's Kremlin – Kremlin being the Russian term for the fortified heart of a city – which has a good museum and a fine 11th-century Byzantine cathedral. From it a footbridge over the river leads to Yaroslav's Court. There is a cathedral within the court which dates from the 12th century.

Tver, the next city on the road, was a stopping point on the journey of Catherine the Great. Here she built the Putevoy Dvorets (literally the 'Road Palace'), a palace that still stands among the city's classier houses. Tver (the name changed back from Kalinin in 1990) stands on the Volga, Russia's longest river and one embedded deep in the Russian psyche. The crossing of the river is one of the highlights of the journey.

The next city is Moscow, capital of the Soviet state since 1918 and also of the new Russia. It is not an attractive place, the ugly concrete blocks of Stalin's utilitarian city creating a depressing sprawl. But dotted about in the faceless city are odd gems – onion-domed churches, ancient monasteries and buildings such as Yaroslavl Station, built in 1902-4. The station is the terminus of the Trans-Siberian Railway.

At the heart of Moscow are the Kremlin and Red Square, a centre of which any city would be proud. From the bridge over the Moskva River south of the square, the view of the gold onion domes of the Kremlin's cathedrals and of the multi-coloured domes of St Basil's Cathedral is superb. Your overnight stop in Moscow might be in a hotel close to Red Square. If not, a journey into the centre will allow you a visit to another of the city's highlights, the Metro. Built under the direction of Khruschev with the aim of showing that Russian engineering and architecture could rival that of any other country, the Metro stations are a remarkable mix of marble columns and platforms, cut-glass chandeliers, and escalators that are longer, and quicker, than any you will have experienced.

Red Square will probably seem smaller than it appeared on Western television during the May Day military processions of the Soviet era. At its southern end is St Basil's Cathedral, one of the world's most beautiful buildings. Built in 1552 by Ivan the Terrible to celebrate the capture of the Khanate stronghold of Kazan, the cathedral is named for Basil the Blessed, a 'Holy Fool', an ascetic who died in the same year and is buried inside. The domes – turbans, pineapples and swirling onions – were painted in the 17th century. For many years the cathedral was closed to the public, but you may now see the gloriously painted interior.

North of the cathedral the Square is hemmed in between the Kremlin's eastern wall and the GUM department store. The raised circular stone dais is the Lobnoye Mesto, the Palace of Skulls, site of public executions in tsarist Russia. Beside the Kremlin's wall is Lenin's tomb. The queue to see the Father of the Revolution is shorter now than in Soviet times, and eventually the wax-like body may be moved from view. So if the queue is

ABOVE, *the exuberant colours of St Basil's Cathedral in Moscow were based on traditional designs of Russian timber churches*

FAR LEFT, *the Spasskaia Tower is one of 20 which surround the Kremlin; the red star at the top of the spire replaced the double eagle of the Tsar in 1935*

RIGHT, *Kiev is divided by the River Dnepr; the right bank is hilly and the left a broad plain*

FAR RIGHT, *Odessa enjoys a Mediterranean climate, protected by the mountains*

still there, join it for what may be your only chance of a somewhat macabre view of one of the 20th century's most influential figures. At present the guard at the tomb is changed every hour, a worthwhile sight in its own right.

Ahead now is the History Museum, built in fine 19th-century Russian style and housing the country's most important museum to the evolution of Russia and the Russian people.

Go left at the end of the Kremlin's wall to reach its main entrance. Within the citadel there are no fewer than four cathedrals, together with another church, the palace of the Tsars, fine gardens and the offices of state. The whole is dominated by the Borovitsky Tower at the south-eastern corner and the gold onion-domed bell-tower of Ivan the Great. Of the cathedrals, that of the Annunciation, with its collection of gold onion domes and marble façade, is the most exquisite. The State Armoury, a vast but elegant building, houses the treasury of the Tsars with some of the richest insignia in the world.

Finally, the Kremlin has its curios. The Emperor Bell is the largest ever cast, but was never rung. It cracked after falling from its belfry during a fire, and the piece that stands beside it fell out during another fire. The bell, cast in 1735, weighs 210 tonnes. The cracked piece alone weighs 11.5 tonnes. The Emperor's Cannon, on the other side of Ivan's bell tower, is the word's largest cannon, with a 17 foot (5 m) barrel of calibre 35 inches (88cm). It was cast in 1586 for Tsar Fyodor I. It has probably never been fired and the cannonballs beside it are certainly too large for its barrel.

BELOW RIGHT, *the Golden Gate at Kiev, built in 1037 as part of the city's fortifications, is surmounted by a tiny church*

BELOW, *the Emperor's Cannon, cast in bronze and weighing 40 tons, was designed to fire crushed stone at invaders*

South to the Steppes of the Cossacks

Southward, the road travels through the seemingly endless suburbs of Moscow before opening out to the glorious Steppes, so famous in Russian history. Beyond Tula at Yasnoya Polyana – just a short distance from the road – you can visit a museum to Leo Tolstoy, housed where the writer was born and lived. Tolstoy was of noble birth, his family having an estate close to the village, but he eventually tired of estate life and moved away in 1910. He lived the peasant's life his heart treasured for only a few months before he died of pneumonia. He is buried on the estate.

Further south, and also very close to the road, is Spasskoe Lutovinova, where the writer Turgenev lived after being exiled from St Petersburg for his provocative writings. His house is also a museum. At Orel, further on, there is another museum to Turgenev, and a statue of the writer overlooking the River Oka. The town's prosperous days are behind it, but it still has a fine array of houses dating from the period in the 19th century when it was the seat of many families of minor Russian nobility. Turgenev wrote about these folk in his book *A Nest of Gentry*; the subjects of the book were so taken with it that they named a park in the city after it and raised a bust of Turgenev there, so that a walk around Orel seems like a visit to an extended shrine to the writer.

The journey from Orel to Kiev will take you about eight hours, perhaps more with the formalities of crossing the Ukrainian border. Ukraine is endless steppe; this is the land of the Cossacks, the name deriving from the Turkish *kazac* which means horseman, outlaw or free man, depending upon its context. Ukraine suffered badly during its time as a Soviet republic,

Practical Information

■ Independent travel in Russia is not easy. Intourist still attempt to control the journeys and accommodation of travellers, but this has the advantage that Intourist will organize the necessary visas and car hire. Intourist will only allow you to drive 312 miles (500 km) each day. However, this is unlikely to be a problem as 200 miles (320 km) on Russian roads is usually enough.

■ Petrol stations are about every 60 miles (96 km), but it is advisable to fill up at every opportunity. Speed limits are 37-62 mph (60-100 kph).

■ The best time to follow the road is summer.

and its relationship with Russia is still uneasy. You will be treated well, however, and can expect to enjoy the visit, particularly to Kiev, where the restaurants are guaranteed to offer chicken Kiev, the quality of which will be variable. The city has an enviable site on the River Dnepr (Dnieper), and an equally enviable history, claiming to be the founding city of the true Russia and having been at one time a brother state of Constantinople. The latter link is obvious in the cathedral of St Sophia, named after the Cathedral of Hagia Sophia in Istanbul and built in Byzantine style. Also worth seeing are the elegant church of St Andrew, built of green and white stone reminiscent of St Petersburg's Hermitage, and the Golden Gate, another work inspired by Byzantium. Finally, if you have the time, you should visit the Caves Monastery, about 2 miles (3 km) south of the city. As the name implies the monastery is underground; the monks live in a series of tunnels beneath a wooded hill above the Dnepr. Visitors can wander through the tunnels, coming very close to the preserved bodies of the monks laid to rest on ledges. As the fame and prosperity of the monastery increased, a series of gold domed churches were built on the wooded hill, adding a breathtaking beauty to a fascinating site.

The highway heads south from Kiev, away from Chernobyl, Ukraine's most infamous town, which lies 60 miles (96 km) to the north. It is a day's travel now to Odessa and the Black Sea, the last part through a land of mudflats that were once estuaries of the Dnepr and Dnestr rivers, between which Odessa sits. The mud is reputedly a cure for all ills, and many come to the city to take mud baths. Odessa was a part of Ottoman Turkey until Ukraine fell to the Russians. With its development as a naval base it soon grew to be Russia's second port, after St Petersburg, and third city. It was also influential in the Revolution, a workers' uprising in 1905 being supported by the crew of the battleship *Potemkin.* Although the uprising was crushed, it sowed the seeds for the successful uprising in 1917. Sergei Eisenstein's famous film on the incident was made in the city in 1925. As a visitor's city, Odessa has little to offer. The Potemkin Steps are in the grand style, the statue of the mutineers has historical interest, and that of the Duc de Richelieu mystery value – what is he doing here? The prosaic answer is that he governed the city for ten years after fleeing the Revolution in France. But for most visitors, and especially those who have travelled virtually the length of Russia, the city's most enticing attraction is a relaxing stroll along the shores of the Black Sea.

BELOW, *the Monastery of the Caves at Kiev, founded in 1051, consists of a series of museums and churches above extensive cave systems*

The Silk Road
Overland from the Orient

ROSEMARY BURTON

ABOVE, *silkworms in Jiangsu museum industriously producing the raw material for silk*

During the first century BC, China and the Roman Empire began to trade, sending goods 4000 miles (6400 km) overland by baggage train across some of the most difficult and dangerous terrain in the world. Hundreds of years later this route was named the Silk Road. It's a poetic title which conjures up exotic images, but the reality is rather different: other commodities were traded as well as silk and there was not one Silk Road, but several. Yet the idea of the Silk Road has become a romantic metaphor, symbolising commercial and cultural contact between East and West.

DID THE PEOPLE who drove laden camel trains along the Silk Road 2000 years ago think of themselves as taking part in a romantic adventure? It seems unlikely – the harsh conditions of the journey must have left little time or energy for daydreams, and most of the travellers and animal handlers worked only one section of the 4000-mile (6400-km) trans-continental trail, transferring goods from one baggage train to another at fixed points along the way. Even the evocative name for the ancient trade route between China and the west turns out to be a 19th-century invention, dating from the time when reports of cities buried in the desert sands of Tartary began to intrigue European adventurers.

ABOVE, *Xi'an, where the Silk Road begins, became famous worldwide in 1974 when the Terracotta Army was discovered*

It was a German scholar, Ferdinand von Richthofen, who came up with the name 'Silk Road' in the 1870s, and the title is now firmly rooted in popular imagination, although it only celebrates one aspect of a route which saw trade in numerous commodities besides silk and allowed for commerce and exchange of ideas between Chinese and Europeans and between Jews, Hindus, Moslems, Zoroastrians and Buddhists.

Like the early travellers whose footsteps they tried to trace, 20th-century explorers such as Sven Hedin, Peter Fleming and Ella Maillart had to cope with storms of sand, salt and snow, with shifting sand dunes and a river which alters course, with altitude sickness, snow blindness and desperate extremes of temperature. Even if they managed to withstand all the natural hazards, there have always been other dangers awaiting aliens crossing foreign lands, where borders might be in dispute

ABOVE, *snow lies on the Karakoram highway, near the China–Pakistan border*

Although the Silk Road is more of a romantic concept than a geographical reality, it is possible to track several routes along which goods from the East were transported to the West. The Silk Road begins in Xi'an, China, and continues to Lanzhou where there was a choice of routes around the Taklimakan desert. One option was to go north through Hami, Turpan, Yanqi and Aksu, and the other south via Miran, Yutian, Hotan and Shache, skirting the Kunlun Shan. The two routes converged at Kashi, then continued northwards to Fergana and Tashkent and thence to Samarkand; but it was also possible to divert before reaching Kashi, at Shache and travel a southerly route along the borders of Afghanistan, close to the Hindu Kush. Beyond Samarkand, the route continues to Tehran via Mary (or Merv), then on to Hamadan and Baghdad. To reach the shores of the Mediterranean, the travellers journeyed on through Dimashq (Damascus) to Beyrouth (Beirut) or turned north to Halab (Aleppo). From here they might take ship to Rome from Antioch (Hatay) or Tyre (Soûr). Another Silk Road ended at the Black Sea, crossing overland to Constantinople (Istanbul).

ABOVE, *at Dunhuang in Gansu province, the 'Singing Sand-dunes' seem poised to engulf the road*

or fiercely guarded, and where bands of thieves might pounce at any time. Given the isolation and the ordeals to be endured, it is hardly surprising that over the centuries people crossing the barren wildernesses of Central Asia have told stories of supernatural forces with disembodied voices which tried to lure them away from their proper path.

THE TAKLIMAKAN

Today provision is beginning to be made for tourists eager to experience the romance of the Silk Road but, despite the introduction of package tours, much of the way remains barren and inhospitable. For some people the hardships are an essential part of the attraction, of course, but anyone tempted by visions of caravanserais and baggage trains weighed down with bales of colourful silks should not forget that the journey requires them to negotiate a desert called Taklimakan, which translates roughly as 'You go in, but you do not come out'.

Faced with such an obstacle, where progress is complicated by the fact that the sand dunes move, as does the course of the Tarim, the glacier-fed river which crosses the entire region, the answer would seem to be not to go in at all but to go round, and travellers have tended to do exactly that. Merchants discovered that, by keeping to the northern or southern edges of this vast western Chinese wasteland, their chances of survival (and of living to see the profits of their trade), were greater, and gradually oasis towns developed to serve the traffic making the hazardous expedition between East and West.

However, the routes skirting the Taklimakan could hardly be described as an easy option. The desert is bordered to north, south and west by some of the highest mountains in the world, while to the east lies the Gobi Desert and the Lop Nur, a huge lake of fluctuating size surrounded by salt marshes. The Lop Nur region is remote enough and barren enough for the Chinese authorities to use it as a nuclear testing site.

Despite the Taklimakan, or indeed because of it, many people have been drawn to explore the Silk Road, but they did not all follow exactly the same route. Around the Taklimakan, and to the west of it, there is no one strictly defined 'Silk Road', but rather a number of choices. Traders and explorers have always had to tailor their progress according to the specific geographical, climatic and political conditions which they encountered; and it is only necessary to reflect on the recent politics of Iraq and Iran, of the former

Soviet states, of Afghanistan and of China itself to realize that a trans-continental journey in search of the Silk Road may be a complex business.

THE START OF THE SILK TRADE

From the Western viewpoint, Xi'an (ancient Ch'ang-an), a city in Shaanxi Province which became famous in recent years after the discovery near by of a buried army of terracotta warriors, is regarded as the origin of the Silk Road, and Rome is often cited as the Western terminus, because silks and spices for the Roman Empire were among the most valued commodities traded along the route. However, Chinese silks and spices were valued in other places too, and there were silk routes which led to Damascus (Dimashq) and Baghdād, while some writers trace the Western end to Constantinople (Istanbul), because that city literally and symbolically links Europe and Asia. Others picture a silk route leading to Venice, because that was the home of Marco Polo, who travelled part of the route in the 13th century and brought startling news of China back to the West.

From the Eastern point of view, Xi'an was simply the ancient capital city of a resolutely self-sufficient Chinese empire – a city from which traders were accustomed to travel westwards for some 300 miles within the Empire along a well-maintained imperial highway long before the foreign silk trade was developed. Before the silk trade began, jade and gold were the precious commodities brought eastwards into Xi'an along this route from a distant part of the Tarim river basin and from mountains south of Hotan (Khotan) – a town on what is now known as the southern Silk Road.

In time China sent silk, spices, bronze and porcelain out to the West along the imperial

INSET ABOVE, *near to the 'Singing Sand-dunes' is the oasis of the Crescent Moon lake and temple*

MAIN PICTURE, *the desert presents a formidable obstacle to travellers today, just as it did to camel trains on the Silk Road*

ABOVE, *a remote border crossing at the border of China and Pakistan on the Silk Road*

highway and in return the Western traders brought a wealth of European and Middle Eastern goods including metals, jewels, pistachio nuts and a renowned breed of horses from Fergana (in modern Uzbekistan). According to some estimates, Chinese silk took three years to travel to Rome, and the fact that it was priced almost as highly as gold on arrival says much about the costs of the journey and the mystery of silk creation.

Silk was certainly cultivated in China during the third millennium BC and probably even earlier than that, but knowledge of this apparently miraculous material seems only to have reached the West towards the end of the Roman Republican era. The Romans knew vaguely about China as a distant Eastern land whose people they called Seres, but their introduction to silk seems to have been as late as 53BC when, at the battle of Carrhae, a Roman army was dazzled by Parthian forces waving shimmering silken flags. Although they were defeated, the Romans obtained some of the exotic cloth and learned that the Parthians had traded for it with the Chinese. Before long the new material, rumoured to grow on trees, had become the height of fashion in Rome. The popularity of silk caused offence to Roman moralists, who saw it as a symbol of unacceptable effeminacy and decadence, and there were even attempts to prohibit men from wearing it.

BELOW, *the snowy peaks of the Qilian Shan mountains in Gansu Province provide a dramatic backdrop to a fort*

Despite the surrounding mountain ranges – the Pamirs and the Hindu Kush to the west and the Karakorams and Kunlun Shan to the south, all with passes many thousands of feet high – the city of Hotan itself was just about within the reach of traders who occasionally ventured north from India or east from Turkey and Persia. In this way lines of communication began to be opened up and Western and Eastern peoples gradually began to learn something of one another around two and a half thousand years ago. Perhaps the Chinese were tantalized by garbled stories of strange Westerners, perhaps they were eager to assess the strength of the Huns who lived beyond their western borders, and perhaps, too, they began to realize that there might be wealth to be gained from abandoning their age-old policy of insularity.

Chinese Exploration

Whatever the reasons, during the second century BC, the Chinese Han dynasty emperor, Wudi, sent an ambassador to travel beyond Hotan to Fergana and the territory of the Massagetes, who led a nomadic existence in the region between the Caspian and Aral seas. An account of the adventures of this ambassador, Zhang-qian, survives in a contemporary Chinese chronicle, which reveals that he was detained for 10 years by the Huns, before escaping westwards to Fergana and exploring the lands of Bactria and Parthia, which were crossed by the key trade routes to the West.

Eventually Zhang-qian reported back to his

emperor and, according to the chronicle, before long the leaders of China and Bactria were talking to one another with the result that trade caravans began to make their way from East to West. These animal trains were often made up of hundreds of two-humped Bactrian camels, although mules and horses were also used and yaks were best suited to the icy and precarious terrain of the high mountain passes.

There were periods during which China lost supremacy over the Tarim basin, and complex alliances among the oasis towns and increasing Hun domination meant that traffic was often interrupted, but the market for Chinese goods had been established in the West and threats to supplies simply added to the rarity and desirability of the items from the East. After a period of severe decline from the beginning of the 3rd century, the route enjoyed a revival under the Tang dynasty in the 7th century, only to suffer eclipse again as Mongol and Tibetan struggles for supremacy made safe passage impossible.

At the beginning of the 13th century an alliance of nomadic Mongol tribes was formed under the leadership of Genghis Khan, and after further decades of upheaval a Mongol empire brought stability and unity to the region and traders again felt confident about travelling along the ancient route. At the same time, new overland itineraries were beginning to be favoured, far to the north of the original silk routes, while Western countries were becoming increasingly competent at manufacturing their own silk. Trade in other commodities would naturally continue between China and Europe, but before very long sea routes would be established and more and more goods would travel by boat.

ABOVE, *Kazakh people of the 'heavenly mountains' in Xinjiang province, north-east of Xi'an*

WAYS AROUND THE TAKLIMAKAN

Even in the earliest days, traders leaving the cosmopolitan city of Xi'an had a choice of routes. The caravans seem to have stayed together for the crossing of the Gobi desert via Lanzhou, but on reaching the Dunhuang oasis some opted for the northern and others for the southern route around the Taklimakan. The northern route went through the Jade Gate in China's Great Wall (a name commemorating the fact that jade was brought to the capital that way) and then through a sequence of oasis settlements in the foothills of the Tien Shan (the 'heavenly mountains'). Travellers who favoured this northern route around the Taklimakan kept to the mountain slopes between the towns of Hami, Turfan (Turpan, China's hottest city, equipped with an

BELOW, *the Maijishan Buddhist grotto occupies a commanding position high on a mountain at Tianshui*

ABOVE, *goods on display at a Sunday market in Kashgar (Kashi), where the northern and southern Silk Roads diverged*

extraordinary network of underground irrigation canals), Karashahr (now Yanqi), Kuqa, Aksu and Tumshuk, finally reaching Kashgar (Kashi), where people who had opted for the southern route might also arrive after a journey through Miran, Cherchen, Keriya (Yu-Otian), Khotan (Hotan) and Yarkant (Shache).

There was also a rather more direct, and even more hazardous, middle route which actually ventured into the desert from Dunhuang via the city of Loulan, before joining the northern peripheral route west of Turfan. Loulan itself was once an important Silk Route staging post which seems to have vanished beneath shifting salt marshes and sand dunes some time in the fourth century, and was only rediscovered by Sven Hedin in the twentieth.

Marco Polo's experience of the Silk Road dates from long after the height of the trade, and long after Loulan's disappearance, but his description reveals the conditions encountered by any traveller, ancient or modern, attempting to cross this huge wilderness: '. . .travellers who intend to cross the desert rest . . . for a week in order to refresh themselves and their beasts. At the end of a week they stock up with a month's provisions. . . This desert is reported to be so long that it would take a year to go from end to end; and at the narrowest point it takes a month to cross it. It consists entirely of mountains and sand and valleys. There is nothing at all to eat. . . And all the way through the desert you must go for a day and a night before you find water.'

Beyond Kashgar (Kashi), which became an influential independent kingdom and today remains a predominantly Islamic city with an appealing medieval centre, the Silk Road traveller had to cross the Pamir mountains and then make a choice between several possible routes to pursue the journey westward. A northern route continued via Fergana, Tashkent, Samarkand and Bukhara to Merv. Archaeologists are currently excavating at Merv (now called Mary), in modern Turkmenistan, and they have discovered a series of walled cities here, including an early Islamic one which was once the eastern capital of the Seljuk empire.

A southern silk route also went through Merv via Yarkant (Shache) and Balkh. From this point traffic might continue south of the Caspian Sea, through Ecbatana (Hamadān), and on to Baghdād, Palmyra (Tadmur), Aleppo (Halāb) and the coast, where goods could be taken by ship to Rome from Antioch (Hatay) or Tyre (Soûr). An alternative route took traders on an overland journey to Constantinople (Istanbul).

FAR RIGHT, *traditional means of transport in use along the Silk Road near Kashgar*

BELOW, *although much Buddhist art of the area has been destroyed, these statues can still be seen in the Mogao caves at Dunhuang*

THE ARRIVAL OF THE WESTERN EXPLORERS

It is the Taklimakan desert section of the Silk Road which seems to have exerted the greatest fascination over Western travellers and explorers in the 19th and 20th centuries, partly because it is the region least known in the West and perhaps also because surviving the desert is an experience which puts everything else in the shade. The name of the whole area, which has remained predominantly Moslem since the 10th century, has changed countless times. Currently it is known as the Sinkiang Uighur Autonomous Region of the People's Republic of China, but in other eras it has been Chinese Central Asia, Chinese Tartary, Kasgaria and Serindia. The discoveries which were made here in the 19th century were prompted by reports of a great Buddhist civilization, whose relics were said to have been buried under sand and hidden in hundreds of caves in the foothills of the Tian Shan and Kunlun mountain ranges for over a thousand years.

Buddhism was established in Central Asia by missionaries travelling from India some time after the third century BC. The growing numbers of Buddhist converts, who were better able than most people to endure hardship and isolation because of their teachings and their meditative techniques, made themselves cave dwellings in the mountain foothills and carved temples and monastic complexes out of the rock face. These holy buildings were approached by long flights of man-made steps, and were richly painted inside with scenes from Buddhist scriptures and furnished with fine sculpture, painted silken banners and precious manuscripts. It was contrary to Buddhist practice for monks to have any personal wealth – they had to beg for alms and it seems that prosperous Silk Road merchants responded to their requests, perhaps believing that generosity and reverence would be rewarded with a safe journey and further riches. The extraordinary quality of the temple art certainly indicates the existence of wealthy patrons resident in, or travelling through, the area over a long period of time.

By the early years of the 20th century scholars of several different nations were at work in the region, among them Sven Hedin of Sweden, who conducted a series of expeditions into the Taklimakan and nearly died in his attempts to map the region. Hedin left graphic descriptions of his ordeals. At one stage, with only a single surviving companion and too weak to talk, he writes: 'Still we toiled on for life – bare life. Then imagine our surprise, our amazement, when on the long sloping surface of a dune we perceived human footsteps imprinted in the sand! We followed up the trail till we came to the top of a dune, where the sand was driven together in a hard compact mass, and the footprints could be more distinctly made out. Kasim dropped on his knees; then cried in a scarcely audible voice, "they are our own footsteps!".' After this Hedin recounts how something (perhaps the bewitching effect of the moon) made him change direction and, in a desperately dehydrated state, he found some water which saved his life.

Hedin succeeded in producing the first accurate maps of the Tarim Basin, and these were of vital service to many other explorers. One who benefited was Aurel Stein, a British archaeologist who is remembered for his investigations of the huge Mogao Cave temple complex near Dunhuang. Stein negotiated with a Taoist priest there to obtain thousands of Buddhist and other manuscripts from a hidden cave library. The manuscripts were removed to the British Museum and their complexity was such that they took 50 years to catalogue. Two German academics, Albert Grunwedel and Albert von Le Coq, also carried out extensive archaeological investigations, and their work during and after four Royal Prussian Turpan expeditions led to the establishment of an outstanding collection of Central Asian Buddhist art at the Museum for Indische Kunst in Berlin, and to the discovery of unique manuscripts belonging to the Manichaean and Nestorian religious sects, whose influence was revealed to be far more widespread than had previously been thought.

These manuscripts, like the ones obtained by Aurel Stein, were genuine but some others were not. At one stage, when foreign fervour for ancient documents was at its height, enterprizing local salesmen went into business manufacturing ancient papers, and even inventing scripts and languages which scholars attempted to decipher.

Buddhism was suppressed following the Moslem conquest in the 10th century, and its images were often defaced because they offended the beliefs of the new rulers. Some 20th-century explorers reported with sorrow on the lack of regard shown for the Buddhist art and manuscripts by the native people they encountered on their expeditions. Stories of priceless historical documents being used as a convenient source of vegetable fertilizer, and evidence of continuing neglect and desecration of Buddhist art, no doubt helped some Europeans to justify the extreme measures which they employed to remove their finds and transport them to their own countries.

There is a degree of irony in the fact that manuscripts, sculpture and paintings were packed up and transported to Europe in much the same way as bales of silk had travelled in ancient times. The display of these artefacts in Europe encouraged Western scholars and tourists to make the return journey to Turkestan – and so Silk Road travel continues.

PRACTICAL INFORMATION

■ In October 1994, 20 nations along the Silk Road including Turkey, Russia, Iran, Uzbekistan, Kyrgyzstan (Kirghizia) and China, signed the Samarkand Declaration to facilitate easier border crossings and a relaxation of currency and visa regulations. There are also plans to provide tourist facilities where few or none now exist.
Thomas Cook offer a rail tour of the Silk Route – for information Tel: 01733 33255.

■ The following books are useful sources of practical hints: Dominic Streatfeild-James's book *Silk Route by Rail* (Trailblazer Publications) is detailed and entertaining, Judy Bonavia's *Introduction to the Silk Road* (Odyssey, Hong Kong) concentrates on the Chinese section of the journey, and *Night Train to Turkestan* (Paladin), Stuart Steven's amusing account of adventures along China's Silk Road, presents some of the bureaucratic and practical problems

ABOVE, *decorative buildings like this pagoda can be found amid Kyoto's modern architecture*

The Old Tokaido Road from Tokyo to Kyoto

DAVID SCOTT

The Tokaido, literally the Eastern Sea Road, was for two centuries the main route between Edo (now Tokyo), the political and military capital of Japan, and Kyoto, the religious capital and home of the emperor and his court. The journey on foot took several weeks – nowadays the old road is paralleled by the Tokaido Shinkansen (bullet train) railway track and is itself overlaid by a modern highway. However, parts of the original road are still to be found in the Hakone National Park and a feel of the changing landscapes along the route may still be experienced today.

THE OLD TOKAIDO ROAD had a total of 53 post stations, where the samurai, merchants, priests, pilgrims and the noble lords who travelled the road could buy food, stay overnight and find entertainment. These were illustrated by Hiroshige (1797–1858), probably the best known of the great Japanese wood-block print artists, in his collection of landscapes, *Fifty-three Stages of the Tokaido.* The drawings for these were collected on a journey in 1832. Hiroshige made the trip as part of the entourage of a Japanese noble family. The collection was published and quickly became successful popular art.

In the Tokaido series Hiroshige showed himself to be an artist with a precise and clear eye. His drawings are not limited by the ritualized rules of Chinese painting then popular with Japanese intellectuals. He drew with a clear vision and simple humanity that was appreciated and understood by the common man. Breaking away

from the stylized conventions of the time, the people, buildings and landscapes in his prints are real and recognizable. His subject matter was concerned with the ordinary business of the Tokaido and did not include impressions of the ceremonial pomp of the procession he was travelling with. This independent view was unique within the formal order of early 19th-century Japan. His subject matter and style reflected a wider feeling of change in the old order of things. Hiroshige's Tokaido series invests the ordinary with an extraordinary quality.

TOKYO – ECONOMIC CENTRE OF JAPAN

Of the original 53 stations, 23 still exist, and can be visited on the route. The first of these is also the largest. Tokyo is home to almost 12 million people, one of the world's largest cities and the capital, and economic and cultural centre of Japan. Unlike the historic city of Kyoto, it is not a place of classic sights and traditional charms, since few buildings survived the earthquake of 1923 and the Allied bombing during World War II. It is, however, a city of global influence, wealth and creative energy.

For the first time visitor, Tokyo may appear as a disappointing jumble of high rise buildings, concrete flyovers and crowded sidewalks, a city without any particular distinguishing features. However, a more careful investigation, such as an exploration on foot away from modern thoroughfares, reveals it to be a complex metropolis of interconnected towns, each with

ABOVE, *a print in the series '53 Stations of the Tokaido', entitled 'Sunrise at Shinagawa'*

BELOW, *girls at a local festival in Kyoto, dressed in brightly coloured traditional costumes*

The Old Tokaido Road goes between Tokyo in the east and Kyoto, to the west. Since most visitors to Japan base themselves in Tokyo, our journey starts from there. Nihonbashi Bridge in the middle of town is the first subject of Hiroshige's famous Tokaido series of wood-block prints and an appropriate starting point for this journey. From Tokyo the road runs along the Pacific coastline, passing through Yokohama and close by Kamakura, one of the most beautiful and historic towns in Japan and worth a detour. From here the road crosses the top of the Izu Peninsula (Izu-hanto) and along the coastal fringe of the Fuji–Hakone–Izu National Park. On a clear day Mount Fuji (Fuji-san) looms repeatedly into view along this stretch of the route. Here you may also visit Hakone-machi and walk on a section of the original Tokaido. The road continues through the tea plantations of Shizuoka and then across flat coastal plain land – a patchwork of rice-growing paddy fields, low roofed villages, urban landscapes, roads, railway tracks and pylons – before turning north-west at Hamamatsu for Nagoya, one of Japan's largest cities. Nagoya is a convenient stopping point and a base for a detour visit to Gifu, famous for its cormorant night-fishing tradition. The road now travels west to Kyoto via Kameyama, Otsu and the southern tip of Lake Biwa (Biwa-ko).

Of the original 53 stopping stations the following places, named after the post station or vice versa, may still be passed on the route, all now towns or cities: Tokyo (Edo), Kawasaki, Yokohama, Fujisawa, Odawara, Hakone-machi, Mishima, Yoshiwara, Shimizu, Shizuoka, Fukuroi, Fujieda, Kanaya, Kakegawa, Fukuroi, Hamamatsu, Okazaki, Chiryu, Nagoya, Kuwana, Yokkaichi, Kameyama, Otsu, Kyoto. The journey from Tokyo to Kyoto covers a distance of 303 miles (485 km).

MAIN PICTURE, *Mount Fuji forms a striking backdrop to the Tomei expressway, seen through the branches of a mandarin orange tree*

their own neighbourhoods of individual character. For those with limited time, the part of Tokyo of most interest and most easily explored is the area bounded by the J R Yamanote loop line. Most of the places you will wish to visit are easily reached by subway, taxi or on foot.

THE ROAD

The Tokaido itself was not very wide and, because no carts used it, was unmetalled. Long stretches were bordered on both sides by rows of tall cedar or pine trees, planted to dissuade travellers from leaving the road and to provide shelter from sun, snow or rain. The end of every district or province was marked by a stone pillar which showed the name of the district and of the owner of the land. Distances were also carefully marked, as this quote from a 17th-century Portuguese traveller illustrates:

'There is no need to enquire about distances because all the leagues are measured out, with a mound and two trees to mark the end of each one. Should it happen that a league ends in the middle of a street, they will do no man a favour by making the measurement either longer or shorter, but pull down the houses there in order to set up the sign.'

Many rivers crossed the Tokaido and they often presented an obstacle to travellers. Ferry boats were used in some places and in others porters carried people and their belongings through the water on their shoulders. The difficulties of these fords, especially that over the river Oigawa, were the subject of several of Hiroshige's prints.

KAMAKURA

The next stopping point on the Tokaido is Kamakura. Between 1192 and 1333 Kamakura was the capital city of Japan. Nowadays, as a result, Kamakura is one of the most interesting places to visit in Japan for its historical temples and shrines (65 Buddhist temples and 19 Shinto shrines). It is also an attractive and prosperous residential town in its own right. It is much smaller than Kyoto, Japan's other religious centre, and easier to find one's way around. The local tourist office (left of the main J R Kamakura station entrance) publishes a convenient map of footpath routes that link the best-known temples. The paths are signposted in English as well as Japanese.

Hakone, lying between Mount Fuji and the ocean, is part of the Fuji–Hakone–Izu National Park. It is an area of high mountains (most over 3500 feet, 1060 m), with Lake Ashino (Ashino-ko) nestling in the centre and Mount Fuji (Fuji-san) nearly always in view to the north-west. Hakone is a very popular day trip from Tokyo and during the summer months roads, cable cars, buses and accommodation in the region are heavily used.

THE LAW OF ALTERNATE ATTENDANCE

The heyday of the Tokaido Road was around the middle of the Edo Period (1600–1868). One of the main reasons for its importance at this time was the Law of Alternate Attendance *(Sankin kotai)*. This was introduced in the early 17th century by the Tokugawa Shogun, Iemitsu, who was both a ruthless soldier and a cunning politician. With it he ensured that the Tokugawa clan would stay in power in Japan for over 200 years. *Sankin kotai* required each of the feudal lords, or daimyo, of Japan's noble families to build a substantial home in Edo (Tokyo) and to then spend alternate years in residence there while in attendance at the Shogun's court. The year in between was to be spent on their own estates. Close family members of the daimyo were restricted at all times to their homes in Edo and the surrounding district. The Shogun, at one stroke, ensured that at any one time half his feudal lords were under his eye at court and for the rest of the time he could, if need be, hold their families hostage. He also required that each daimyo on his journey from his estate to Edo should have with him a stipulated entourage of soldiers, ladies-in-waiting, servants and craftsmen. The size of the entourage was directly proportional to the size of the daimyo's estate. The outlay required to pay for it was designed to ensure that the daimyo never had enough money to finance a rebellion. The Law of Alternate Attendance proved to be most effective in preventing any provincial uprising or court revolution.

This law also meant daimyos had to travel between their estates and Edo once a year. There were five main routes radiating from Edo, and the Tokaido, which followed the eastern seaboard to Kyoto, was the most travelled. It was not only used by nobles from the western provinces, but also by normal traffic journeying between the seat of government and Kyoto.

The journey of a great lord along the Tokaido was an impressive sight. Nobles were carried in beautifully lacquered palanquins. Attendants bore aloft colourful banners, and the marching men and samurai on horseback wore full uniform. The whole effect was designed to illustrate the power and authority of the lord.

A noble procession was heralded well in advance so that post stations and inns could prepare beforehand for the extra provisions, horses and accommodation that would be required. Other travellers who knew of it would also stay clear of the road, both for their own safety and so as not to hinder the progress of the lordly personage. The procession was preceded by horsemen who would shout 'Down! Down!' and people of inferior rank were required to prostrate themselves on the ground as the daimyo passed. Anyone foolish enough to show disrespect and to be unwilling to pay homage in this way was literally chopped down by one of the samurai escorting the lord. Even towards the end of the Tokugawa shogunate this rule applied and foreigners, now starting to re-enter the country, were at risk because of their ignorance of the customs of the country. The following story from *Dr Willis in Japan* by Hugh Cortazzi illustrates the point:

> 'On 14 September, 1862, a Shanghai merchant, Charles L Richardson, in company with a Mrs Borraidaile from Hongkong and two Yokohama residents, Woodthorpe Clarke and William Marshall, were riding along the road between Kanagawa and Kawasaki, not far from Yokohama, when they met the train of the daimyo of Satsuma who bid them stand aside. Ernest Satow described the scene thus: "They passed on at the edge of the road until they came in sight of a palanquin,

INSET BOTTOM LEFT, *seen here from the Ashino-ko Lake, Mount Fuji is the crowning glory of the Hakone National Park*

BELOW, *the Daibutsu (Great Buddha) at Kamakura is more than 36 feet (11 metres) tall and weighs nearly 100 tons*

TOP RIGHT, *the graceful rooftops of Ni-jo Castle, built in 1603, contrast with the modern Kyoto skyline*

FAR RIGHT, *the pavilion of the Kinkaku-ji temple in Kyoto is completely covered in gleaming gold foil*

BELOW, *the castle at Nagoya, where a display of 'dolls' formed from crysanthemum bushes can be seen from September to November*

occupied by Shimazu Saburo, father of the Prince of Satsuma. They were now ordered to turn back and, as they were wheeling their horses in obedience, were suddenly set upon by several armed men belonging to the train, who hacked at them with their sharp-edged swords. Richardson fell from his horse in a dying state, and the other two men were so severely wounded that they called out to the lady: 'Ride on, we can do nothing for you.' She got safely back to Yokohama and gave the alarm. Everybody in the settlement who possessed a pony and a revolver at once armed himself and galloped off towards the scene of slaughter."'

Nobles and Daimyo

Apart from the processions of feudal lords the Tokaido was regularly travelled, like any other road of the day, by a colourful stream of merchants, priests, peddlers, entertainers, religious pilgrims, thieves and con-men. They all journeyed on foot since only the nobility were entitled to travel on horseback or by palanquin. These box-like structures, called *kago* in Japanese, were very ornate, but by today's standards extremely small. They were suspended from a long pole which the bearers, six to eight of them, carried on their shoulders.

Carriages drawn by oxen were the sole privilege of the imperial court and would normally only be seen in and around Kyoto. This could be the cause of some consternation for the procession of a daimyo entering Kyoto. If the daimyo's procession crossed the path of the carriage of an aristocrat from the Imperial Palace, the daimyo himself would have to get out of his palanquin and prostrate himself on the ground. This was obligatory, even though the aristocrat might be impoverished and have no political power. To avoid this embarrassing situation the daimyo would send a guard ahead to offer gifts of money to travelling aristocrats with the suggestion that it was a good time to stop for refreshments.

Sekisho (Barrier Gates)

Good communication was necessary between Edo and Kyoto, but this also presented a problem for the Shogun, since he wanted to restrict freedom of movement. The solution was to maintain a system of barriers along the Tokaido through which all travellers were obliged to pass. It was a serious offence to avoid the control points and the numbers and movements of travellers were kept under constant observation. The barriers also ensured that none of the daimyo could move any of their families out of Edo without permission. This especially applied to womenfolk, and any woman travelling with a procession was subjected to the closest scrutiny. She had to carry a certificate of authorization and to it was attached a detailed physical description to make sure she did not swap places with another woman along the way. The higher her rank the more a woman would be examined and interrogated at each of the barriers. This obviously discouraged travel, but it also gave rise to many Japanese stories of intrigue, adventure and thwarted love.

One of the most important barrier gates on the old Tokaido was on the shores of Lake Ashino, at

Hakone-machi, and here several miles of the cobbled and surprisingly narrow Tokaido have been preserved. There is also a reconstruction of the original barrier guardhouse which displays very realistic life-size mannequins of guards and travellers, samurai suits of armour and weapons, and some early macabre photographs of crucified, beheaded criminals. There is also another stretch of the preserved Tokaido at nearby Moto-Hakone. The 1 mile (1.5 km) length of road ends near the Amazaka no chaya teahouse – a good place to stop for refreshment before continuing along the road to Nagoya.

NAGOYA

Nagoya has a long history, but it was razed to the ground by Allied bombing during World War II. It was rebuilt and has since become the fourth largest city in Japan. Nagoya has few historical attractions for the visitor, except its two national treasures – Nagoya-jo Castle and the Atsuta Jingu Shrine. It is, however, a convenient base for visiting Gifu, famous for the cormorant fishing on the Nagara-gawa River. This takes place every evening between May and October, and before and after the actual fishing, which is over quite quickly, the Japanese gather on the banks of the river and indulge in much drinking and eating. It is very definitely a tourist event, but still a lot of fun. The tourist office at the station will give you details of how to get to the river, and book accommodation for you.

From Nagoya, the Tokaido continues to the ancient city of Kyoto, the final stopping place.

KYOTO – THE HEART OF JAPAN

Kyoto was established in AD794 and remained the centre of civilization in Japan for over 1000 years. Even today, although the capital has now moved to Tokyo, Kyoto retains its unique position as the country's historical and cultural centre. 'Nihon no furusato', The Heart of Japan, is how the Japanese describe Kyoto. Fortunately, the Allies spared Kyoto from bombing during World War II (thanks, it is said, to the timely intervention of the French orientalist, Elisseeff). Thus it remains a living museum to Japan's great artistic heritage, home to numerous historical and religious sites and a vast wealth of traditional art, crafts and architecture.

More than 30 million tourists a year visit the city, but there is so much to do (nearly 2000 temples and shrines alone) that crowds tend to form only at the most popular places. Avoid Kyoto on public holidays and the best known sites at weekends if you do not like crowds. Major attractions are the Kyoto Imperial Palace, Ni-jo Castle and gardens, Daitoku-ji Temple with its numerous sub temples, Ginkaku-ji (Temple of the Silver Pavilion), Kinkaku-ji (Temple of the Golden Pavilion), the sand and rock Zen garden at Ryoan-ji Temple, the major Shinto shrine Heian and Kiyomizudera Temple, built on a steep hillside with wonderful views over the city.

Kyoto also has numerous museums and a botanical and zoological garden, and there are many popular annual festivals held here. They are normally associated with the changing of the seasons or with religious occasions. For the three most well known, the Gion (16–17 July), Jidai (22 October) and Aoi (15 May) festivals, hotel bookings should be made well in advance.

Kyoto is further renowned for traditional Japanese crafts, especially pottery, lacquerware, wood-block prints, fans, Yuzen silk dyeing and Nishiju silk weaving. Major schools of the tea ceremony, flower arranging, classical dance and Noh drama have their headquarters here.

PRACTICAL INFORMATION

- Car hire is widely available in Japan and you may reserve a car through Avis or Hertz, both of which have offices in Tokyo. The traffic drives on the left. Speed limits vary, but generally the limit is 50 mph (80 kph) on highways and 25 mph (40 kph) in urban areas.
- The journey will take from two to four days, depending upon your itinerary. The best times to travel are in the spring and autumn.
- The Tokyo Travel Information Centre, run by the Japanese National Tourist Office, is at Kotani Building, 1-6-6 Yurakucho, Chiyoda-ku.

Skippers Canyon – a Rocky Road to Gold

BEN DAVIES

From the Coronet Mountain Range on New Zealand's South Island, Skippers Road hugs the magnificent Skippers Canyon, winding its way past gorges and precipitous drops into the heart of the old gold mining country. Here, amidst wild and dramatic scenery, you'll find a world of ruined 19th-century cottages, abandoned mining claims and memories of one of the country's biggest gold rushes.

ABOVE, *a four-wheel drive vehicle is essential for driving in Skippers Canyon*

RIGHT, *Queenstown, on the shore of Lake Wakatipu, and the Remarkables*

INSET RIGHT, *the road from Queenstown follows the Shotover River north towards Skippers Canyon*

TWENTY MINUTES driving time north of Queenstown the green foothills of the Coronet Mountain Range give way to jagged outcrops and gullies, a bleak splendour which marks the land as far as the eye can see. Here and there a scattering of tussock and speargrass clings to the mountainside against the distant outline of Lake Wakatipu. This is the sign that you are near the Skippers Canyon.

To begin this magnificent route you must head out on Arthurs Point Road then take the small left turning off Skippers Road at the junction with Coronet Peak Road, which climbs steeply, twisting past rocks formed by giant glaciers to the highest point, known as Skippers Saddle. From here the Skippers Road snakes its way past Green Gate Creek to the township 11 miles (17 km) further on.

Little more than a century ago, thousands of gold prospectors battled their way over these cliffs on a precarious bridle track, lured by the promise of instant wealth. Living in tents and shanties, they tolerated extraordinary hardship, suffered from dysentery, were attacked by brigands and overcome by sudden floods. Some made their fortunes overnight, but many died along the way.

These days, as you descend Long Gully through this barren countryside, you will find plenty of reminders of those early days. To the east of Skippers Road, below the strange shaped rocks known by locals as 'Winnie the Pooh' and the 'Upside Down Elephant', the narrow outline of the old bridle path is still visible, marking the spot where prospectors traipsed across some of the most treacherous terrain known to man.

From Queenstown, drive north for 14 km along Gorge Road, Arthurs Point Road and Skippers Road in the direction of Coronet Peak Road until you see a small turning on your left, signposted to Skippers Canyon. From here it's an 11 mile (17 km) drive along a narrow stony track to the abandoned Skippers township, which marks the end of the road. Sights along the way include the Long Gully Hotel, Pinchers Bluff, Devils Elbow, Pipe Bridge, Maori Point, Wong Gong Creek, Skippers Bridge and the old Skippers township.

Drivers should be aware that the road is extremely hazardous. There are no barriers on the corners and few places to pass other vehicles.

Along with Ninety Mile Beach in Northland, the Skippers Road is not covered by travel insurance. From Skippers there is no alternative route back, so you must retrace the road to the junction with Coronet Peak Road and on to Queenstown.

Near Skippers there are plenty of other attractions. At Arrowtown, a picturesque old mining village some 9 miles (15 km) away, you can still see the former homes of gold prospectors as well as the old gaol with its gun racks and heavy iron doors. In the western part of town is Ah Lum's store, built in 1870 and one of the few original Chinese buildings. There's also a fine little museum known as the Lakes District Centennial Museum, with a wealth of information on gold mining.

More energetic visitors will want to go power boat racing or paragliding over beautiful Lake Wakatipu, or bungy jumping in the nearby canyon. Between May and September skiers head up to Coronet Peak and The Remarkables, which offer an extensive network of ski lifts. Transport can be arranged in Queenstown, which is beautifully situated on the shore of Lake Wakatipu.

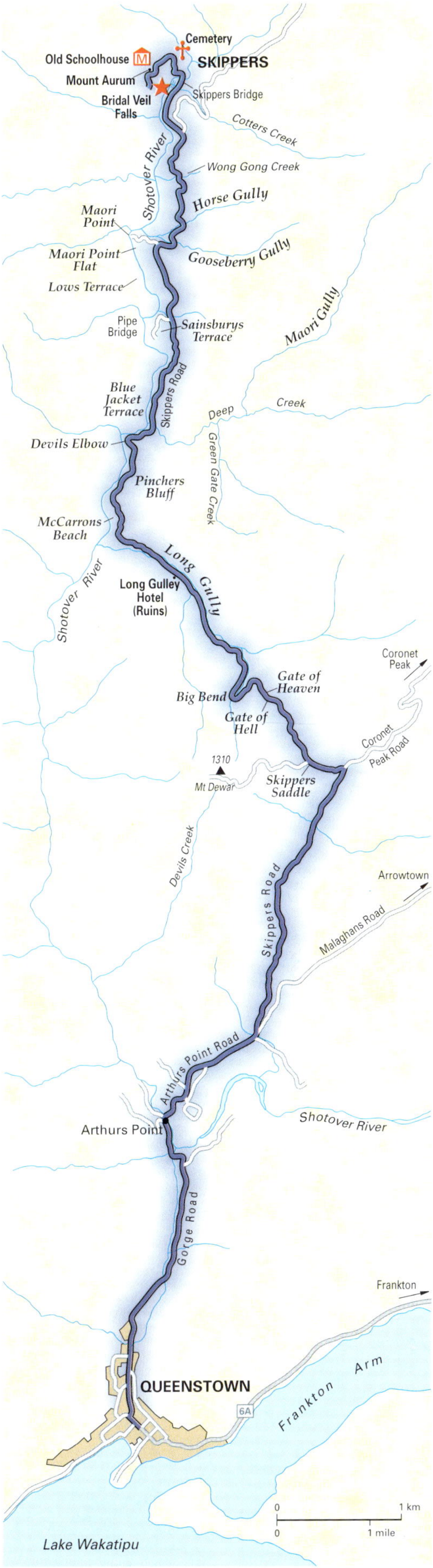

ABOVE, *a tour group pauses for a break in Long Gully, where the old bridle path can still be seen*

Continuing down Long Gully for about half a mile (1 km), you will reach the first of the great engineering feats. When British surveyors explored the Skippers area in 1882, they discovered a giant wall of rock blocking the way. It took workers eight months to cut through the rock face using metal hand drills, hammers and crowbars. Those who survived called it simply the 'Gate of Hell'.

Some 160 feet (50 m) further, beyond a sharp twisting bend, you will find another celebrated landmark, rising sheer above the ravine. Chinese labourers, however, took just three months to carve their way through the offending bluff and it was subsequently christened the 'Gate of Heaven'.

Beyond the 'Gate of Heaven', the landscape is dominated by rugged mountain peaks stretching as far as the eye can see. Here and there vast primordial rocks stand like sentinels along the route, silent witnesses of those pioneering days.

GOLD FEVER

Between 1862 and 1900, some 65 million ounces of gold were extracted from the Shotover River, which runs through Skippers Canyon, representing almost one ounce of gold for each foot of river bed. Locals proclaimed the Shotover River 'the richest river in the world'. Sir Julius Vogel even prophesied that by the year 2000, gold would be extracted by the ton.

But within 30 years of its discovery, much of Skippers Canyon was abandoned, leaving behind only vast heaps of slag, tumble-down cottages and the ghosts of its former inhabitants. Until 1992 a lone dredger produced some gold in the Shotover River. Today, the canyon is silent and deserted, but for the memories of former times.

At the bottom of Long Gully, where the route curves gently round towards Green Gate Creek, two old buildings still cling to the barren hillside. The first was constructed in 1890 and inhabited by an old retired couple who settled here to be with their gold prospecting friends; the second is known as the Long Gully Hotel and was built in 1885, although little is left now but a couple of chimneys and some skeletal ruins.

Prior to the gold rush not even hotels graced this unutterably stark landscape. When William Gilbert Rees came here in 1859, the only sign of life was the abundant thorn bushes. 'Speargrass,

RIGHT, *Arrowtown is popular with tourists seeking to capture the authentic atmosphere of the Gold Rush*

FAR RIGHT, *the road through the Canyon is extremely precipitous*

often more than three feet high, and masses of matagouri constantly impeded us,' wrote the unhappy man. 'Our trousers from the thighs downwards were filled with blood and it was with the greatest difficulty that our poor horses and pack mules could be urged to move forward.'

There was however some consolation. In 1862 two sheriffs working for Rees discovered gold in the Shotover River during one of their days off. Although both sheriffs were sworn to secrecy, the word soon got out and within weeks thousands of prospectors invaded the area in search of the ubiquitous nuggets.

It took another 20 years, however, before a new road could be put through alongside the slippery old bridle path. In all, the road took six years to build, using four construction teams and costing thousands of pounds, paid for out of a special gold tax. In 1888 the stony track was finally opened for pack horses and ox carts.

THE MODERN ROAD

Nowadays, although the narrow road has in theory been turned into a public highway, there is still no shortage of obstacles. As you descend the road beyond Big Bend, beware the notorious Bus Scrape Corner, where a jutting piece of rock has taken the paint off many an unwary motor vehicle.

Scrapes, however, are not the only problem. Three years ago a father and son were killed when their car went over the edge of a precipice. In an earlier incident a driver survived a fall into the gully and managed to climb back up to the road, only to die of a heart attack.

During the late 19th century, travellers had plenty of other things to worry about. Whilst many a horse slipped off the side of the road, far greater numbers of gold prospectors were held up and robbed at gun point. Few of the thieves were ever caught, and those that were habitually escaped from their makeshift jail in nearby Arrowtown, by merely lifting the logs to which they were chained and sauntering off.

Beyond Bus Scrape Corner, as the road sweeps around the mountainside, you will catch your first view of the Shotover River as it winds its way through sheer gorges and crags towards McCarrons Beach. It was near here that some of the biggest gold finds were made, using dredgers stationed on the river bank. The course of the Shotover was even diverted in places at a cost of thousands of pounds in order to allow the prospectors to explore the riverbed.

At Pinchers Bluff, half a mile (1 km) further down the route, Chinese labourers achieved an even more awesome feat when they cut the road into the sheer rock face by dangling at the end of 300 foot (91 m) pieces of rope. In all it took two

ABOVE, *adventure seekers can try bungy jumping from Skippers Bridge*

ABOVE RIGHT, *the school house at Skippers township has been restored and is now a museum*

BELOW, *a headstone in the cemetery at Skippers is a poignant reminder of a young life lost in the mine*

years to complete this section, under the direction of the infamous German engineer Pincher.

From Pinchers Bluff, the road traverses Deep Creek, curving around Devils Elbow towards Sainsburys Terrace. A small left turning leads from here to Pipe Bridge, a narrow wooden structure which spans the Shotover River. Ever since it opened in 1994, bungy jumpers by the thousand have dived off the bridge with only a piece of rubber cord tied around their ankles. Adherents of the sport claim that bungy jumping is the greatest invention since the advent of the parachute. Those with less extreme tendencies can enjoy the incongruous sight of bungy jumpers hanging upside down above the river after their perilous 330 foot (100 m) leap.

Gold miners got their kicks in different ways. The first prospectors simply used pannikins and a butcher's knife to extract gold by the handful. Others opted for digging with picks and shovels, then filling a pan with washdirt and water and rotating it in a circular motion until the specks of gold were left in the bottom of the dish. By the late 1870s the miners had progressed to using cradles, sluice boxes and even quartz mining to extract the precious metal.

From Pipe Bridge you must follow the small turning around until it rejoins the Skippers Road, curving spectacularly round the canyon past the distant outline of Lows Terrace. In places, the entire mountainside has been carved away, as miners gouged deeper to extract the metal trapped when the river was at a higher level. A short distance before you get to Horse Gully, the road descends to Maori Point Flat, where a sluice spills down to the river below. In 1885 the first hydro-electric generator was installed near here to sluice the pay dirt and drive a powerful crushing mill. But by 1907, the long-suffering promoters were forced to close the machinery down due to the prohibitive costs involved.

Against this wild backdrop, legends thrived. One of the most notorious characters around Skippers was a man named Captain William Henry Hayes, widely known as 'the barbarous barber'. An American by nationality and a pirate by profession, Hayes became the scourge of the region, terrorizing its inhabitants, before ending his life in a brawl on board a ship in the Marshall Islands. No less colourful was the group of Irishmen known as the 'Tipperary Men', whose speciality was to force prospectors off their claims before fleeing the scene with as much gold as their packhorses could carry.

A legend of another kind is remembered at Maori Point, just a short way beyond Gooseberry Gully, where a small sign marks the scene of one of the most staggering gold finds. In 1862 two Maoris, Dan Erihana and Hakaraia Haeroa,

jumped into the river to rescue their dog, which had been swept downstream. By the time they discovered the bedraggled animal, its fur was covered in gold flakes from the surrounding rock crevices. Legend recounts that the two men were able to recover more than 25 lb (11 kg) of gold before nightfall. Locals quip that the dog may even have been the country's first golden retriever.

It's just a two minute drive on from Maori Point to Wong Gong Creek, where another of the region's most notorious characters thrived. Wong Gong, an immigrant from the Sexip region of China, made his fortune prospecting for gold, before turning his hand to vegetables. Not only did he become notorious for his cabbages, but he also achieved acclaim as a rabbiter and a storekeeper in Arrowtown. Life, however, was short and in 1909 Wong died aged 49, and was buried in the Queenstown Cemetery.

The industrious and frugal Chinese workers made their mark in other ways too. In 1889 one enterprising digger named Sew Hoy started a dredging operation in the Shotover and managed to extract gold worth more than £5000, despite the fact that the area had already been mined by Europeans. Their success came at a price, though. In 1867 the *Dunstan Times* called for locals to attack the miserable looking Orientals with pickhandles. Other officials accused the Chinese of gambling and opium smoking. The president of the Arrowtown Miners' Association even went as far as calling them 'slaves' and 'Mongolians'. In 1881 a £10 poll tax was levied on all Chinese immigrants, a tax which was to increase in subsequent years.

From Wong Gong Creek the road continues past the delightful little waterfall known as Bridal Veil before crossing the Shotover River, hemmed in by sheer walls of rock. The original Skippers Bridge was built in 1866 and stretched 345 feet (105 m) across the river. Weakened by floods and battered by winds, it was subsequently replaced in 1871 and again in 1901. The bridge is now most famous as the first home of commercial bungy jumping, although these days Pipe Bridge is a more popular alternative.

SKIPPERS TOWNSHIP

Beyond Skippers Bridge the road turns west, curving through pine trees and gorse bushes for about half a mile (1 km) until you reach the old Skippers township, nestling amidst tranquil pastures. There is little left of the thriving community though, except the old Mount Aurum homestead and the charming old school house, recently rebuilt and turned into a museum.

Leaving your vehicle at the school, it's a short walk to nearby Skippers graveyard, where 20 simple gravestones recall some of those early pioneers for whom the dreams of riches turned to tragedy. Among the headstones placed in memory of European prospectors, one lone Chinese grave remains in this tranquil setting, left behind when others were taken for reburial in their native lands.

But whilst the cemetery acts as a sombre reminder of the transience of life, Skippers Canyon is far from dead and buried. Indeed, since the late 1980s there has been a new gold rush. It is called tourism, and it encompasses bungy jumping, river rafting, helicopter rides and power boat racing.

From Skippers township, you have little choice but to retrace the route along the narrow canyon, back to the main road. From here it's a pleasant 9 mile (14 km) drive to Queenstown, a prosperous little town sitting plumb on Lake Wakatipu with hundreds of hotels, guest houses, restaurants and tour agents – the hallmarks of the latest bounty hunters.

PRACTICAL INFORMATION

- You will have problems hiring a car to Skippers. Driving on these roads is no fun anyway, since the authorities will not insure vehicles. For a safer outing, take a tour with Nomad Safaris (Tel.: 442 6699) or any other agent in Queenstown.
- The best months to view Skippers are from October to May. From June to September the road may be closed because of snow and ice.
- Regular flights run from Auckland to Queenstown, which is the ideal base from which to explore Skippers Canyon.
- Bungy jumping, helicopter rides, rafting and power boat racing can be booked through any Queenstown tour agent.
- With thanks to Murray at Nomad Safaris, Queenstown.

BELOW, *snow-capped peaks seen from the top of Skippers Canyon*

Across Australia's Red Heart from Adelaide to Darwin

ANNE MATTHEWS

The Stuart Highway is named after the explorer John McDouall Stuart, the first white man to traverse the Australian continent (and return alive!) in 1861–2. The highway crosses the nation's 'Red Heart' and passes through an ancient, incredibly rugged landscape. This is a land of wide open horizons, and fascinating Aboriginal and European history. The people who live here tolerate isolation, extremes of temperature, and an existence that relies on bore water and a constant influx of supplies. The Highway provides a vital link between isolated settlements – a narrow strip of civilization that crosses some of Australia's most remote country.

ABOVE, *outback driving means mile after mile of red dust and bush, under the wide Australian sky*

RIGHT, *a signpost at Alice Springs gives an idea of the sheer distances involved when touring in the Red Centre*

BELOW, *Adelaide, on the River Torrens, is famous for its many parks which provide a wide range of recreation opportunities*

THE EUROPEAN STORY of the Stuart Highway – affectionately known as 'The Track' – goes back to 1836 when the first settlers arrived at Glenelg, Adelaide, to found the state of South Australia. The Aborigines, who had already inhabited this land for around 40,000 years, naturally had their own 'highways'. The centre of Australia is criss-crossed with trails along which Aboriginal people have journeyed throughout the ages.

South Australia claimed the rugged country to its north in 1863, but this vast tract of land became known as the Northern Territory in 1911. Although Port Darwin was discovered (and named after Charles Darwin) in 1839 by the crew of the *Beagle,* serious overland exploration from the south did not begin until the mid 1840s. One of these adventurous explorers was John McDouall Stuart, a Scottish-born surveyor who had arrived in South Australia in 1839.

Although it is likely that your journey will start from Adelaide, the highway really begins at Port Augusta, 193 miles (309 km) to the north. From here it is 581 miles (930 km) to the Northern Territory Border, then a further 1114 miles (1782 km) to Darwin. Driving in Australia's Outback requires special care. Most minor roads are unsealed and a four-wheel drive vehicle is essential if you intend going well off the beaten track – be sure to have plenty of water and fuel, as well as a repair kit and spare parts. You may not meet another vehicle for several hours at a time, so it pays to be self-sufficient. Hazards include stray sheep, cattle and kangaroos, while 'road trains' of up to 55 yards (50 m) long should be treated with respect. After Port Augusta there are few settlements of any size. South Australia is the country's most arid state: the Outback takes up 80 per cent of its area, but just 0.75 per cent of the population lives here. The highway later leads to the Northern Territory border, past small roadhouse outposts. There are plenty of these modern oases en route, offering petrol, mechanical repairs, water, food and accommodation. The longest stretch without fuel is the 157 miles (251 km) from Glendambo to Coober Pedy. The terrain is just as rugged north of the border, but Alice Springs is relatively sophisticated. The scenery eventually becomes less arid and there is much to see. Detours take you to the World Heritage wonders of Ayers Rock and The Olgas, Kakadu National Park and, finally, the Stuart Highway leads into the heart of tropical Darwin.

From 1858 onwards, Stuart made six voyages of exploration into the interior, and by 1860 a race to cross the continent from south to north had developed: Adelaide-based Stuart versus Robert O'Hara Burke and William John Wills, who were backed by the state of Victoria. Although Burke and Wills reached the Gulf of Carpentaria in February 1861, they perished in the Outback and never completed the return journey. Stuart finally crossed the continent, reaching Point Stuart, near present-day Darwin, on 24 July 1862. He named many places *en route* and found suitable sites for settlement, before returning to Adelaide in January 1863. His vision badly impaired and his health ruined, this most tenacious of Australian explorers died in England (in his early fifties) just three years later.

Stuart's persistence had finally opened up the route north – an achievement of great importance to the South Australian Government, who

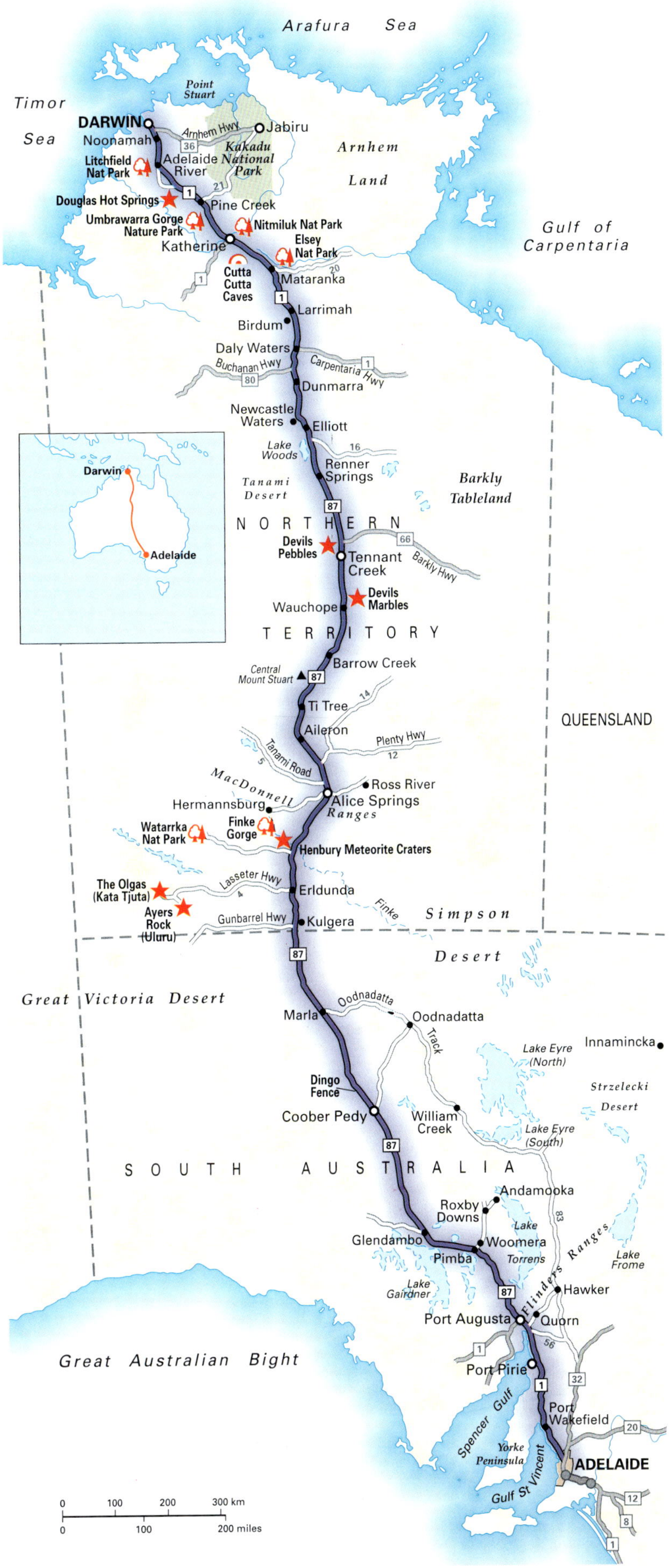

ABOVE, *there is always a risk of hitting a kangaroo, especially at night*
BELOW, *the name of Palm Valley in the Finke Gorge National Park recalls native plants such as the primitive cycad*

claimed this land for cattle and sheep farming. Then, in 1870, the government agreed to construct a telegraph cable line to Darwin, to link up with the British–Australia Telegraph Company London–Java cable.

Surveys in 1870 followed Stuart's route, and work began on the line from Port Augusta to Darwin. The ambitious project included the construction of 11 transmitter stations. Alice Springs, Tennant Creek and other modern settlements began life as Overland Telegraph outposts. Much of the transportation work was carried out by camels and their 'Afghan' drivers, who played a vital role in developing the Outback until the 1930s motor age. The final link in the 1985 mile (3175 km) line was made in August 1872.

By 1911, a highway of sorts extended from Darwin to Adelaide River, and work began on roads in the Alice Springs region. Until the late 1930s the development of the Stuart Highway was rather haphazard. The route generally followed the Overland Telegraph Line, but had to be relocated after each wet season. Progress, however, became vital for defence reasons during World War II. The road was then upgraded between Darwin and Alice Springs, via the military centre of Tennant Creek, but it was not until 1987–8 that the entire highway was realigned, reconstructed and sealed, and for the first time in Australia's history there was a reliable, all-weather road from Adelaide to Darwin.

ADELAIDE TO THE NORTHERN TERRITORY BORDER

Stuart Highway journeys usually begin at Adelaide, the gracious capital of South Australia. Surrounded by parkland and carefully planned by its founders in 1836, Adelaide is home to just over a million people and is renowned for its good-living, fine architecture and artistic ventures. From here to Port Augusta, you travel along Highway 1 through farmland and undulating country, with Gulf St Vincent to the west. At the head of the gulf, Port Wakefield grew up

as a port for the Yorke Peninsula mining region.

The route then passes through farmland, east of the industrial and commercial centre of Port Pirie, and past the South Flinders Ranges to reach Port Augusta, at the apex of Spencer Gulf and the gateway to South Australia's north. This modern city serves the Outback through its Royal Flying Doctor Service base, School of the Air and commercial services. Also here is the interesting Wadlata Outback Centre, which interprets the Outback and its Aboriginal heritage.

At Stirling North, just before Port Augusta, there is a turn-off to the historic railway towns of Quorn and Hawker and the magnificent Flinders Ranges, one of South Australia's natural wonders. If you have time, a detour to this region of rugged mountains and gorges, Aboriginal history and exceptional wildlife is well worthwhile.

North of Port Augusta, the Stuart Highway passes through woodland before reaching the desolate Arcoona Plateau, a region of stony ground, grassy plains and few trees. This area also contains lagoons and salt lakes, and you are likely to see kangaroos and other roadside wildlife. This section of the highway was the last to be sealed.

Just over 100 miles (160 km) from Port Augusta, and off the highway, is the small settlement of Pimba, a stopover point for passengers on the Indian–Pacific railway from Adelaide to Perth, and a supply base for road travellers. It is north of here that South Australia's vast desert region truly begins. From Pimba the highway passes through the Woomera Prohibited Area (named after the Aboriginal throwing stick), a stony, treeless region that was established as a British–Australian experimental rocket and missile launching base in 1947. The base closed in 1980, but the region is still administered by the Department of Defence. This vast area also encompasses the rather sinister Maralinga nuclear weapons testing site, which operated during the 1950s and 1960s. Although undoubtedly contaminated, much of this land is inhabited by Aboriginal people.

Although you can drive into the town of Woomera, with its Missile Park and Heritage Centre 3 miles (5 km) off the highway, entry to the Area itself and

MAIN PICTURE, *the extraordinary rock formations of the Olgas, rich in Aboriginal mythology, near Uluru in the centre of Australia*

BELOW, *the pristine landscape of Emily Gap, near Alice Springs*

ABOVE, *desert roads are often unsealed, and a four-wheel drive vehicle may be required to drive on them*

the Aboriginal land in this region is allowed only with a permit. Travellers should not stray far off the highway between Woomera and Coober Pedy. You can, however, travel north of Pimba to Roxby Downs, built in the early 1980s to accommodate staff of the vast Olympic Dam mine, where gold, silver, copper and uranium are extracted in huge quantities. It is also possible to drive on to the opal mining settlement of Andamooka, 66 miles (106 km) from Woomera.

From Pimba it is a dry and dusty drive to the town of Coober Pedy, 229 miles (366 km) away, past the usually dry salt lakes of Island Lagoon and Lake Hart, and the roadhouse at Glendamb. With a population of around 2400, arid Coober Pedy (Aboriginal for 'hole in the ground') is, by Outback standards, a large town. The reason is the presence of high quality opals, mined since 1915 by prospectors who endure temperatures up to 122°F (50°C), lack of water and incredible isolation. This is a most interesting frontier town, with eccentric locals, a mining museum, ingenious cool underground homes and shops, and the chance to buy opals. You can also visit a working mine and sample outback life in the raw.

BELOW, *at Coober Pedy opals are found in rock called Bulldog Shale, deposited by the sea during the Cretaceous period*

Although this is true desert country, cattle and sheep are farmed here and the region contains one of the world's largest cattle stations – 11,580 square mile (30,000 square km) Anna Creek. You may also see emus and red kangaroos in this area. To the east lie the dry, rocky Strzelecki Desert and Lake Eyre National Park. The lake rarely contains water, and the park is a vast and little-visited expanse of desert and salt pans.

From Coober Pedy to the Northern Territory border there are few major points of interest. North of town the Stuart Range, with its flat-topped hills, provides some scenic relief among the mulga (drought resistant trees and grasses) and gibber (rock strewn) plains. You will also pass the 1400 mile (2240 km) long South Australian Dingo Fence, designed to keep wild native dogs from roaming into sheep farming lands.

There are some impossibly remote settlements in this eastern region. Innamincka, near the Queensland border, is famous as the spot where explorers Burke and Wills perished in 1861, while Oodnadatta was once an important 'Ghan' railway town on the line to Alice Springs. The famed Oodnadatta Track, which follows Stuart's original route north, links this town with William Creek and Marla, 146 miles (234 km) from Coober Pedy and the next main highway settlement.

Marla is a new town and an important Stuart Highway service centre. Accommodation, a medical clinic, petrol, food and other supplies are available here – the last before Kulgera, over the border. You can make a short excursion from Marla to Mintabie, a major opal mining centre a few miles to the west. From Marla the road stretches another 99 miles (158 km) through arid Anangu Pitjantjatjara Aboriginal land, the habitat of kangaroos and emus, to the Northern Territory border.

THE NORTHERN TERRITORY BORDER TO TENNANT CREEK

Just over the border you will cross the famous Gunbarrel Highway, a rough stock route to the western deserts, and then reach the highway village of Kulgera. This is cattle country and the point where the prickly spinifex grasslands, which so frustrated the early explorers, begin.

A further 46 miles (74 km) on lies Erldunda. There is little but a roadhouse here, but the site is important for the road heading west, the 156 mile (250 km) Lasseter Highway, which leads many thousands of visitors each year to two of Australia's most important landmarks. Ayers Rock, or Uluru, is the world's largest monolith – 1140 feet (348 m) high, with an incredible 6 mile (9 km) circumference. Along with the nearby

ABOVE, *an isolated settler's house is a reminder of the hard life of the pioneers*

Olgas (Kata Tjuta), Uluru is the tip of a vast underground sandstone mountain, some 600 million years old. These wonderful sites, with their extraordinary aboriginal history, are an absolute must for any Stuart Highway traveller.

Between Erldunda and Alice Springs a turn-off to the west leads to Watarrka National Park, a 178,000 acre (72,000 ha) reserve which contains the spectacular sandstone gorge of King's Canyon. A short distance off this road are the strange Henbury Meteorite Craters. These large indentations are attributed to a meteorite plummeting to earth 5000 years ago.

After crossing the Finke River, named by Stuart for one of his patrons, the highway now leads you between low mountain ranges and through a narrow opening known as 'The Gap' in the MacDonnell Ranges to Alice Springs. This oasis at the heart of the continent was the site of one of the Overland Telegraph repeater stations. 'The Alice', originally known as Stuart, has developed from its remote beginnings in 1872 into an important Outback town with many attractions. Although still a rather rough and ready place, Alice Springs is relatively sophisticated by Red Centre standards and lives well from its tourism, mining and cattle rearing income.

Alice is dominated by ancient quartzite hills, the MacDonnell Ranges, which run in a broken line to the south of town. The eastern section contains Trephina Gorge Nature Park, historic Ross River Homestead (which offers camel rides), and the Arltunga Historical Reserve, where gold was discovered in 1887. Highlights of the Western MacDonnells are Simpson's Gap National Park and Standley Chasm, with their spectacular gorges, Finke Gorge National Park and the lovely Palm Valley oasis, and the old Aboriginal mission town of Hermannsburg.

Alice Springs itself is most interesting. From visiting the casino to touring the Royal Flying Doctor Service base, sampling the produce of the local winery to exploring the carefully restored Old Telegraph Station, visiting the Ghan Preservation Society with its steam train and railway museum, or the Aboriginal Strehlow Research Centre, there is much for the visitor to enjoy here.

A few miles north of Alice Springs the Tanami Road leads to the distant Western Australian border, while a further 31 miles (50 km) along, the Plenty Highway heads east to central Queensland. You then come to the small villages of Aileron and Ti Tree and, to the left of the highway, Central Mount Stuart. This is the spot where John McDouall Stuart stood in 1860, declaring it (almost correctly) to be the centre of Australia. Further north there is hilly country around Barrow Creek. The village was named by Stuart and contains a telegraph station dating from 1872. This is the beginning of the end of the Red Centre's dry, dark-coloured country. The scenery now becomes progressively greener as you head towards the tropical 'Top End'.

Just off the highway, 70 miles (112 km) north and beyond the small settlement of Wauchope, are the curious Devils Marbles. These rounded boulders vary in size from massive to small and are

RIGHT, *an astonishing variety of native plants grow in the red sand, and Aboriginal people still make use of 'bush tucker'*

balanced precariously on one another. Aboriginal legend has it that the marbles are the eggs of the Rainbow Serpent, but geology says they are the remnants of an ancient granite outcrop.

Sixty-two miles (99 km) further on, through mulga and spinifex country where huge termite mounds are a common sight, you come to the town of Tennant Creek. Set in the McDouall Ranges, this was originally another Overland Telegraph Station. The present-day town is a few miles from the old station buildings, at the site where gold was struck in the 1930s. North of town, the Devils Pebbles are miniature versions of the Devils Marbles.

TENNANT CREEK TO DARWIN

North of Tennant Creek you will pass the Barkly Highway turn-off and the John Flynn Memorial. This obelisk commemorates the remarkable founder of the Australian Inland Mission and Royal Flying Doctor Service. There is another memorial at Attack Creek, this time to John McDouall Stuart who turned back here after a skirmish with Aborigines, on his first attempt to cross the continent in 1860. To the west is the vast sandy Tanami Desert. Although largely waterless there are several Aboriginal settlements here. East of the highway, the flat, river-dissected Barkly Tableland slopes to the Gulf of Carpentaria.

FAR RIGHT, *it may be advisable to pull over when a massive road train appears in your mirror*

BELOW, *the Devils Marbles, in the Davenport Ranges, are formed from volcanic granite*

After travelling beside the Ashburton Range you reach Renner Springs, generally regarded as the dividing line between the Red Centre and Top End, and then Lake Woods with its prolific birdlife. Next is the small township of Elliott, which has long been a stopping place for travellers, although there was just a dusty track through town until the 1940s. South of Dunmarra there is a memorial to Sir Charles Todd, the South Australia Postmaster-General, who oversaw the construction of the Overland Telegraph. It was in this area that the north- and south-bound wires met in August 1872. Further north, Daly Waters was one of the Overland Telegraph Station sites. In those days supplies were brought in from Darwin once a year by camel and horse teams – the journey took up to five months.

At Mataranka a lush oasis contains a thermal pool with a constant 93°F (34°C) temperature. The springs and pool are located in Elsey National Park, and near by are the 1916 Mataranka Homestead, an historic cemetery and the Museum of the Never Never – the unofficial name of this region.

The highway then takes you past Aboriginal lands, the large Tindal RAAF Base and into Katherine, where the biggest draw is the superb, Aboriginal-owned Nitmiluk (Katherine Gorge) National Park. Here the Katherine River has carved its way through the ancient sandstone to create a spectacular 7½ mile (12 km) long series of 13 gorges. The walls are up to 195 feet (59 m) high and boat tours take visitors to view Aboriginal wall paintings and the local wildlife. Freshwater crocodiles (the harmless-to-humans variety) and many other reptile species are found here. Also within the park are the delightful Edith Falls and their natural swimming pool.

Katherine has been an important highway

town since the 1870s, and the railway later brought growth. Nowadays around 5700 people live here, most of whom are engaged in the tourism and cattle industries. Town attractions include the Low Level Nature Reserve, with its prolific birdlife, a School of the Air, the Katherine and railway museums, and Springvale (1879), the Territory's oldest house.

Gold was discovered at Pine Creek in 1872 and a decade later the town became the terminus of the North Australian Railway. The days when there was a large, predominantly Chinese, population have long gone, but the town still mines gold and attracts its fair share of tourists. The Old Railway Station museum is interesting, as are the guided mine tours, and nearby Umbrawarra Gorge Nature Park, with its crystal-clear pools, is a charming spot.

From here, the Kakadu Highway leads to the town of Jabiru and Kakadu National Park – there is no better reason to travel the Stuart Highway than to take a right just out of Pine Creek! Covering 7720 square miles (20,000 square km), this is a place of spectacular scenery and evidence of at least 25,000 years of Aboriginal occupation. Rich birdlife, the sheer walls of the Arnhem Land escarpment, waterfalls, estuarine crocodiles and the extraordinary Aboriginal art are just some of the highlights of Kakadu.

North of Pine Creek, an alternative, scenic route to the west covers a 32 mile (51 km) loop of the old Stuart Highway. This detour takes you to the Douglas Hot Springs, rejoining the main road at the town of Adelaide River. This large World War II military centre was one of the few places in Australia to be bombed. Almost 500 people were killed during the 1942–3 Japanese air raids and a visit to the War Cemetery is of interest. This area is the start of 'salty' (estuarine or saltwater crocodile) territory, so stay away from the river's edge.

Just 29 miles (46 km) from journey's end, and in cultivated farming country, you can take the Berry Springs turn-off to meet native wildlife at the Territory Wildlife Park. Back on the highway, past Noonamah, a stop at the Darwin Crocodile Farm is also worthwhile. Beyond here, the Arnhem Highway is the most popular route to Kakadu and Aboriginal-occupied Arnhem Land.

And so to tropical Darwin, the relaxed Northern Territory capital which is home to people of almost 50 nationalities. Although bombed in 1942 and flattened again by Cyclone Tracy in 1974, the isolated port city has re-created itself and has much to offer. Perhaps the most enjoyable aspect for Stuart Highway travellers, however, is the location – on Port Darwin and facing out to the Timor Sea. A world away from sedate Adelaide and the long, landlocked journey!

Practical Information

- To cover the distance comfortably including a few stops, you will need to allow two weeks, while to include the Flinders Ranges, Ayers Rock and Kakadu National Park, three weeks would be ideal.

- The best time to undertake this journey is during the cooler months from April–May to September, which is also the dry period in the tropical north. At other times of year, heavy rain can make the latter part of the trip unpleasant.

- A variety of operators offer guided tours along the Stuart Highway, such as Travelmarvel or AAT King's. Contact the South Australia Travel Centre, 1 King William Street, Adelaide. Tel: 8 212 1505

The Garden Route across the foot of Africa

TONY PINCHUCK

There's only one better trip in South Africa than a quick half-day drive along the Garden Route: a slow leisurely one. The relatively brief 142 mile (227 km) journey between Mossel Bay and Storms River packs in mountains, rivers, gorges, indigenous forests, bays and some of the best sandy beaches in the world. A first-rate tarred highway speeds you along, but the best way to enjoy the area is to wander off the main road and explore the coastal towns and national parks, or to head for the hills.

ABOVE, *the Kirstenbosch Botanical Gardens near Cape Town are planted with over 6000 of South Africa's 20,000 species of flora*

BELOW, *Cape Town's City Hall is the setting for a daily flower market*

AT THE FOOT OF AFRICA lies the lush forested belt of the Garden Route – one of the world's most beautiful journeys. On one side it is bounded by a series of mountain ranges; on the other, the Indian Ocean comes crashing in. For most people the route is a section of the longer journey between the harbour cities of Cape Town, where the first European settlement was established in 1652, and Port Elizabeth.

Heading east from Cape Town the N2 follows the route taken by European settlers as they expanded into South Africa. The highway takes you past a series of long-established towns with elegant Cape Dutch buildings, wide streets and sombre churches. It skirts past Somerset West and the Cape winelands, established by French Huguenots who arrived in the 1680s. It passes in the shadow of hazy mountains overlooking large wine estates, whose whitewashed homesteads and slave bells recall another South Africa. The highway then veers inland through Swellendam, Heidelberg and Albertinia until, 242 miles (388 km) later, it again meets the ocean at Mossel Bay – the starting point for the Garden Route.

The summer holiday months (December and January) bring many South Africans to the dozens of unspoilt coastal resorts along the Garden

Route. They come for the blend of mountains, forests, lakes and lagoons, but most of all for the sandy beaches that rival any in the world.

FOLLOWING THE FOOTSTEPS OF THE SETTLERS

In the centuries after the Europeans put down roots in Cape Town settlers began to move out, drifting off or leaving in large organized treks. Some, who headed north-east, discovered hardship in the parched valleys of the Little Karoo and on the baking plains of the Great Karoo. The more fortunate ones who headed east along the coast found hardwood forests carpeted with strange-looking plants, dripping with vines and teeming with wildlife.

Along the Garden Route, Dutch, French and later English settlers established woodcutting settlements, ports, trading stations and mining towns – enslaving, displacing and exterminating the indigenous Khoi people, whose ancestral roots in the area reached back some 12,000 years. Little remains today of these first South Africans, apart

ABOVE, *the Garden Route runs between the sea and a series of mountain ranges*

Nothing could be simpler than motoring along the Garden Route. Most people start in Cape Town, ending their trip in Port Elizabeth (or vice versa). Well signposted and well maintained, the N2 can be negotiated throughout the year. Most resorts and places of interest are clearly signposted and a short distance off the highway.

For the start of the route, follow the N2 from Cape Town for 242 miles (388 km), when a turnoff to the right takes you into Mossel Bay.

34 miles (54 km) further along the highway turn left on to the R29, which after 2 miles (3 km) brings you to George (before it continues to Oudtshoorn). The N2 cuts straight through the centre of Knysna, 31 miles (50 km) beyond George. Plettenberg Bay, 20 miles (32 km) later, and Keurbooms River, 4 miles (6 km) on, are just off the N2. To avoid the toll gate along the stretch beyond Keurbooms River, turn right and take the tortuous but beautiful route through the Grootrivier and Bloukrans passes. The road into the Tsitsikamma National Park is to the right, 32 miles (51 km) after Plettenberg Bay. A further 6 miles (10 km) later is Storms River (Stormsrivier) – the end of the Garden Route – and Port Elizabeth is 116 miles (186 km) beyond that.

You can drive selected sections by finding an alternative way of getting there and hiring a vehicle on arrival. Express coaches run between Cape Town and Port Elizabeth, stopping at the main Garden Route towns, and a scheduled steam train connects George and Knysna. Although regular train services between Cape Town and Port Elizabeth ended in the 1980s, these have been replaced by luxury rail tours.

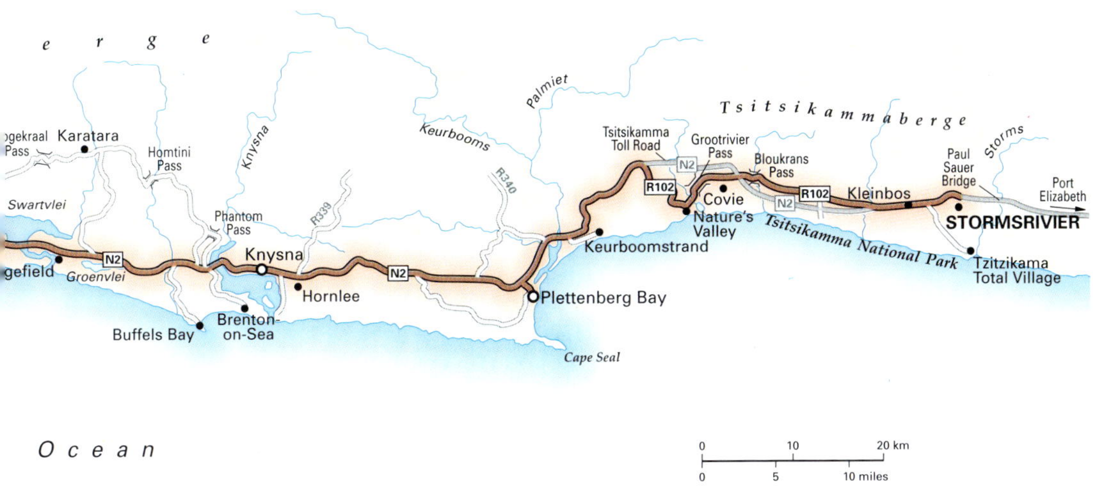

ABOVE, *the climate of the Cape is well suited to grape production, and South Africa's wines are marketed worldwide*

from artefacts, archaeological finds and the names they gave to mountains, rivers and forests.

Mossel Bay and the Outeniqua Mountains (Outeniekwaberge) mark the beginning of the Garden Route. In the Khoi language Outeniqua means 'a man laden with honey', and archaeological relics at Mossel Bay indicate that, for the Khoi, the Garden Route was truly a land of milk and honey. They herded cattle and lived on an enviable diet that included seafood, fruits of the forest and game.

Mossel Bay is also where the first Europeans – Portuguese sailors – set foot in southern Africa in 1497. Here began the painful history of contact between black and white in the region, when the Europeans traded for cattle with the Khoi. Because of its freshwater springs the bay became a regular port of call. A tree at Mossel Bay was used as a postal station by seamen for centuries. Today history and tourism have united and letters posted in a nearby pillarbox are specially franked: 'The Old Post Office Tree'.

'JAWS' COUNTRY

Shark lovers and fans of the movie can come face to face with 'Jaws' – or at least, a great white shark – at Mossel Bay. This so-called 'close encounter of the death defying kind' involves a trip out to sea, where a bloody hunk of meat is attached to a float. Once a shark has caught the scent (you know this because the water gets churned up), the bait is reeled in and you are submerged in a steel cage to see the action at first hand. Perhaps there's some comfort for shark phobics in the knowledge that two-day outings are recommended to avoid disappointment.

Leaving Mossel Bay, the N2 bypasses a number of small and pleasant coastal resorts – Hartenbos, Little Brak River (Klein-Brakrivier), Great Brak River (Groot Brakrivier), Glentana and Herolds Bay – all of which come to life for a couple of holiday months a year.

Thirty five miles (56 km) later is George, which bills itself as the capital of the Garden Route. Founded in 1811, it was named after the reigning British king, George III. Sixty-six years later the novelist Anthony Trollope was moved to describe it as 'the prettiest village on the face of the earth'. No one would make quite such extravagant claims today, but it still remains a green and pleasant place.

For travellers, one of the best things about the town is the sheer number of ways you can leave it. Flying is perhaps the least romantic, but most of the other options are along gorgeous routes. The road north out of town heads through the mountains to Oudtshoorn, the ostrich centre of South Africa. Regular trains used to follow a similar route on their way between Cape Town

BELOW, *rock pools above the beach at Mossel Bay invite exploration*

and Port Elizabeth, and it was reckoned to be one of the most dramatic sections of railroad in the world. After leaving George the line curved and climbed more than 1000 feet (303 m) during one remarkable 16 mile (26 km) section.

A steam train aimed at tourists, the Outeniqua Choo-Tjoe (never mind the name, enjoy the view) runs east to Knysna and crosses some memorable countryside. At certain points the tracks span wide lagoons, perched on columns in the water. The three-and-a-quarter-hour journey takes in views of beaches, lakes and forests.

Yet another way to travel to Knysna is on foot. The Outeniqua Hiking Trail is one of the hundreds of officially designated walking routes in South Africa. It passes through mountain scenery, pine plantations, indigenous forest and the ghost village of Millwood – a deserted remnant of the 1886 Knysna goldrush. The trenches, foundations and shafts have long been overgrown, but minute amounts of gold are said to remain. To complete the trail you'll need to be fit and have plenty of time. The entire trek takes eight days and covers 86 meandering miles (138 km). In contrast, the 38 miles (61 km) by road should not take more than an hour, though you can easily spend several days lingering in the attractive little seaside towns or heading off into the mountains.

The Passes Route from George to Knysna avoids the coast and follows an old wagon trail, first laid in the 1860s. Most of its 50 miles (80 km) trundle through mountain forests, rising then winding down into a series of river valleys and gorges.

KNYSNA

Knysna's extensive lagoon used to serve as an ideal harbour. This, and its position in the middle of the forest, made the town that developed on the water's edge ideally placed as a centre for the timber trade of the 19th and early 20th century. In the 1940s uncontrolled wood cutting was stopped and Knysna, by virtue of its exceptional beauty, relaxed comfortably into its current role as a thriving holiday resort, trading – at least partially – on local mythology.

A heady mix of royalty and elephants have fuelled the mystique of Knysna. George Rex, who lived here for 35 years, was reputed by locals to be

ABOVE, *driving through the Seweweekspoort Pass in Little Karoo, near Knysna*

BELOW, *scenic bridges add to the enjoyment of a ride on the Outeniqua Choo-Tjoe steam train*

the illegitimate son of George III. In 1804 Rex left Cape Town for a farm he had bought on the lagoon. He travelled along the Garden Route in a coach sporting an impressive coat of arms and drawn by six horses, accompanied by a large retinue of friends. Backwoods bystanders were dazzled by this unaccustomed passing splendour, and in no time the erroneous rumour of Rex's regal origins had spread like a forest fire through the area. He died in 1839 after a prosperous career as a local merchant and is buried in Knysna.

The Knysna elephants, on the other hand, miraculously still survive in the forests near the town. As the industrial culture of men like Rex took root and grew in the wilderness of the southern Cape, the wildlife – lions, buffaloes and elephants – began to disappear. Although many smaller animals remain, by 1993 all that was left of the big game was four Knysna elephants. They were rarely seen and their future seemed in doubt. In 1994, three female calves were introduced to the forest and everyone crossed their fingers. By the end of the year the good news was out – the youngsters had been accepted into the adult herd.

Like the elephants, the Knysna forest too has been saved from destruction. The wanton felling that wiped out nearly a third of the Garden Route forests has now been replaced by conservationist policies ensuring they will remain the largest indigenous forests in the sub-continent. There are over 60 species of hardwood here, and none is harder than the ironwood. It was used in pioneering days for railway sleepers because it produced virtually the only timber that was resistant to relentless termites.

Some of South Africa's best antique furniture, elegant in its simplicity, is made of glowing yellowwood – as is the woodwork in many colonial buildings in the Cape. Large shopping malls of antique and craft shops make Knysna one of the best places to pick up small wooden knick-knacks or some really beautiful old timber objects.

BELOW, *Knysna is a favoured spot for rock fishing, and oysters are a local speciality*

WHALE-WATCHING IN PLET

Twenty miles (32 km) on is Plettenberg Bay, known to the locals as 'Plet'. Some people call it 'the South African Riviera'. The comparison must be based on glitz rather than geographical similarity. The town is unquestionably southern Africa's premier luxury resort. Large amounts of Johannesburg wealth have turned up in Plet, an extensive development of second houses, timeshares, multi star hotels, shops, restaurants and discos. If this frenzy of things-to-do seems at odds with the natural tranquillity of sea and mountain, then take comfort that the resort replaced a Norwegian whaling station, abandoned in the 1920s.

Plettenberg Bay is perhaps the best place along the southern coast for whales. The mountain-encircled bay provides the undisturbed peace they need to court and calve. And for voyeuristic humans it offers fine lookouts from the land.

Largest of South Africa's marine visitors are the southern right whales. For commercial whalers they were the 'right' kind of whale: not difficult to spot, easy to kill and, conveniently for their hunters, their bodies floated. By 1940, when whaling was stopped in these waters, there were fewer than 40 adult females. Since then their numbers have swelled to 10 times that, with the entire population now totalling 1600. Southern rights are particularly rewarding to watch because they revel in play. During their spectacular breaching displays they leap from the water in an arching movement before falling back on their sides.

Spring (September to November in the southern hemisphere) is the best time to see the whales, but May to July are also good months. There are a number of lookouts at Plettenberg Bay. Settle down with a drink at the Beacon Island Hotel, where picture windows overlook the water, or get away from the urban buzz and take off for Keurbooms River on the opposite and less developed side of the bay, with equally good observation points.

Just beyond Keurboomstrand the N2 touches the edge of the Tsitsikamma National Park. Its Khoi name means 'place of abundant water' and the park has sections of rainforest as well as a 50 mile (80 km) coastline, and extends 3 miles (5 km) into the sea. In the 1960s it became the first marine reserve in Africa.

The coast is at some points rocky and wild, and at others fringed with sandy beaches. The rich plant life includes ferns, orchids, proteas and lilies. Some of its yellowwoods are estimated to be 800 years old, and the 210 bird species include the colourful Knysna lourie. A variety of antelope shares the forest with badgers, baboons and vervet monkeys. Two reclusive cats – karakuls and leopards – are present but rarely seen.

Compared with the more developed resorts of the Garden Route, Tsitsikamma is low-key eco-tourist country. Over a dozen hiking trails, varying from a couple of hours to the five-day Otter Trail (named after the Cape clawless otter), provide access to the forest. The entrance to the park is on its far eastern side.

Just 6 miles (10 km) beyond is the Garden Route's edge – a spectacular gorge carved into the landscape by the Storms River. The best way to mark the end of southern Africa's most beautiful journey is from the restaurant of the Tzitzikama Total Village. A wooden deck juts out towards the chasm, providing dizzying views into its depths and of the 623 foot (190 m) bridge that carries the N2 on to Port Elizabeth. The service at the Total Village is notoriously slow. But with this view, who cares?

PRACTICAL INFORMATION

■ The Garden Route is popular and finding accommodation may be a problem during the peak season (November to March).

■ Scheduled flights connect Johannesburg, Cape Town, Port Elizabeth and Durban with George, making it an ideal base. Hire cars are available at Mossel Bay, George and Plettenberg Bay.

■ Complete packages, including flights from Britain, can be arranged through Southern Africa Travel, 1 Pioneer Business Park, Amy Johnson Way, York YO3 8TN.

■ If you just want a Garden Route mini-package then contact SARtravel, 266 Regent Street, London W1R 5DA. Alternatively, Abercrombie and Kent, Sloane Square House, Holbein Place, London SW1 8NS can arrange packages; Tel: 0171 730 9600, or from USA Tel: 708 954 2944 or: 1 800 323 7308.

ABOVE, *the magnificent scenery of Nature's Valley in the Tsitsikamma National Park*

ABOVE, *the entrance to the Mamba Crocodile Village, at the north end of the Nyali–Bamburi beach in Kenya*

The Swahili Coast – Dar es Salaam to Lamu

MELISSA SHALES

While Rome ruled the Western world, Arab traders were already sailing round the horn of Africa, in search of ivory, rhino horn, tortoiseshell and slaves. They found lush forest, glittering sands, and rich blue harbours, where the ferocious Indian Ocean waves were tempered to a gentle swell by coral reefs. By the 7th century they were staying to inter-marry, converting the locals to Islam, while a new hybrid lifestyle and language known as Swahili evolved (from the word *sahel* meaning 'coast'). This led to the birth of one of Africa's greatest civilizations .

RIGHT, *many graceful buildings survive from Zanzibar's wealthy past, including the Old Dispensary*

OPPOSITE ABOVE, *travelling from Dar es Salaam towards the port of Tanga, an important centre of the sisal industry*

OPPOSITE BELOW, *Arab dhows still ply the quiet waters of the harbour at Dar es Salaam in Tanzania*

IT IS HOT AND HUMID on the East African coast. For centuries it was considered a fever trap. Nor are there any great towering cliffs or crashing waves to stir the senses. Yet it is still one of the most beautiful and welcoming shores in the world. Instead of high drama, there is a wall of coral reefs gleaming with fish of a million psychedelic hues. Beyond it is the kingdom of the great predators – marlin and barracuda, swordfish and shark. Inside the reef the sea is gentle, washing daintily onto an endless ribbon of silvery palm-fringed beaches, beloved of small pink crabs and large pink tourists. At intervals this postcard-perfect vista is broken by sparkling turquoise creeks and inlets, ideal havens for the tiny village fishing fleets, or by veined rivulets which weave tortuously through tangled mangrove swamps, accessible only by dugout canoe. A short way upstream, hippos and crocodiles lounge yawning on the sandbanks while elephants and buffalo crash through the dense forest, watched from the branches by monkeys and a thousand multi-coloured birds. On the banks of the inlets and in forest clearings, small villages cluster in a patchwork of tiny plots of maize and cassava and banana trees, while chickens and dogs, children and goats play together in the dust.

It seems like a rural idyll, yet travellers have found that the country's real heart is in its cities. The coast of East Africa is a meeting point of cultures, where traders from all points of the compass have mingled for thousands of years, adapting and creating a new culture immeasurably richer than any of its component parts.

Dar es Salaam, starting point of the highway, is in fact the newest city along the route, founded in 1866 by Sultan Majid bin Said of Zanzibar. Its development really only took off in the 1890s, when it became the capital of German and later

This route hugs the coast for some 400 miles (650 km), from Dar es Salaam in Tanzania north to Lamu in Kenya. The road varies from rutted dirt track to impeccable highway.

From Dar es Salaam visit Zanzibar and Pemba Islands, by air or sea. It is about 45 miles (75 km) north on a poorly maintained road to Bagamoyo. From here, the coast road becomes virtually impassable, so cut inland or return to Dar es Salaam and take the main road to Tanga via Msata. From Tanga, the road to the Tanzanian border at Horohoro is dire. The Kenyan border at Lunga Lunga is 4 miles (6 km) further.

It is about 80 miles (130 km) from the border to Mombasa along a well-paved road, passing Shimoni, the Shimba Hills National Park and the Diani Beach resort strip. The Likoni Ferry runs a shuttle service across the harbour into Mombasa City.

The 40 mile (65 km) stretch from Mombasa to Malindi, past Nyali Beach, Watamu and Gedi, is one of the best roads in Kenya. Both Mtapwa Creek and Kilifi Creek are now crossed via smart Japanese-built bridges.

Beyond Malindi the final 125 miles (200 km) to Lamu are along a pot-holed dirt road. Half-way, the massive Tana River is crossed by ferry at Garsen, 20 miles (32 km) inland. If the river is in flood, the nearest crossing may well be Garissa, a desert outpost 140 miles (224 km) upstream. From Garsen, the road runs north via Witu to Mokowe, where you leave your car in the care of the local askari (watchman) and take a passenger ferry to Lamu Island.

ABOVE, *market traders display their wares on the ground in Zanzibar, Tanzania*

British Tanganyika and the first railways to the interior opened up the farms and mines of central Africa. Today it is a huge and largely run-down city, a crucial trading port which lacks charm or sophistication and which has lost its capital status to inland Dodoma.

ZANZIBAR

The real history of the Swahili coast begins offshore on the islands of Zanzibar and Pemba. As early as the second century AD, the Greek geographer Ptolemy talked of thriving trade with the Zanj people of the Azania coast. It was the inter-marriage of these black African Bantu tribes (described by the author of the *Periplus of the Erythraean Sea* as having 'very large bodies and piratical habits') with the seventh and eighth century Arabic traders that created the distinctive Swahili culture. Based on a deep-seated belief in Islam, thriving trade with the Middle East and the African interior, and a sophisticated taste for fine living, it resulted in some spectacular architecture.

OPPOSITE, *Mount Kilimanjaro rises into the clouds above the acacia trees in Amboseli National Park, Kenya*

Zanzibar is now a gentle backwater, as any real political and commercial significance was removed in 1964 when the Sultan stepped down and merged his kingdom with newly independent Tanzania. Zanzibaris now regret their actions and are lobbying for independence, but aesthetically it has saved the city, whose shabby historic buildings are potent reminders of the city's many incarnations, dating back to its medieval golden age which lasted until the arrival of Vasco da Gama in 1498.

For the next two centuries the entire coast was battered by a series of wars and skirmishes as the Arabs and Europeans battled for supremacy over lucrative trading routes. By the late-17th century, the Omanis gained the upper hand and the Portuguese retired to lick their wounds. Zanzibar flourished once again, this time as part of the Omani kingdom. By 1832 the island was so important that the Sultan of Oman decided to move his capital here.

Zanzibar and nearby Pemba are most famous today for their clove trees – at one stage, they supplied 75% of the world market. However, it was the gruesome trade in human flesh that provided the coast's real wealth. By the mid-19th century it is estimated that up to 50,000 slaves a year were sold in Zanzibar alone, and by the time the trade was finally outlawed in 1873, it is said that 1.5 million people had been sold, while as many as 15 million died in chains on the march to the coast. Many more, of course, later died at sea.

The 19th century also saw the arrival of the British and Germans. Livingstone, Stanley, Burton and Speke were amongst the many explorers to set out from Zanzibar and Mombasa on a quest for knowledge, new markets and souls to save. Following hard on their heels were the missionaries and the charter companies, who leased narrow strips of coastal land from the sultans and built trading posts to use as a springboard for colonising the hinterland. The Germans built their capital in the 14th century slaving port of Bagamoyo, just north of Dar es Salaam. Once the mainland terminus of the slave caravans, its poignant name means 'lay down your heart'. In 1891 the Germans moved to Dar es Salaam and today Bagamoyo's historic buildings are crumbling.

The main road north heads past turnings for the small Sadani Game Reserve, the delightful coastal village of Pangani, with white-sand beaches and pristine coral reefs, and the Tongoni Ruins, a religious complex with a mosque and some 40 tombs. Tanga, the last large town before the Kenyan border, was developed along with the railway because of its natural deep-water harbour. It still has a sleepy, colonial air and is, surprisingly, the second largest port in Tanzania. Five miles (8 km) north are the limestone Amboni Caves, the largest cave system in East Africa, with chambers up to 43 feet (13 m) high, stalactites and stalagmites, and cave paintings.

RIGHT, *the Roman Catholic mission in Bagamoyo, Tanzania, infamous in former times as a slaving port*

INTO KENYA

Border formalities can be protracted in this part of the world, so start early. Once across, anyone wishing to head straight for Mombasa can be there in under two hours. Alternatively, 22 miles (35 km) beyond the border, shortly before Ramisi, turn right to Shimoni, once a slaving port and later the first headquarters of the Imperial British East Africa Company. Its name means 'place of the hole' and you can visit the 9 mile (15 km) long cave once used as a slave pen, but the town is now redesigning itself as an off-beat holiday resort. This is the mainland access to Wasini Island and, more importantly, the Kisite Marine National Park and the Mpunguti National Reserve. Together, these protect one of the most spectacular stretches of coral reef in Africa, with magnificent possibilities for diving and snorkelling away from the crowd.

Back on the main road, you pass one of East Africa's largest coconut factories, with vast fields of copra laid out to dry in the sun. A turning to the right leads to another small slave town, Msambweni. Just beyond this, a turning to the left marks the entrance to the densely forested Shimba Hills National Park, the only really good wildlife sanctuary right on the route. With a luxury tree hotel built above a salt pan and water hole for night viewing, there are chances to see an elusive leopard, as well as Kenya's only herd of elegant sable antelope.

INSET BELOW, *the arid bush country of the Tsavo National Park in Kenya, near the Tanzania border*

RIGHT, *a form of local transport called a* matutu, *from the Swahili word for three; in colonial days the standard fare was three shillings*

BELOW, *beyond Mombasa, the well-made road passes this beautiful beach at Watamu*

Turn right at Ukunda and there couldn't be a greater contrast, for this bill-board clad road marks the entrance to Diani Beach, heartland of the packaged tourist trade – a glittering 6 mile (10 km) parade backed by a chain of wall-to-wall resort hotels, complete with beach umbrellas, cocktails with paper parasols, and carefully orchestrated displays of tribal dancing.

The road north to Mombasa currently grinds to a halt at Likoni, a bustling market town on the southern shore of Kilindini Creek, where a constant shuffle of car ferries moves traffic to and from the city across the entrance to Kilindini Harbour, a vast modern container port tucked virtually out of sight behind the island. The old Mombasa Harbour was a small affair, designed to cope with sailing dhows, while early steamers anchored off-shore. In 1896 work began on the Mombasa–Uganda Railway and Kilindini was founded to cope with the massive machinery and heavy construction materials arriving from England. Winston Churchill described his journey along the 585 mile (935 km) 'Lunatic Line', chugging out of Mombasa seated on a garden bench firmly roped onto the cow catcher. It was an extraordinary venture. No one could fathom any possible reason for a

railway to cross 10,000 foot (3000 m) mountains and one of the most dramatic sections of the great African Rift Valley to Lake Victoria, through virgin bush the whole way. In fact, it proved one of the Empire's most profitable ventures, opening up the rich highland farmlands and leading directly to the colonization of the interior. Today, the train still rattles over the great plains of Tsavo, while first class passengers dine on a four-course meal worthy of Mrs Beeton, with brown soup, grilled fish, meat and two veg and stodgy English pudding.

Those who really wish to see some of Africa's most glorious wildlife should make the 125 mile (200 km) detour west to the vast, arid Tsavo National Park, home to some of the world's largest remaining elephant herds, and to little Amboseli, where wildebeest play in emerald green swamps beneath an achingly perfect view of Mt Kilimanjaro. Africa's highest mountain, at 19,454 feet (5895 m), hangs in the air, wreathed in cloud and topped by creamy glaciers and snowfields.

MOMBASA

By the 1920s Mombasa had become the first port of call for the flood of new, and often titled, settlers who flocked out to Kenya. Among them was Karen Blixen. In *Out of Africa,* she wrote that 'Mombasa has all the look of a picture of Paradise, painted by a small child'. It may be Kenya's second city, but it still feels like the same small, low-rise town surrounded by sea 'as blue as a cornflower' that she described, filled with charming old buildings of coral rock, most of them unfortunately now stuffed to the gunwales with souvenir shops. Like Zanzibar, the city is built on an island, and it too began life as a Swahili trading port, as far back as the 8th century. By the late 15th century, when the Portuguese arrived, the merchants were said to be so rich that they dressed habitually in cloth of gold.

The Portuguese were rather more successful here than in Zanzibar and by 1589 had Mombasa firmly under their control. It was ruled from Goa, almost directly opposite on the far side of the Indian Ocean. Their most enduring legacy is the massively forbidding, mushroom-pink Fort Jesus, which still looms over the old town, in spite of the many times it has been besieged. The 17th century was marked by constant warring, with the Portuguese eventually succumbing to an all-out attack and prolonged siege by a Turkish fleet in 1696. They left the coast for the last time in 1720 and a period of relative calm followed, broken only by a bloody squabble when the local Mazrui governors declared independence from the Omani court.

In the mid-19th century the British were constant visitors and by 1873 they had enough power to force an end to the slave trade. The local economy virtually collapsed and in 1886 they signed a treaty with Germany, carving up East Africa with scant regard to the now enfeebled local rulers. The Imperial British East Africa Company was formed in 1888, and shortly thereafter moved its headquarters to Mombasa. By 1907, however, Nairobi had taken over as the capital of British East Africa and Mombasa sank back into relative obscurity, to be rescued only by its port and its thriving tourist trade.

The earliest tourist developments were just north of the city in Nyali, where the elegant Nyali Beach Hotel, the seaside playground of the settlers, is still one of the most popular resorts in an area filled with hotels, snake and crocodile farms, discos and souvenir stands. In recent years it became the base for the American airlift to Somalia.

The road, now a superhighway by African standards, sweeps north to Kilifi, a quiet little town bright with flowers and popular with retired

ABOVE, *Fort Jesus is an imposing monument to the Portuguese occupation of Mombasa in the 16th century*

ABOVE, *rooftops in Lamu Town; walls in the houses were built of coral two feet thick*

ABOVE, *a woman of the nomadic Masai people, who live in the Rift Valley area of Kenya and Tanzania*

OPPOSITE ABOVE, *an ancient mosque minaret in the Shela district of Lamu*

colonials and international 'yachties'. Nearby Takaungu is one of the most charming, untouched villages along the coast, perched between a golden beach and a rich blue creek, where the village boys squeal as they swim amongst their mothers' laundry. On the south side of Kilifi Creek are the Mnarani Ruins, last vestiges of a small town utterly destroyed by invading inland tribes in the 18th century.

These days, in the sunny calm, it seems hard to imagine the devastation faced by this northern stretch of the coast when successive waves of ferocious Galla and Zimba tribes swept south from the Somali Desert, obliterating everyone and everything in their wake. The next stop, Watamu, is best known now for its marine national park, with some of the finest coral along the coast, and the underwater Tewa Caves, where divers can hand-feed a colony of gentle, giant rock cod, up to 7 feet (2 m) long and 800 lb (400 kg) in weight. Here too, however, are the tumbled ruins of Gedi, a once wealthy trading port whose name means 'precious' in Galla. Archaeological evidence proves that it thrived until the 18th century, with finds from China, Persia and even Venice amongst the ruined houses which sprawl beneath the shadowy canopy of the Arabuko Sokoke Forest. It is a true ghost town, decimated almost overnight and now colonized only by monkeys.

Another 10 miles (16 km) further you reach Malindi, the second largest resort along the coast, filled with hotels, the odd disco and pizza parlours, usually run by Italians. There is little to do but sunbathe now, but Malindi was once a powerful city state. The kings were also markedly friendlier than those of Mombasa and Zanzibar. In 1414 the great Chinese explorer Zheng He visited the city. The following year the king of Malindi sent a present to the Chinese Emperor of an oryx, a zebra and a giraffe, a beast so impressive that it was adopted as the Chinese emblem of Perfect Virtue, Perfect Government and Perfect Harmony. Nearly a century later, in 1498, Vasco da Gama sailed into port. Although rebuffed further south, Malindi welcomed him, gave the Portuguese land for a trading post and their first toehold in East Africa – something the king probably regretted later. The explorer's visits to the town are still commemorated by the simple stone cross at the entrance to the bay, erected originally in 1499, and by a tiny thatched church on the seafront, built in the early 16th century and thought to be the earliest Christian church in East Africa.

LAMU

North of Malindi, you fall abruptly off the good roads, on to corrugated and pot-holed *murram*. At times, it seems as if you have also fallen off the edge of the known world. There are towns and villages to the north, but this is very remote territory, where the desert begins to encroach on

to the coastal strip and the sea is striped brown by the powerful muddy delta of the Tana River. It is probably sensible to avoid potential problems and fly the last section up to Lamu – where cars are forbidden anyway. The governor's Land Rover is the only motorized vehicle on the island and he only has a mile (2 km) of road on which to drive it.

Lamu is the most perfectly preserved of the Swahili towns, saved by its off-shore location from the ravages of the Somali tribes and virtually forgotten for over a century. It is an entrancing close-knit web of narrow alleys, just wide enough for a donkey laden with panniers to pass, lined by coral-block courtyard houses, some over 500 years old with elaborately carved wooden doorways. The original waterfront is now a block inland, replaced by a line of elegant colonial mansions. In the 1930s astonished guests at the eccentric Petley's Inn had to cook their own meals, and complained of rats big enough to eat the tiny local cats. In the 1970s the magnificent beaches around Shela, on the southern shore, gained notoriety as a hotbed of drugs, nude bathing and free sex on the hippy trail – all anathema to the Muslim locals. These days the great Omani fort, the elegant British District Commissioner's residence and the finest Swahili houses have all been carefully restored and are now home to excellent museums. The town has cleaned up its act and welcomes tourists, although fortunately the difficulty of getting there and purchasing alcohol, and the tiny number of upmarket hotel rooms, have stopped any real mass market encroachment.

As a perfect end to your journey, head for one of the simple seafront restaurants, where you can sip fresh lime juice and dine on lobster as you watch the little sailing dhows unload their cargos onto a fleet of donkeys or creaking wooden hand-carts. The journey has led back 500 years to a scene that would have gladdened the hearts of the early explorers. May it never change.

Practical Information

- It is always hot and humid in this region. It rains in November and April–May. You should allow from three days to a fortnight to travel the route. Always carry spare fuel and water, emergency food supplies, a blanket and at least one good spare tyre.
- Local tourist offices are not helpful; it is advisable to do detailed research before leaving and to take a good guidebook.
- The Kenya Tourist Office is at 25 Brooks Mews, London W1Y 1LG. Tel: 0171 355 3144 The Tourist Office for Tanzania is at 43 Hertford St, London W1Y 7TF. Tel: 0171 407 0566
- Only the final leg from Malindi to Lamu may not be secure. There have been incursions by Somali bandits and it may be safer to fly. Check the current situation with locals.

LEFT, *Lamu is a busy port, but the waterfront has an air of tranquillity*

The Golden Road to Samarkand is not an existing road, but a journey from a poem by James Elroy Flecker (1884–1915). Whilst Flecker wrote his poem from imagination, the route does exist. It starts in Baghdad in modern Iraq and travels north to join the ancient Silk Road from China to the West. It is unlikely that merchants really transported Indian carpets to Samarkand via Baghdad, rather than using a direct route through India. However, the Golden Road still possesses a romance that causes people to make the journey to Samarkand even today.

The route begins in Baghdad, and then travels eastward, up into the Zāgros mountain range (along the modern Iraq–Iran border), through the Khanqin pass and on to Kermanshah (Bākhtarān) and Ecbatana (Hamadān). It then travels along the northern edge of the Iranian Plateau, around the southern deserts and the foothills of the Elburz Mountains. It continues to Tehran and Mashhad and crosses into Turkmenistan, to Merv (today named Mary). From there the road passes into Uzbekistan, to Bukhara and thus to Samarkand.

The Golden Road to Samarkand

Rosemary Burton

The name of Samarkand has come to stand for all that is magnificent, exotic and even inaccessible. Among the many writers who have felt the fascination of this Central Asian city and contributed to its fabled image, the English poet Flecker has perhaps done most to give Samarkand its place in the popular imagination. Flecker wrote his account of the Golden Road purely from imagination – he never visited Samarkand. However, the modern traveller can still trace out part of the route, and capture at least the spirit of the Golden Road to Samarkand.

Very few people read the works of James Elroy Flecker today, but a line from one of his poems, written in the summer of 1911, remains instantly recognizable: 'the golden road to Samarkand'. The title of Flecker's poem is actually 'The Golden Journey to Samarkand' and it has two parts, a prologue and an epilogue, with the 'golden road' line appearing only in the latter. But what was the golden road? Was it a real route which can be explored today, or simply a poetic image? For Flecker it was a journey undertaken in the imagination only, for he never visited Samarkand himself, but his half-remembered lines have probably accounted for many a modern tourist's journey to inspect the mosques and tombs of this Central Asian city. Reading the poem can be the start of various journeys: literal, historical, literary and imaginative.

In his poem Flecker imagines merchants and pilgrims setting out with laden camel trains from Baghdad to Samarkand. Samarkand lay on the ancient silk roads between China and the West, and merchants from the area of Baghdad in Mesopotamia are known to have established trade routes linking their home region with the main

THE GOLDEN JOURNEY TO SAMARKAND

PROLOGUE
We who with songs beguile your pilgrimage
And swear that Beauty lives though lilies die,
We Poets of the proud old lineage
Who sing to find your hearts, we know not why, –

What shall we tell you? Tales, marvellous tales
Of ships and stars and isles where good men rest,
Where nevermore the rose of sunset pales,
And winds and shadows fall towards the West:

And there the world's first huge white-bearded kings
In dim glades sleeping, murmur in their sleep,
And closer round their breasts the ivy clings,
Cutting its pathway slow and red and deep.

II
And how beguile you? Death has no repose
Warmer and deeper than that Orient sand
Which hides the beauty and bright faith of those
Who made the Golden Journey to Samarkand.

And now they wait and whiten peaceably,
Those conquerors, those poets, those so fair:
They know time comes, not only you and I,
But the whole world shall whiten, here or there;

When those long caravans that cross the plain
With dauntless feet and sound of silver bells
Put forth no more for glory or for gain,
Take no more solace from the palm-girt wells,

When the great markets by the sea shut fast
All that calm Sunday that goes on and on:
When even lovers find their peace at last,
And earth is but a star, that once had shone.

EPILOGUE
(At the Gate of the Sun, Bagdad, in olden time)
The Merchants (together)
Away, for we are ready to a man!
Our camels sniff the evening and are glad.
Lead on, O Master of the Caravan:
Lead on the Merchant-Princes of Bagdad.

The Chief Draper
Have we not Indian carpets dark as wine,
Turbans and sashes, gowns and bows and veils,
And broideries of intricate design,
And printed hangings in enormous bales?

The Chief Grocer
We have rose-candy, we have spikenard,
Mastic and terebinth and oil and spice,
And such sweet jams meticulously jarred
As God's own Prophet eats in Paradise.

The Principal Jews
And we have manuscripts in peacock styles
By Ali of Damascus; we have swords
Engraved with storks and apes and crocodiles,
And heavy beaten necklaces, for Lords.

The Master of the Caravan
But you are nothing but a lot of Jews.

The Principal Jews
Sir, even dogs have daylight, and we pay.

The Master of the Caravan
But who are ye in rags and rotten shoes,
You dirty-bearded, blocking up the way?

The Pilgrims
We are the Pilgrims, Master; we shall go
Always a little further: it may be
Beyond that last blue mountain barred with snow,
Across that angry or that glimmering sea,
White on a throne or guarded in a cave
There lives a prophet who can understand
Why men were born: but surely we are brave,
Who make the Golden Journey to Samarkand.

The Chief Merchant
We gnaw the nail of hurry. Master, away!

One of the Women
O turn your eyes to where your children stand
Is not Bagdad the beautiful? O stay!

The Merchants (in chorus)
We take the Golden Road to Samarkand

An Old Man
Have you not girls and garlands in your homes,
Eunuchs and Syrian boys at your command?
Seek not excess: God hateth him who roams!

The Merchants (in chorus)
We make the Golden Journey to Samarkand

A Pilgrim with a Beautiful Voice
Sweet to ride forth at evening from the wells
When shadows pass gigantic on the sand,
And softly through the silence beat the bells
Along the Golden Road to Samarkand

A Merchant
We travel not for trafficking alone:
By hotter winds our fiery hearts are fanned:
For lust of knowing what should not be known
We make the Golden Journey to Samarkand.

The Master of the Caravan
Open the gate, O watchman of the night!

The Watchman
Ho, travellers, I open. For what land
Leave you the dim-moon city of delight?

The Merchants (with a shout)
We make the Golden Journey to Samarkand.

[The Caravan passes through the gate]

The Watchman (consoling the women)
What would ye, ladies? It was ever thus.
Men are unwise and curiously planned.

A Woman
They have their dreams, and do not think of us.

Voices of the Caravan
(in the distance, singing)
We make the Golden Journey to Samarkand.

ABOVE, *Marco Polo travelling to China; a detail from a Catalan atlas drawn in 1375 for Charles V of Spain*

silk road traffic further north. Baghdad itself, situated on the river Tigris at a point where the Euphrates is only some 20 miles (32 km) distant, was not founded until AD762, long after the first silk routes were opened up, but archaeological evidence has shown that there were other settlements on the site hundreds of years before. Anyone travelling from Baghdad to Samarkand would be travelling on a branch of the Silk Route, and Flecker's poem is full of details which bring the journey to life. The 'Orient sand', the 'palm-girt wells' and the 'great markets by the sea', can easily be visualized, as can the merchants' opulent goods, their 'turbans and sashes, gowns and bows and veils', their 'swords engraved with storks and apes and crocodiles'.

In the poem, the merchants and pilgrims (whose 'rags and rotten shoes' contrast with the splendour of the exotic trade goods) gather at, and then pass through, the Gate of the Sun in Baghdad. The name suggests that this is an eastern gate and from it the merchants would have travelled eastward, climbing up into the Zāgros mountain range, (Kuhha-ye-Zāgros, rising to 11,000 feet, 3330 m, and marking the Iraq–Iran border today), through the Khanaqin Pass and on to Kermanshah and Ecbatana (Hamadān). The next stage of the journey would take them along the northern edge of the Iranian Plateau, avoiding the southern deserts and skirting the foothills of the Elburz Mountains (Reshteh-yeh-Alborz); and then perhaps they would continue via Tehran and Mashhad to Merv (now Mary), Bukhara and Samarkand.

BELOW, *merchants who had to cross the Zāgros mountain range would have hurried to avoid the onset of winter*

DIM-MOON CITY OF DELIGHT, BAGHDAD

Baghdad (Flecker's 'dim-moon city of delight') is not at the present time an accessible or recommended destination for Western visitors, and Iraq has not joined other countries in signing the Samarkand Declaration, intended to assist Silk Route travellers. For the time being the city, which is remembered as the setting for the tales of the *Arabian Nights*, is one which can be visited in the imagination only.

The original 8th-century city of Baghdad was built by Caliph al-Mans_r and known as Mad_nat al-Sal_m or 'City of Peace'. The plan of this round city was remarkable, with three concentric circular walls, four roads radiating from the centre, leading to four gates, and a surrounding network of canals. As the city grew, new settlements were built beyond the walls and in the 9th century a university of international importance was established. A period of decline saw the destruction of the round city, followed by its rebuilding and expansion and, from the mid-12th to the mid-13th century, construction of some outstanding mosques, tombs and *madrasas* (colleges, usually with two-storey, arcaded buildings around a central quadrangle). War and rapid 20th-century expansion have destroyed some of Baghdad's historic quarters, but magnificent examples of Islamic architecture survive.

SAMARKAND

Samarkand, which is now in the independent (former Soviet) state of Uzbekistan, is easily accessible to visitors, although today's travellers are more likely to fly or take the iron road (the railway) rather than a golden one. The city became the fabulously wealthy capital of the Turkic prince Timur (Tamburlaine) in 1369, but long before that it had become a major staging post for Silk Route caravans. Flecker's description of 'those

ABOVE, *the city of Tehran lies in the shadow of the Elburz mountains*

LEFT, *Baghdad, the romantic point of departure of Flecker's poem, is currently inaccessible to modern travellers*

ABOVE, *the Kalyan Minaret in Bokhara was built in 1127 and rises to 150 feet (46 m)*

CENTRE, *the road from Tehran to Ramsar climbs into the mountains*

long caravans that cross the plain/ With dauntless feet and sound of silver bells' says in the space of a couple of lines almost all that needs to be said about silk trade camel trains.

Marco Polo talks about Samarkand in his *Travels*, but a far more detailed account was written by Ruy Gonzalez de Clavijo, ambassador of the King of Castile and Léon, who travelled to the court of Timur in 1403. His descriptions of magnificent buildings and a courtly life which involved a great deal of feasting in pleasure gardens were published in an English translation by the Hakluyt Society in 1859, and this may have been known to Flecker. It is easy to see why the idea of this exotic city appealed to the poetic imagination. To cope with the trade in foreign goods, whole streets were roofed over and turned into a huge bazaar running the length of the city. De Clavijo remarks that the 'city is so large, and so abundantly supplied, that it is wonderful . . . Russia and Tartary send linen and skins; China sends silks, which are the best in the world (more especially the satins), and musk, which is found in no other part of the world, rubies and diamonds, pearls and rhubarb'. He describes the decorative brick and tile work which can still be seen in Samarkand today and generally creates a picture of overwhelming opulence:

> 'This garden had a very lofty and handsome entrance, made of bricks, and adorned with tiles in blue and gold, arranged in various patterns . . . In the centre of the garden there was a very beautiful house, built in the shape of a cross, and very richly adorned with ornaments. In the middle of it there were three chambers, for placing beds and carpets in, and the walls were covered with glazed tiles.
>
> 'Opposite the entrance, in the largest of the chambers, there was a silver gilt table, as high as a man, and three arms broad, on the top of which there was a bed of silk cloths, embroidered with gold, placed one on top of the other, and here the lord was seated. The walls were hung with rose-coloured silk cloths, ornamented with plates of silver gilt, set with emeralds, pearls and other precious stones, tastefully arranged.'

RIGHT, *the mausoleum of Ismael Samani in Bokhara*

FAR RIGHT, *the Khangah of Nadir Divanbeg at Bokhara is richly decorated with mosaic tiles*

Today Samarkand has the traffic, noise and urban sprawl common to most cities, but at its heart the magnificent Registan Square is preserved. The square is on a vast scale and bordered by three *madrasas* and a mosque. The Ulug Bek *madrasa*, which accommodated some 200 students of arts and sciences, dates from the beginning of the 15th century and was built by Timur's grandson. Two hundred years later the Shir Dor *madrasa* was built directly opposite, and the mosque and another *madrasa* were added shortly afterwards. Some heavy restoration and rebuilding work has been undertaken, but the elaborate ceramic tiles and patterned brickwork still make it difficult to disagree with Lord

Curzon, who described the Registan as 'the noblest of all squares'.

A poem, however, is not a route map. The more literal-minded reader might ask what sort of curious itinerary Flecker's merchants are following which involves them in transporting 'Indian carpets dark as wine' from Baghdad to Samarkand, when there would have been a far more direct route from India to Central Asia. The best answer might be a poetic itinerary. Metaphorically, Flecker's golden road can stand for all manner of roads and journeys. In an essay about the skills of literary critics he even discusses the word 'road' and says that, for someone interpreting a poem, 'road' must mean 'not merely one particular road but all the roads in the world whereon men walk like pilgrims from the grey of dawn to the terror of the sunset'.

Flecker's ability to capture the magic and exoticism of the Orient, demonstrated in so much of his verse, can be seen partly as a product of his knowledge of Persian and Turkish poetry, but it was a skill which even he could not fully explain. He lived in the Near East for some time – after a Classics degree at Oxford and two years studying oriental languages at Cambridge he worked for the British consular service in Turkey and the Lebanon – but he claimed to hate the foreign environment. In one letter he says, 'I loathe the East and the Easterns and spent all my time there dreaming of Oxford. Yet it seems – even to hardened orientalists – that I understand.' Douglas Goldring, one of Flecker's publishers and the author of an early memoir, agrees with this in a comment about a poem called *The Gates of Damascus*. 'All through', he says, 'we have the East, the real East, as it is given us nowhere else in English poetry.' The truth seems to have been that Flecker, whose grandparents were Central European Jews, but who was brought up in a strict evangelical Protestant household, was restless wherever he was, longing for England when abroad and for abroad when in England. In the end, after months of pain and ineffective high altitude treatment for tuberculosis, he died in Switzerland but was buried in Cheltenham where he had grown up. 'Seek not excess: God hateth him who roams!' is the cry of an old man to the merchants and pilgrims in the Epilogue section of 'The Golden Journey', but Flecker rather liked excess and it is impossible to tell if he would ever have arrived at his own 'Samarkand' if congenial employment, a sufficient income and good health had been available to him.

PRACTICAL INFORMATION

- Travel to Iraq and Baghdad is not advisable at the time of writing.

- Samarkand, in Uzbekistan, features in numerous organized tours (often involving a flight to Tashkent) and tour companies are also able to organize the necessary visas. A few specialist companies provide small-group and tailor-made travel packages taking in this part of the Silk Route and in general the newly-signed Samarkand Declaration is intended to make travel along the entire route easier than it has been.

- Flecker's work is not easily obtainable, but most anthologies of English verse print 'The Golden Journey to Samarkand' and sometimes one or two other poems.

The Jerusalem Corridor to Tel-Aviv-Yafo

ELIZABETH CRUWYS AND BEAU RIFFENBURGH

ABOVE, *an 'evil eye' above the door of a house in the Yemenite Quarter of Tel-Aviv-Yafo*

Winding from Jerusalem's golden domes and spires to the modern bustle of Tel-Aviv-Yafo, Israel's Jerusalem Corridor passes dusty desert, rolling hills and richly scented orange groves. It once provided the only access from Tel-Aviv-Yafo to the capital, and the route is crammed with history. Rusting tanks squat at the roadside, a grim reminder of Israel's recent wars, while crumbling fortresses and convents date from the Crusaders' bloody wars in the Holy Land. The battles between the Israelites and the Philistines also took place here long ago.

FAR RIGHT, *the olive trees in the garden of the Basilica of Gethsemane are said to have stood since the time of Jesus*

BELOW, *the Dome of the Rock in Jerusalem stands on the Temple Mount, a flat plateau built up by Herod in the first century* BC

THE MAJESTIC Dome of the Rock gleaming gold in the sun, the peaceful Garden of Gethsemane with its scrubby olive trees, the mighty Damascus Gate, black-garbed crowds at the Wailing Wall, tiny shops in narrow alleys crammed with brighly coloured wares in the old city – Jerusalem is a city that conjures up many images. By contrast, Tel-Aviv was founded in 1909 as a suburb of Yafo (Jaffa), and is a noisy, busy modern city, providing about a quarter of Israel's population with homes and work. It would be difficult to imagine two more different cities, and the road that runs between them offers an equally varied fare of ancient and modern history, desert and cultivated land, old Arab villages and modern Jewish settlements.

JERUSALEM

The journey begins in Jerusalem, one of the most important sites for the world's three great monotheistic religions, and boasting 5,000 years of history since its founding by the Canaanites.

In around 996 BC, King David chose Jerusalem to be his capital, and his successor Solomon began to build a temple and walls to the city. Other kings

continued to fortify Jerusalem, subjected to a series of violent attacks during the next 1000 years by Assyrians, then Babylonians, Persians, Greeks under Alexander and, finally, Romans under Pompey. Constantine the Great declared Jerusalem a holy city in AD324, and shrines and churches were built on traditional sites, such as Jesus's tomb and the Mount of Olives. From AD638 Muslims held Jerusalem until it was retaken by the armies of the First Crusade in 1099. It passed back and forth between Christians, Mamelukes, Muslims and Turks until British rule began in 1917.

Violence was always seething just below the surface, and when British forces left Palestine in 1948 a war erupted between Arab and Jew. Egyptian and Jordanian armies isolated Jewish Jerusalem, leaving its inhabitants short of water and food. In June 1948 the Israeli army forced a passage between Jerusalem and the rest of Israel – the Jerusalem Corridor. Jerusalem remained divided between Israel and Jordan until 1967, when Israeli forces united it after heavy fighting. Sadly, there is still tension in this beautiful old city, and periodic outbreaks of violence.

The heart of Jerusalem is the Old City, enclosed by walls broken by seven fine gates. The Golden Gate has been blocked since the Crusades, and, according to Jewish tradition, will open

Route 1 leads from Jerusalem to Tel-Aviv-Yafo through hills and valleys, a distance of 38 miles (60 km). Leaving Jerusalem and heading north-west, the Yafo (Jaffa) Road becomes the Route 1 Expressway. It heads out towards the Judean Hills, past an enormous cemetery and some small settlements, before beginning to rise in a series of hairpin bends. The road descends into a pleasant valley, from which a short excursion to Aqua Bella reveals a Crusader convent set among pomegranate trees. Back on the main road, the route travels past the Sha'ar ha-Gay Gorge, and the Martyrs' Forest, in which trees have been planted to commemorate Jews who were killed in the Holocaust. After this limestone gorge, two roads lead to Tel-Aviv-Yafo: Route 1 and Route 38/44. Route 1 continues through the fertile Ayyalon Valley ('Emeq Ayyalon), where the Trappist abbey is worth visiting, especially for those interested in purchasing the fine wines made by the monks. At the far end of the valley, it meets Route 40, which goes to Lod and Ben Gurion Airport. The ancient town of Lod is worth a diversion, and is said to be the birthplace of the dragon-slaying St George. Route 1 continues north-west through citrus fruit groves, which give way to the rolling suburbs of Tel-Aviv-Yafo. Alternatively, Route 38 leads through pine-cloaked slopes to the Shimshon Junction and along the 'Heroes Road', built under enemy fire in the 1940s. Meeting Route 44, it continues through the Nahshon Junction, passing vineyards on the way to Ramla, with its picturesque White Mosque. It is worth making the 3 mile (5 km) diversion to Gezer. Route 44 enters Tel-Aviv-Yafo past the industrial area at Holon and the small town of Azor, with its curious nine-domed mosque.

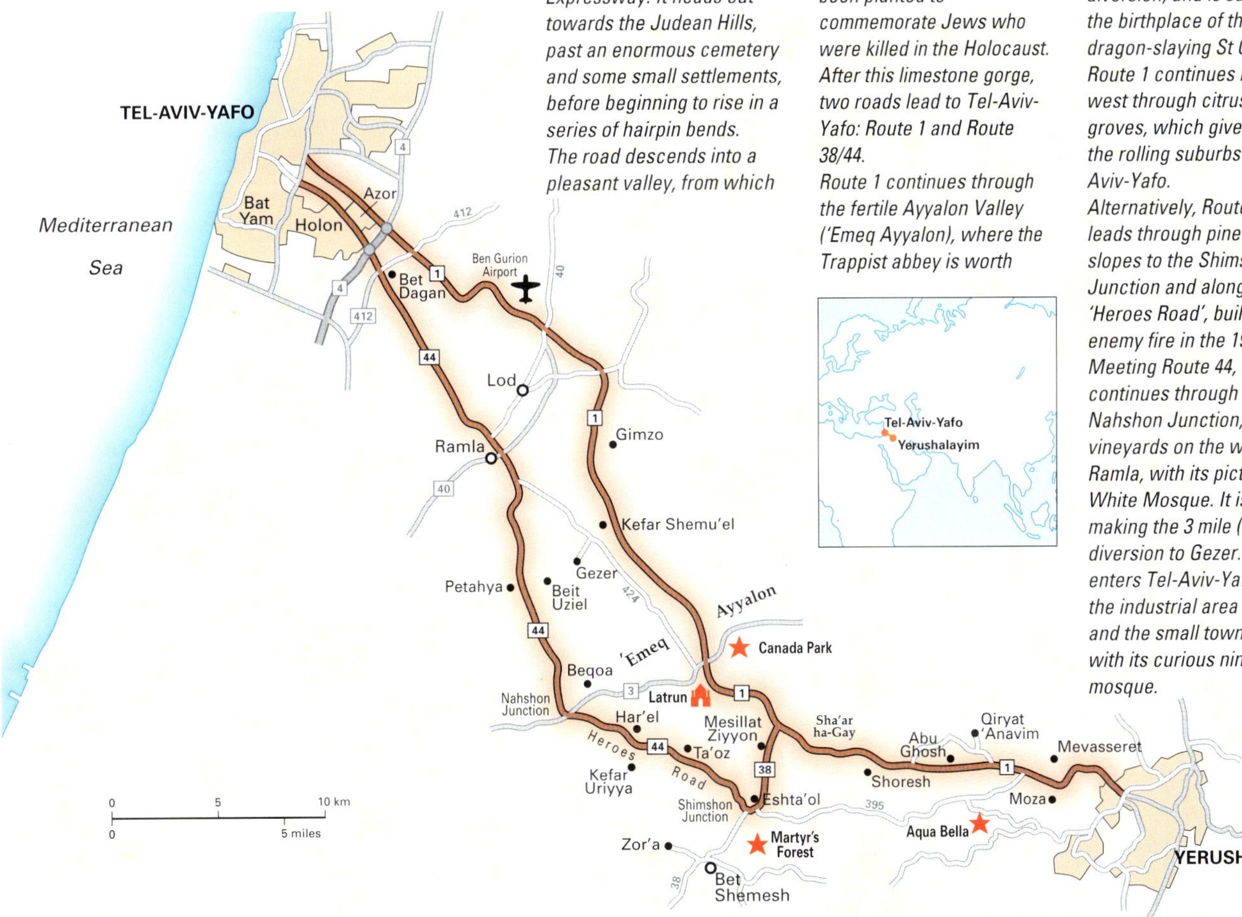

RIGHT, *the road to Tel-Aviv-Yafo speeds through the Judean Hills*

BELOW, *the most elaborate gate in the city wall is the Damascus Gate; a path winds between the saw-toothed battlements*

when the Messiah comes; on the opposite side stands the splendid Citadel, some parts dating from the first century BC. Christian sites include the Via Dolorosa, or the Way of the Cross, which begins near the glorious blue and gold Dome of the Rock and ends at the beautiful Church of the Holy Sepulchre. The Old City is still divided into quarters – Muslim, Jewish, Armenian and Christian – each with its own distinct character, reflecting different historical and religious backgrounds.

Outside the Old City, the hills and valleys are also packed with history. The Last Supper is said to have taken place on Mount Zion, and David's Tomb, an elaborate sarcophagus covered with an embroidered cloth, is also here. The Mount of Olives stands opposite the closed Golden Gate, and the peace of the Garden of Gethsemane at sunset contrasts starkly with the traffic roaring along the Jericho Road below.

The road through the Jerusalem Corridor begins at the Jaffa Gate, built by Suleiman the Magnificent in 1538. The road itself is more recent, being specially built for a visit by Kaiser Wilhelm II in 1898, so that he would not have to get out of his carriage as he entered the city.

The Road Towards the Mediterranean

The Yafo Road heads north-west towards the coast, past the Hall of Heroism, and out into the

modern suburbs where it becomes Route 1, the Jerusalem / Tel-Aviv-Yafo Expressway. In the early 19th century, the population of Jerusalem was only around 8,000, but recent history has swollen these numbers to just under half a million.

The radio mast at the city of Ramla can just be glimpsed in the distance off to the right before the road runs down the western slopes of the Judean Hills, through newly planted forest and citrus groves.

A series of hairpin bends through this attractive countryside leads to Moza Zion, dominated by Qastel Hill, named after the 12th-century crusader fort that once stood on its summit. An Arab stronghold here in 1948 harried traffic travelling along the road, causing some bitter battles. Eventually, the Har'el Pass leads into a pleasant valley, where Qiryat 'Anavim, a large kibbutz, farms cattle and poultry near the site where King David kept the Ark of the Covenant for 20 years before carrying it triumphantly to Jerusalem.

To the left, a road leads to the Aqua Bella Nature Reserve, where the ruins of a Crusader convent nestle among terebinth and pomegranate trees on the banks of a gurgling stream. To the right is the small town of Abu Ghosh, founded on the site of a Roman fort. The Crusaders built a church here, which was lovingly restored by French Benedictines. Higher up the hill stands a 20th-century church topped with a vast statue of Our Lady of the Ark of the Covenant, which dominates the surrounding landscape.

ABOVE, *the Western Wall is the only surviving relic of the second temple built by Herod, and is the most sacred of all Jewish sites*

Route 1 descends from the dolomite limestone Sha'ar ha-Gay Gorge through chalky foothills to a point where the road divides, offering two possible routes to Tel-Aviv-Yafo.

ROUTE 1: TEL-AVIV-YAFO VIA BEN GURION AIRPORT

Route 1 is the faster of the two roads that lead to Tel-Aviv-Yafo. It winds through the fertile Ayyalon Valley ('Emeq Ayyalon), flanked by rolling hills. Many armies have marched here over the last 4,000 years. Between 1948 and 1967, the valley was virtually a 'no man's land', and a tank mounted on a concrete platform serves as a monument to those who died during this bloody period in Israel's history. The British under General Allenby advanced on Jerusalem through the Ayyalon Valley in 1917, and the Crusaders

BELOW, *a site of archaeological interest near Imaus – a place of special significance for Christians*

ABOVE, *Tel-Aviv-Yafo, formerly a small Arab town, has now become a major resort city*

were here from the 11th century until the fall of the Crusader Kingdom in the 1290s. Earlier still, it was in the Ayyalon Valley that Joshua is said to have ordered the sun to stand still while he routed the Canaanites.

The road then passes Canada Park, a large area of playgrounds and sports fields, and Imaus (Emmaus), the site where Jesus is said to have eaten with two of his disciples after his death. Nearby is the Trappist monastery at Latrun, built on the site of a 12th-century castle. The monks make wines from the vineyards in the valley, and visitors can stop to buy some, and view parts of the monastery.

BELOW, *the rounded contours of the Judean Hills, seen in springtime*

Winding north and west, Route 1 continues through the gently undulating countryside until it meets Route 40. The land is dry and dusty, but the groves of fruit trees that fringe the hills are a testament to the ingenuity of those who have been able to turn arid land into viable farmland. It is well worth turning left on Route 40 and travelling the 2 miles (3 km) to the ancient town of Lod. Lod's chief claim to fame is as the burial place of the legendary dragon-slayer, St George. Richard the Lionheart built a cathedral at Lod, and the Church of St George that can be visited today was built on these ruins in 1870. St George was decanonized by the Catholic church in recent years, but this minor setback does not seem to have affected Lod's veneration of him.

For the remaining few miles, the air is rich with the scent of fruit trees, especially in the spring when they are in blossom. This is one of the main orange-growing areas – the Jaffa oranges of which Israel is so justly proud. Ben Gurion International Airport lies to the right, by which time Route 1 is already skirting the first suburbs of Tel-Aviv-Yafo.

ROUTES 38 AND 44: TEL-AVIV-YAFO VIA RAMLA

Route 38 winds between tree-covered slopes towards the Shimshon Junction, so named because Sampson was thought to have been born near here at Zor'a. The Martyrs' Forest was planted here in memory of those who died in the Holocaust, and a gateway leads to a cave where the names of some of the Jewish communities that were destroyed are written.

A 1½ mile (2.5 km) diversion down Route 38 leads to Bet Shemesh, an industrial town founded in 1895; David is supposed to have fought Goliath on a site just to the south. The tree-lined section of Route 38 between the Shimshon and Nahshon Junctions is known as Heroes Road, because it was built under heavy fire during the War of Independence.

At Shimshon Junction, Route 38 meets Route 44, the attractive vineyard-lined road to Ramla. A diversion of about 3 miles (5 km) leads to the ancient town of Gezer, an important trading centre in the 15th century BC, which saw some bitter fighting in the War of Independence. King Solomon was given Gezer as a gift when he married a pharaoh's daughter.

Ramla, founded in AD716 by the Caliph Suleiman, is 6 miles (10 km) on from Gezer through rolling farmland. Napoleon made Ramla his headquarters in this area, and is said to have directed operations from the top of the impressive 100 foot (30 m) high, 14th-century Tower of the White Mosque. The Crusaders mistakenly believed that Ramla was Arimathea, and founded a church in honour of St Joseph, which can still be visited. Also impressive is St Helena's Cisterns, vast underground water storage chambers which have been used as both a lunatic asylum and a centre for the Muslim whirling dervishes. They are also said to be able to water 24 camels simultaneously; occasionally boat trips are available, allowing the visitor to drift under the vast ribbed vaults of these silent, dripping caverns.

After Ramla, Route 44 passes some military camps and the industrial suburb of Holon, which lies to the left. The city of Azor, once a separate town but now subsumed into the sprawling Tel-Aviv-Yafo complex, has an interesting nine-domed 16th-century mosque.

TEL-AVIV-YAFO

When asked where the nightlife of Jerusalem can be found, the half-joking response is 'on the road to Tel-Aviv'. This busy modern city teems with life and energy, and with its orchestra, theatres, restaurants and nightclubs is distinctly more lively than Jerusalem. Tel-Aviv was founded by Zionist immigrants in 1909, adjoining the ancient Arab town of Yafo (Jaffa), and because both settlements are now firmly intertwined, the official name for the city is Tel-Aviv-Yafo.

Yafo's origins stretch back in time to the 15th century BC, when it was captured by the Egyptians. Jonah began the voyage that included a sojourn inside a whale from Yafo, and by the first century AD the city was a thriving seaport. Christian tradition maintains that St Peter raised a woman from the dead in Yafo. In 1798 Napoleon seized the city in an attempt to conquer Egypt. The old city boasts the Mah-mudiye Mosque, built in 1810, with its elegant inner courtyard. There is also the 17th-century Armenian monastery that Napoleon used as a military hospital, and a house where St Peter is said to have stayed.

Tel-Aviv was founded as a garden suburb of the ancient Yafo, but the modern city grew at an incredible rate after the founding of the State of Israel in 1948. Many of the Arab residents left, and today Tel-Aviv-Yafo's population is predominantly Jewish. It is Israel's major financial and commercial centre, bursting with energy, noise, traffic and people. The modern city offers a wide range of attractions to the visitor. The Cultural Center complex houses a museum of modern art and the Habimah Theatre, while various museums display exhibitions on the history of Israel, glass, science and technology, coins, ethnography and archaeology.

Modern Tel-Aviv is not all concrete tower blocks, and offers an impressive variety of architectural styles. The narrow streets of the Yemenite Quarter, settled in the 1920s and 1930s by Jews from Yemen, contrasts vividly with the soaring Shalom Tower with its many shops, restaurants and offices. An observation point at the top of the tower affords fine views across the Judean Hills and the Mediterranean coast.

The journey proper must end at the jumble of winding little streets in Yafo, overlooking the glittering blue of the Mediterranean Sea, where the atmosphere of timelessness makes it almost possible to believe that this ancient port was founded by Noah's son Japheth after the Flood.

PRACTICAL INFORMATION

- The addresses of the Israeli Government Tourist Offices in Jerusalem and Tel-Aviv-Yafo are: 24 King George Street, Jerusalem, and 7 Mendele Street, Tel-Aviv-Yafo.
- Express buses travel frequently between Jerusalem and Tel-Aviv-Yafo, but visitors wishing to get off to see places along the way should take the local buses that leave roughly once an hour.
- The journey between Jerusalem and Tel-Aviv-Yafo takes about an hour without stops.
- The main highway is good, but the other roads are two-lane only. Great care should be exercised when driving in Israel, especially when approaching blind bends.

BELOW, *the ancient city of Yafo overlooking the Mediterranean, with Tel-Aviv in the background*

About the Authors

Dr John M Baxter trained as a biologist and is now working for Scottish Natural Heritage, to ensure the protection of Scotland's natural heritage while enabling people to continue to live and work there. He has considerable knowledge of both Northern Ireland and Scotland, has written a guide to Britain's sea shores, and is a major contributor to the AA's *Natural Wonders of the World.*

Rosemary Burton is a freelance writer and editor. She studied Classics at Oxford University before working on the literary magazine *Quarto*, and then at *Punch.* AA publications she has contributed to include *Wonders of the World* and *Journeys of the Great Explorers.*

Dr Elizabeth Cruwys is a member of the department of Zoology at the University of Cambridge and a Fellow of Wolfson College. She has travelled extensively in Europe, Asia, Africa, the polar regions and North America, and is a contributor to the AA's *Houses of Treasure* and *Natural Wonders of the World.* Co-author with Beau Riffenburgh of *Explore Britain's Castles,* she is currently working on a major new guide to Britain.

Ben Davies is a freelance journalist and photographer who has covered almost every country in Asia. Currently living in Bangkok, he has contributed articles to publications including *Euromoney, The International Herald Tribune* and *The Phnom Penh Post* (Cambodia). He is the author of two recent guides to Thailand, a guide on Bali, Java and Lombok in the AA's *Thomas Cook Travellers* series, and has contributed to several other travel books including the AA's *Train Journeys of the World.*

Adi Kraus is a freelance writer and photographer who has a considerable involvement in research for the AA's travel guides. Born in Austria, he has spent many years in England, working actively in travel and tourism. He is the author of the *AA Tourguides* to Germany and Austria, and is a contributor to the AA's *Train Journeys of the World* in his capacity as a photographer.

Pip Leahy is a freelance writer and researcher. She has contributed to the *Sunday Times Magazine, The Observer* and *Woman,* and has worked extensively on travel guides for the AA. She now combines feature writing and researching with marriage to a photographer and looking after a daughter, a dog and two cats in a small Wiltshire town.

After exploring Europe and Asia in her early twenties, English-born **Anne Matthews** became fascinated with Australia well before it became fashionable. She emigrated in 1979 and spent 7 years in Sydney working in the adventure travel industry, including an extended period of living in India and Nepal. After returning to Sydney in 1986, she became a travel writer and photographer, specialising in brochures and guidebooks – she has worked on 7 projects for the AA including *Essential Sydney*, the *Tour Guide to Australia* and *Sydney and New South Wales* in the *Thomas Cook Travellers* series.

Tony Pinchuck is a freelance writer and designer, born in South Africa and now living in England. He has contributed to the AA's *Train Journeys of the World*, and was co-author of the *Rough Guide* to Zimbabwe and Botswana; he was both author and illustrator of *Mandela for Beginners.* He is the director of an editorial and design company in London.

Dr Beau Riffenburgh lectures in History at the University of Cambridge and is the editor of *Polar Record,* the journal of the Scott Polar Research Institute. A journalist for 10 years before moving to England from Los Angeles, he has written hundreds of journal, magazine and newspaper articles and books on subjects as diverse as the history of exploration, the development of the Anglo-American press, and American football. Co-author with Elizabeth Cruwys of *Explore Britain's Castles* , he is also a contributor to *Natural Wonders of the World.*

Richard Sale was trained as a physicist and has a PhD from Bristol University; he has done research into X-ray astronomy and glaciology. He has climbed in alpine regions including Austria, and was a member of the 1993 International Everest North Ridge Expedition. He has written or contributed to over 25 books on travel and the outdoor life, such as *Arctic Odyssey* and the AA's *European Regional Guides* to Provence and the Italian Lakes, and *Train Journeys of the World.*

David Scott has written many books on Japan, health and cookery, including *Japanese Cooking, The Demi-veg Cookbook* and the *AA Essential Guide to Japan* . He was a co-author on a guide to the martial arts, and is a Fifth Dan. He lives in Liverpool, studies Zen, and is co-owner of a restaurant.

Melissa Shales is a magazine editor and freelance travel writer who has a particular interest in Africa and India; a consultant for the AA's *Thomas Cook Travellers* series, she is the author of guides to Kenya and Delhi, Agra and Rajasthan, and is currently writing an AA *Explorer* guide to South Africa. She has written the first post-independence guide to Zimbabwe, where she was brought up.

The Automobile Association would like to thank the following photographers, libraries and associations for their assistance in the preparation of this book.

ANCIENT ART & ARCHITECTURE COLLECTION 12a Horace 65BC, 12b The Aurelian Walls of Rome, 13a Beneventum Arch of Trajan, 13b Via Appia Antica, 14a View of Quirinal Hill, 14b Via Appia Antica, 16a, 16b Tomb of Cecilia Metella, 17 Theatre of Maxentius, 18b Lekytus vase, Taranto Archeological Museum, 19 Brindisi, 20a St James Santiago de Compostela, 23a Chapel on Pilgrim Route, 24b Tomb Santo Domingo de la Calzada
K BASSINDALE 82 Mt Everest
P BOOZ/BILDBRUKET PICTURE WORKS 78b, 85c Itinerant monk Lhasa, 137a Karakoram highway, 140a Border China & Pakistan, 142b Mogao Caves, Dunhuang, 143 Road Kashgar
THE BRIDGEMAN ART LIBRARY 145a Hiroshige: TH Riches 1916 Shinagawa: Departure of a Daimyo (Fitzwilliam Museum, University of Cambridge)
B DAVIES 86a Grand Palace Bangkok, 88a Ranong, 150a Skippers Canyon, 151 Queenstown, 152a, 153 Skippers Canyon, 154a Pipe Bridge Skippers Canyon, 154b Skippers Graveyard, 155a School buildings Skippers Township, 155b View Skippers Canyon
J HENDERSON 28 Tomintoul, 29 Old Bridge of Avon, 30 Glen Livet, 31b Strathisla Distillery
CHRIS HILL PHOTOGRAPHIC LIBRARY 36a Larne, 36b Cushendun, 37 Coast road Ballgalley, 38a Carnlough, 38b Glenarm, 39a Glendun Viaduct, 39b Cushendun, 40a Carrick-a-Rede, 40/a Giants Causeway
THE HUTCHINSON LIBRARY 2/3 Road from Jerusalem, Judean Hills, 71a Rice paddies Mangalore, 72b Threshing rice, Mangalore, 186/7 Road from Jerusalem, Judean Hills
IMAGES COLOUR LIBRARY6/7 California road, Eastern Sierras
JAPAN NATIONAL TOURIST ORGANISATION 148 Nagoya Castle
A KRAUS 68a Heiligenblut church altar
I MOREJOHN/BILDBRUKET PICTURE WORKS 78a Prayer flags & wheels Lhasa, 80b Jokhang Temple, 82b Kumbum Palkhor Chodë Monastery, 83 Tashilhunpo Monastery, 136a Silk worms, 136b Terracotta Army, 138 Dunhuang "Singing Sand-dunes", 139a Dunhuang Camels, 140b Fort & Qilian Shan Mountains, 141a Kazakh people of the "heavenly mountain", 141b Maijishan Buddhist grotto, 142a Kashgar Sunday market
C OSBORNE/MEP 180 Iran, Zagros Mountains, 181a Elburz Mountains
ANN & BURY PEERLESS -SLIDE RESOURCES & PICTURE LIBRARY 70b Kerala palms
PICTURES COLOUR LIBRARY 1 California Marin County, 6 California Highway 1 Big Sur, 34a Glenfiddich Distillery, 64a Edelweiss, 85a Kathmandu, Bodnath Buddhist Stupa, 89 Phuket, 91b Penang Kek Lok Si Temple, 97 Lake Laberge, 104 St John's Harbour, 105 Château Frontenac, Quebec, 106 Saskatchewan, 108/9 Moraine Lake, 110a San Francisco cable car, 111 Hollywood Freeway, 112/3 Big Sur, 116a Saguaro Cactus, 119a St Louis, 121 Arizona sign, 123a Santa Monica Freeway, 124b Andean foothills, 127a Machupicchu ruins, 128 Cuzco, 172a Zanzibar, Tanzania
THE RUSSIA REPUBLIC'S PHOTOLIBRARY 132b The Kremlin
R SALE 81 Ploughing with yaks
SPECTRUM COLOUR LIBRARY California Highway 5, 15 Old Roman Road – Appian Way, 16c Pilgrims route 'pigeon cote', 24/5 Puenta la Reina, 26 Church of St Martín, Fromista, 27b Santiago de Compostela, 48a Dinkelsbühl Children's Festival, 49 Romantische Strasse sign, 50a Wies church, 50/1 Augsburg Town Hall Sq, 50b Augsburg statue, 51 Harburg, 54a Nordlingen, 54b Rothenburg, 55 Würzburg, 70a Kathakali dancer, 71b Kerala washing, 72a Kerala fishing nets, 73 Kerala Basilica of Santa Cruz, 75 Kerala loading lorry, 84 Durbar Square, Bhaktapur, 85b Kathmandu, 88b Phet Buri, Phra Nakhon Khiri, 92b Kuala Lumpur,Batu Caves, 102 Totem pole, Vancouver, 103a Trans-Canada Highway 1, 103b Indian, 107a Trans-Canada Highway & Hermit Range, 113a Carmel, 114a Lone Cypress, 116b Painted Desert, 116 Texas signposts, 117a Chicago, 117b Texas signposts, 120a Oklahoma, 120/1 Highway US 60, 122a Taos Pueblo children, 122b Petrified Forest NP, 124a Cuzco, 129b Ponce statue Tiahuanaco, 133 St Basil's Cathedral, 134a Kremlin Emperor Cannon, 145b Kyoto festival,146 Tomei Expressway, 146b Mount Fuji & Lake Ashino-ko, 147 Daibutsu at Kamakura, 149a Ni-jo Castle, 149b Pavilion Kinkaku-ji, Kyoto, 156a Outback road, 156b Adelaide, 157 sign Alice Springs, 159b Emily Gap, 160b Opal mines Coober Pedy, 161 Pioneer Settlers House, 162a flowers, 162b Devils Marbles, 163 Road Train, 164b City Hall Cape Town, 165 Garden Route, 166b Mossel Bay, 167a Seweweekspoort Pass, 167b Garden Route, 168 Knysa Bayble, 169 Tsitsikamma National Park, 170b Zanzibar Old Dispensary, 171a Tanga/Dar Es Salaam road, 171b Boat Dar Es Salaam, 172b RC Mission Bagamoyo, 173a Mt Kilimanjaro, 174b Watamu, 176a Lamu Island, 177a Lamu Mosque Minaret, 177b Lamu, 182a Kalyan Minaret Bokhara,182b Bokhara Mausoleum of Ismael

Index

Samani, 182/3 Tehran/Ramsar road, 183 Khangah of Nadir Divan-beg Bokhara, 185 Jerusalem, Garden of Basilica of Gethsemane, 188a, 189 Tel-Aviv-Jafo
TRAVELPRESS ITALIA 18a Lazio Pv Latina Minturno
TRIP 74a Temple Elephants Aleppey, Kerala, 74b Kerala Backwater, Aleppey & Quilon, 76a Kerala boatrace, 76/7 Kerala Backwater, Aleppey & Quilon, 77a Suchindram Temple, Kannyakumari, 134/5 Kiev, R Dnieper, 134b Kiev, Golden Gate, 135a Odessa, Arcadia beach, 135b Kiev, Monastery of the Caves
YUKON GOV'T PHOTO 94a Gold panning, 94b Klondike Highway, 98 Yukon River, 99a Five Finger Rapids, 99b Klondike Highway, 100 Venus Mine, 101a Dawson City, 101b Dawson City Palace Grand Theatre

ZEFA PICTURES 8/9 Tibet nr Gandon Monastry, 25b Grape picking Rioja, 42a Cagnes-sur-Mer, 42b Road to Monte Carlo, 44 St-Tropez, 45b Cannes, 48b Schloss Neuschwanstein, 54/5 Rothenburg ob der Tauber, 66 Grossglockner Road, 68b Heiligenblut, 79 Potala Palace Lhasa, 80a Lhasa, 90 Nail Island, 91a Pinang Island, 96a Whitehorse Yukon, 96b Yukon Indian burial ground, 107b Banff & Castle Mountain, 108a Calgary, 118 Lake Shore, Chicago, 119b St Louis Gateway Arch, 123b Santa Monica Bay, 125 Cotopaxi Volcano, 126 Quito, 127b Machupicchu,129a Uros women & children, 144 Japan, Kyoto, Pagoda, 164a Kirstenbosch gardens, 166a Kapprovinz, 181b Baghdad Helicoidal Minaret, 187b Emmaus Archeological Site, Latrun, 188b Judean Hills in Spring

All remaining pictures are held in the Association's own library (AA PHOTO LIBRARY) with contributions from the following photographers:
P AITHIE 184a; A BAKER 43, 46a, 46b, 47a, 52/3, 52a, 64–5, 67a, 67b, 69, 158/9, 158a, 158b, 160a; E ELLINGTON 33a; P ENTICKNAP 20b, 21, 22, 23b, 27a; R HOLMES 110b, 114b, 115; P KENWARD 150/1, 152b, 170a, 173b, 174a, 176b; E MEACHER 175; D NOBLE 60b; K PATERSON 56a, 56/7, 57, 59, 92a, 93, 130a, 130b, 131, 132a; C SAWYER 61a, 62a, 62b, 63; M SIEBERT 60a; B SMITH 112a; A SOUTER 184b, 186, 187a; R STRANGE 45a, 47b, 86b, 86/7, 88/9; P TIMMERMANS 109b; R WEIR 31a, 32/3, 34b, 35; P WILSON 58/9; J WYAND 61b